POSITIVE
SCHOOL
LEADERSHIP

POSITIVE SCHOOL LEADERSHIP

Building *Capacity* and Strengthening *Relationships*

Joseph F. Murphy
Karen Seashore Louis

TEACHERS COLLEGE PRESS

TEACHERS COLLEGE | COLUMBIA UNIVERSITY

NEW YORK AND LONDON

Published by Teachers College Press, 1234 Amsterdam Avenue, New York, NY 10027

Copyright © 2018 by Teachers College, Columbia University

Cover photo by Martin Konopka / Getty Images

Library of Congress Cataloging-in-Publication Data is available at loc.gov

Names: Murphy, Joseph, 1949- author. | Louis, Karen Seashore, author.
Title: Positive school leadership : building capacity and strengthening
   relationships / Joseph F. Murphy, Karen Seashore Louis.
Description: New York, NY : Teachers College Press, [2018] | Includes
   bibliographical references and index.
Identifiers: LCCN 2017061240| ISBN 9780807759035 (pbk. : alk. paper) | ISBN
   9780807776896 (ebook)
Subjects: LCSH: School management and organization. | Educational leadership.
   | School administrators--Professional relationships.
Classification: LCC LB2805 .M8175 2018 | DDC 371.2--dc23
LC record available at https://lccn.loc.gov/2017061240

ISBN 978-0-8077-5903-5 (paper)
ISBN 978-0-8077-7689-6-X (ebook)

Printed on acid-free paper
Manufactured in the United States of America

25   24   23   22   21   20   19   18   8   7   6   5   4   3   2   1

We dedicate this book to each other—

In gratitude that we did not come to blows as we negotiated new ways of collaborating that acknowledged our differences and preserved a long and deep professional friendship . . .

We also acknowledge the inspiration that comes from the many effective and engaging educational leaders (and future educational leaders) that we have known throughout our careers. They inspire us, whether they are colleagues, our students/former students, or those who graciously have allowed us to observe and include them in our research. Without them, we could not have written this book.

Finally, we appreciate Dan Bratton's wise editorial comments and patient editing of several of the denser chapters.

Contents

PART II: POSITIVE LEADERSHIP IN ACTION

PART III: THE EFFECTS OF POSITIVE SCHOOL LEADERSHIP

PART I

INTRODUCING THE DNA OF POSITIVE SCHOOL LEADERSHIP

Some magic takes place in the crucible of leadership.

—W. L. Gardner & Schermerhorn, 2004, p. 277

Rather than employees, a purpose-based company has mission-aries.
Instead of customers, it has advocates.
In place of social charity, it avows social conscience.
Instead of loyalty, it aims for love.
   —Carlesi, Hemerling, Kilmann, Meese, & Shipman, 2017, p. 7

The "science" of leadership has progressed since classical writers like Confucius and Plato developed their unique perspectives on the role of philosophers and wise moralists in maintaining stability in the social order. There are many competing perspectives, ranging from modern-day descendants of Machiavelli who focus on the significance of power, to radical constructivists who examine how leadership is invented to make sense of positive and negative events. A Google search of "leadership theory" reveals more than 7 million sources, many of which create typologies or chronologies for competing ideas. In other words, a cacophony of ideas provides rich ground for the endless supply of books advocating strategies for becoming a more successful leader.

Our purpose, and the overall goal of this book, avoids such a comprehensive overview. Instead, we have tried to go deep and to examine a wide array of writers and studies that start from the perspective that the role of leadership is to create positive environments in which human beings can thrive. We are hardly alone in this endeavor and make no pretense at offering a novel theory. Instead, our contribution is to synthesize what we know about positive leadership, which has meant ranging broadly into scholarship associated with a wide array of modern settings, including both private and public sectors. However, we have made our choices among the many studies that we examined by using the filter of their potential for invigorating educational institutions.

To do this thoroughly we had to start with the basics, which is the purpose of Part I of the book. Here we begin by examining what we mean by positive leadership (Chapter 1), make explicit the value base of positive leadership (Chapter 2), and identify the characteristics of positive leadership that are consistent across multiple theories (Chapter 3). Only by clearly laying this foundation were we able to begin to understand some of the behaviors that contribute to the "magic" of positive leadership that we explore in Part II and the known outcomes of positive leadership (Part III).

CHAPTER 1

The Model of Positive School Leadership

Economic hardships and unrelenting changes in today's environment are disrupting organizational dynamics, creating increases in employee anxiety, declines in loyalty, and mistrust of management in far too many work settings. This comes at a time when leadership in our new century is already challenged, perhaps as never before, by forces of globalization, political and social unrest, rapid technological advances, and societal dismay over sensational examples of gross corporate misconduct.
(W. L. Gardner & Schermerhorn, 2004, p. 220)

A new challenge for leaders is to help each other and their employees to grow, develop, and build on their core strengths, competencies, and virtues. (Quick & Quick, 2004, p. 331)

BUILDING OUR THEORY

School leadership is, above all, a moral and ethical task: The lives of children and their families draw us to the work and sustain us when there are excruciating challenges. The purpose of this book is to develop a root construct of Positive School Leadership (PSL). We are proposing a functional and substantive theory of leadership that uncovers core factors and conditions that support the work of scholars who care about what happens to both adults and children, and of the educational leaders we have known who get up every day and work to sustain positive settings. We draw from the existing array of positively grounded models of organizational management that assume that leading organizations well is invariably a value-based calling.[1] Rather than inventing a new ethical framework for school leadership, we identify a logical network of constructs from both educational and other organizational research that characterize Positive Leadership, and relate them to what is known about their causes and consequences (Cooper et al., 2005). We employ qualitative and narrative analysis of existing research in education and other sectors in the quest to identify underlying propositions and to construct a theory that appears "true and real" and that can be subjected to empirical testing in today's schools, which are navigating uncertain and volatile circumstances.

Where We Stand in the Theoretical Thicket

We began with respectful awareness (1) that "leadership research and theory have been criticized as being too segmented" and (2) that previous efforts at greater integration among different approaches have not been fully successful (Owens & Hekman, 2012, p. 806; also see Eisenbeiss, 2012). We also are committed to a theory that provides information about the mechanisms through which leader behavior influences group member behavior, and thus has practical potential (Liden, Wayne, Zhao, & Henderson, 2008). In other words, our purpose focuses on *usable* theory that sustains Positive Leadership that is sensitive to educational settings as a very special workplace context.

In taking up those implicit charges, in full recognition of the magnitude of the task, we do not cry, "behold, I am doing a new thing," or that we are "making a way in the wilderness" (Isaiah 43:19). Rather, we stand on the work of others who have gone before. Our theory pulls essential ideas from other models and weaves them into a macro-level understanding of leadership for leaders in general and for school administrators specifically.

While some new elements appear in our analysis of Positive School Leadership, our review is primarily integrative and synthetic, focusing on the principles and logic that will connect the elements to better outcomes both for individual members and for the achievement of organizational goals. Our methods for determining the "big chunks" drew on reading through different sets of literature and engaging in the "open-coding" principles laid out in Strauss and Corbin's *Basics of Qualitative Research* (1998). During this journey, we were led far from our origins as educational leadership and organizational scholars, and came to rely heavily on Huberman and Miles's (2002) recommendation to look not just at familiar data or congruent findings but also at the plausibility and coherence of the arguments as a basis for theorizing.[2] As we theorized, we kept in mind that in the social sciences a theoretical model must do more than identify the "big chunks," or units of interest. We sought to mine the existing literature to look for congruence in relationships among units and to consider the conditions under which these relationships would hold or become challenging—in other words, the durability of the elements and their relationship over time and context.

Defining Leadership

We start with our borrowed definition of the concept of leadership, that is: "Organizational leaders are individuals who influence the behaviour, thoughts and feelings of a significant number of other people either by word or example" (Forster et al., 1999, p. 11). Obviously, this definition includes those who are in formal positions of authority, but also describes those who have influence because of their expertise, personal attractiveness, or access to critical information (French & Raven, 1959).

Any effort to define leadership is a humbling task. Although our hopes for developing an empirically driven but theoretically justifiable theory of positive leadership continue to drive us, we are sensitive to the complexities of large organized settings. These include our inability to capture "the full set of underlying dimensions" (Cooper et al., 2005, pp. 478–479) implied by all of the different ways in which people demonstrate formal and informal leadership. Even more elusive is the goal of fully reflecting the various levels of leadership, which can occur between individuals, within small groups, in work units, and in the organization as a whole (G. Chen, Kirkman, Kanfer, Allen, & Rosen, 2007; Liden et al., 2008). In addition, it is critical to acknowledge the relatively weak empirical basis for determining which organizational structures or individual behaviors may enhance positivity or other outcomes (Walumbwa, Hartnell, & Oke, 2010).

Since our readers will, undoubtedly, have the same response—that we have set an impossible task—we will, later in this chapter, offer our initial visual roadmap through the thicket, which will be the basis for organizing the remainder of this book. Later chapters address the questions of "how" and "what" and the answers to those queries, or which behaviors may affect followers. The "why" of the leadership narrative unfolds as follows: (1) We begin with an explanation of problems with current understandings of school leadership, (2) move to the forces that are shifting that understanding, and (3) close with the emerging version of a more enriched understanding, that is, Positive School Leadership.

Toward a Theory of Positive School Leadership

First, however, we say a few additional words about the theory development process. Because our focus was not on a meta-analysis of empirical work but on generating a framework from what was already available and in use by scholars and practitioners, our general approach was influenced more by grounded theory methods (Corbin & Strauss, 1990; Glaser & Strauss, 1967) than by models for narrow literature reviews. We used four specific grounded theory processes for searching, coding, and analysis. First, we began our search with the foundation of Positive Psychology and networked into the broader organizational and leadership literature by following the paths of citations. This approach is similar to that of an ethnographer who observes, interviews, and locates additional sites for data collection based on what he or she has seen/heard. This process led us to a wide variety of existing labels for leadership theory that ranged from Appreciative Leadership to Virtuous Leadership (see the Appendix in this chapter for the list of terms used for searching). Second, in perusing the articles and books, we engaged in an *open-coding process*, breaking down the "data" by labeling key illustrative passages in articles that came to our attention as generating insights and concepts. This allowed us to see commonalities and distinctive characteristics across different authors and theories. Third, a*xial coding* was used to create categories and subcategories from the concepts generated. We then returned to the literature to determine whether axial codes were unique to an article or a study, or appeared (with similar or different labels) in other published work. Finally, as saturation was reached, *selective searching and coding* was used to eliminate those themes that were not representative and to deepen our evidentiary base to support the framework that emerged.

Grounded theory expects that the interviewer will interpret meaning in the data and reflect that back to the participant for confirmation or correction (Kvale, 2008). We saw ourselves as the primary participants in the theory generation process and frequently argued with each other about the relevance and utility of each emergent element of the model. While this process was not always pleasant, it required each of us to "own" all elements. We repeated this process in writing the book, which required us to have a "single voice" although we have different approaches to creating a manuscript. We determined that Joseph Murphy would write the first draft and Karen Seashore Louis would be the argumentative colleague who would have the last word and reshape the work and the evidentiary base to reflect her perspectives. In the end, this was an interesting and, for both of us, unique collaborative process.

While the norm in the leadership literature is to set about proving that one's model is distinctive and adds knowledge not found elsewhere (Liden et al., 2008), we were interested in pulling the best from existing models, whether Transformational Leadership, Distributed Leadership, Authentic Leadership, Servant Leadership, or Ethical Leadership. Many of the above have found their way into research and writing about school leadership, but occasionally have drawn a response that leadership theory is accumulating via adjectives.

Our early forays into our work, including preliminary coding, suggested that although the idea of Positive Leadership has established a solid beachhead in organizational literature (e.g., Avolio & Gardner, 2005; Cameron, 2012; Fredrickson, 2001, 2003; Luthans & Youssef, 2007), it has not made its way into the literature on schools and educational leadership in any purposeful and systematic way. Many articles cite the need for "positive school leadership" but do not define what that means in any detail. The idea has much to offer to schools and is clearly appealing, but required development. Indeed, as we report in later chapters, elements of positive leadership examined in educational research are found to have beneficial effects on several critical variables that mediate the relationship between leadership and school outcomes, including self-esteem and motivation in children, and student engagement and student learning outcomes. They have been associated with growth in teacher professional knowledge and social capital. These, in turn, favorably affect the health of the classroom climate and student outcomes. But defining Positive *School* Leadership and how it functions remains an elusive and largely unarticulated task.

As we began coding, another important observation was that scholars who use other labels—Transformational Leadership and Servant Leadership, for example—make frequent reference to the positive orientations and behaviors associated with them. In other words, we saw overlap and the need to incorporate well-known models rather than discarding or replacing them as we searched for a model of Positive School Leadership. Thus, we quickly expanded our search to look for threads from all understandings of leadership that could be woven into a web of positive school leadership.

We draw material from a far-ranging review of perspectives on leadership that highlight positive virtues and values and related leadership behavior. We heed the guidance from others who also have made this effort (Chemers, 1997; Dent et al., 2005) and proceed to develop an integrated theory of leadership that is normative in design (Cooper et al., 2005). In addition, we do not aspire to "colonize" all of the alternative leadership theories, but to enrich our collective consideration of what it means to be a person of influence in schools. This means that while our aim is to put into play the full body of the elements that constitute Positive School Leadership, we also believe that other models of leadership would be advantaged by adding some of the threads from the web of Positive School Leadership to their own perspectives. Second, as will become abundantly clear as we develop our storyline below, the orientations and principles of Positive School Leadership do not fit neatly into boxes. There is overlap among them.

Why This Task at This Time?

There is a sense that we "live in an era of massive institutional failure" (Greenleaf, 1997, p. 343), and that society is plagued by a "seemingly endless parade of ethical lapses" (Avey, Palanski, & Walumbwa, 2011, p. 573)—"ethical moral meltdowns and inauthentic leadership" (p. 573), a "growing lack of confidence in ethical corporate practices" (Hood, 2003, p. 263), and ethics scandals in government, academic, and nonprofit sectors (Xu, Yu, & Shi, 2011). While there is an espousal of "love, harmony, unity, compassion, peace, truth, honesty, understanding, and tolerance in the workplace" (Dent et al., 2005, p. 642), closer examinations often find "greed, cynicism, impatience, self-doubt, envy, and moral decline" (p. 642). The end game, analysts hold, is that the recent upswing in corporate scandals and management malfeasance indicates that a new perspective on leadership is necessary (Dent et al., 2005).

Continuing with the critique, scholars and practitioners alike underscore the seemingly pervasive meltdown of organizations engaged in unscrupulous, unhealthy, and unethical activities (Xu et al., 2011). Their gaze turns toward the questionable to outright illegal activities pursued by some during an era of "corporate scandals" (Lennick & Kiel, 2007, p. 9)—which unfortunately have parallels in the public sector. There is also explicit argumentation about the expanding need for organizational change (Greenleaf, 2002; Harland, Harrison, Jones, & Reiter-Palmon, 2005; S. M. Wilson & Ferch, 2005). Scholars have concluded that organizations are overly concerned with "technical rationality" (Noblit, Rogers, & McCadden, 1995, p. 684; see also Gittell, 2008; Grimshaw, 1986). Consequently, we have limited knowledge about how Positive School Leadership might play out in organizations like schools. As Owens and Hekman (2012) note, "It is simply not known what humble leadership looks like in terms of an overall leadership posture and way of being, what behaviors it involves, what personal and situational factors determine the effectiveness of these behaviors, or how these behaviors might influence important work processes and outcomes" (p. 787). They argue that "since the time of the industrial revolution, managers have tended to view people as objects; institutions have considered workers as cogs within a machine" (Spears, 1998, p. 2), and that the "machine" image of organizations has prevailed (Burnier, 2003; Madden, Duchon, Madden, & Plowman, 2012) even as alternative images have been increasingly available (Bolman & Deal, 1991; Morgan, 1986).[3]

The nearly uniform machine or factory image of schools has become even more embedded in recent years, not only in the United States but in most other countries. Schools today "present accountability models driven by hierarchy and heavy emphasis on rules and regulations that tend not to foster collective values around student and teacher learning" (Neal, 1999, p. 34). Tension is apparent between individual versus collective good (Arjoon, 2000), with organizations, we are told, tilting in the direction of benefiting individuals (Mackay, 2001). While actual policies governing accountability vary enormously between countries, the language of neoliberalism, which views schools as simple organisms that are designed to produce higher tested achievement, is universal (Louis & van Velzen, 2012).

But it feels as if change is coming. Notable public intellectuals, such as Diane Ravitch (2011), have publicly renounced their previous endorsement of the simple machine model of accountability. Scholars have begun to link "soft" development, including both psychological states and social capital, to the health of both individuals and organizations, among both adults (Goleman, 1998; Nahapiet & Ghoshal, 1998) and children (Masten & Coatsworth, 1998). Researchers show us that in education, an appreciation of positive leadership is growing due to (1) the awakening of positive organizational behavior in general and in schools, and (2) a growing acknowledgment that many current models of leadership are inadequate. In other words, there is a palpable need for something better (Fineman, 2006; W. L. Gardner et al., 2005; Harland et al., 2005; Hoy & Tarter, 2011; Luthans, 2002b). Further, there is an initial base of empirical work that suggests that positive organizational behavior "works" as a valid theory and is a productive pathway to valued outcomes, such as commitment and performance (Cerit, 2009; Liden et al., 2008; J. H. Wu, Hoy, & Tarter, 2013). Finally, policies are slowly catching up, with encouragement in the recent Every Student Succeeds Act in the United States[4] as well as similar policy discussions in other countries.

At the same time, there is increasing attention to the potential for organizations to nurture their members as well as to gain from their members' labor. Analysts suggest that the time is ripe "to articulate organizations as reflections of our own best selves—as communities where compassion, support, and positive energy are expected, natural, and normal" (Madden et al., 2012, p. 704). We are advised to "develop effective moral communities, or . . . be doomed to increasing fragmentation" (Chaskin & Rauner, 1995, p. 718). According to Bakker and Schaufeli (2008), our objective is not the "prevailing four D's approach (damage, disease, disorder, and dysfunction) that focuses on preventing poor performance, low motivation, unwell-being, ill-health, and disengagement. Something more is needed—a radical shift, away from the four D's, and this is where *positive organizational behavior* (POB) comes in" (p. 148).

Our interest in Positive School Leadership also develops from the need for greater organizational transparency (W. L. Gardner et al., 2005) and for new organizational forms and dynamics—and because there has been a growing integration of life's private and public domains (Mackay, 2001). Thus, the objective need for positive school organizations is to secure not the appropriate work–life balance but rather their healthy integration. And, of course, Positive Leadership theories and applications grow, as Luthans (2002b) maintains, because of pushback against our penchant for formulating and answering research perspectives in the negative (Mackay, 2001; S. M. Wilson & Ferch, 2005).

> We have focused so much on what's wrong with organizations that we have forgotten how many organizations do not violate ethical standards, whose leaders do care about their communities, and who are consistently trying to do what's right. (May, Chan, Hodges, & Avolio, 2003, p. 248)

Positive School Leadership develops from Positive Organizational Behavior (POB) and Positive Organizational Scholarship (POS), resulting in organizational forms quite different from the norm (Harter, Schmidt, & Hayes, 2002), the topic to which we now turn.

THE MODEL OF POSITIVE SCHOOL LEADERSHIP: AN OVERVIEW

So far, we have discussed the desire to transcend existing institutional models of schooling. We also have argued that forces are arising to create new perspectives. We close here with an advance organizer, "the knowledge that existing frameworks are not sufficient for developing leaders in the future" (Cooper et al., 2005, p. 476) and a snapshot of that future, which we report on in detail in later chapters. According to Liedtka (1996), times have changed and markets have begun to factor in the impacts of positive psychology: A language of care and relationship building has appeared recently with prominence in the business literature, driven by the realities of the marketplace. The push, as Frederickson (2001, 2003) reminds us, is toward a "focus on a wide range of positive behaviors of engaged employees in flourishing organizations" (Bakker & Schaufeli, 2008, p. 148). At the center of the equation are enhanced self-efficacy and organizational performance (Fry, 2003; S. J. Peterson, Galvin, & Lange, 2012; Walumbwa, Avolio, Gardner, Wernsing, & Peterson, 2008; Youssef & Luthans, 2007).

The model of Positive School Leadership that forms the skeleton for the book is visible in Figures 1.1 and 1.2, which we have separated for representational purposes but should be viewed as a whole.

Figure 1.1, which we have labeled Foundations, begins with the characteristics of the person(s) who enacts leadership. It carries us from a focus on the leader's values, virtues, and principles through interactions between "leaders" (who exercise initial influence) and "followers" (who react to and engage with influence). What this figure suggests is the centrality of the development and deepening of interpersonal *trust*. It also shows that *context* continually shapes how action unfolds. While the energy in the model is depicted as flowing from left to right, it is important to note that the model is recursive, with energy flowing often in both directions and feeding back to change elements that initially preceded it.

The earliest piece in the model, *antecedents*, attends to the factors that a leader brings to the process of influencing others. In this section, we concentrate on elements such as personality traits, moral identity, psychological resources and capacities, and cognitive dispositions and capacities. As Judge, Piccolo, and Kosalka (2009) point out, "the leader trait perspective has had a long intellectual tradition, with decades of great prominence in the literature followed by years of skepticism and disinterest," but there is also compelling research to suggest that it should not be ignored (p. 871). We argue that those aspects of individuals have a good deal to say about the viability of positively anchored leadership in schools. Next, we explore the *relational virtues and values* that leaders bring to their work, a topic that is as old as leadership theory itself but that increasingly is addressed by empirical work that considers the moral side of organizations. From there, we unpack the types of *leader behaviors* that foster PSL and elaborate on how they affect individual motivation and engagement.

The importance of cyclical feedback loops as a key feature in our model is even clearer in Figure 1.2, which begins to elaborate the group and

Figure 1.1. Positive School Leadership Model: The Foundations

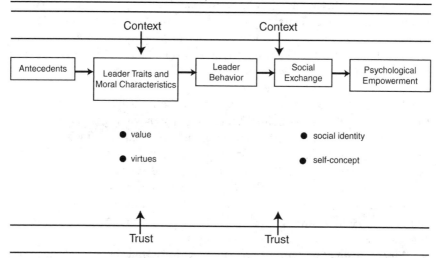

Figure 1.2. Positive Leadership Impacts on the Organization

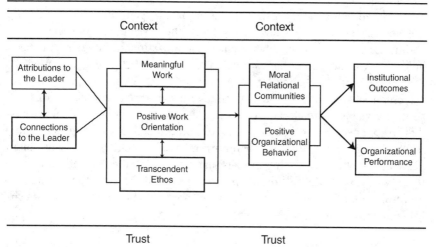

organizational impacts that emerge in Figure 1.1. This means that later variables in the model (such as organizational performance) shape earlier constructs (such as positive work orientation). We begin with the group perceptions of leaders, which form the basis for the development of the "character armor" that reflects the resilience of the school's members. We then move to the interactive core of school settings, the caldron in which leadership resides, which involves crafting relationships at many levels. At the individual level, we link the figures by explaining how Positive School Leadership enhances individual teachers' self-concepts and their integration into school-based communities, and we look at evidence about how leadership shapes positive school cultures that focus on long-term asset building as well as proximate productivity. It is in this interactive phase that we see the essence of leadership in play, because "who is the leader" is often a moving target. Thus, we need to consider how subordinate–leader relationships enhance or diminish trust in school administrators, as well as teachers' attributions of impacts to leaders and their connections to those leaders.

In the middle parts of the model, we direct our analytic spotlight toward the ways in which Positive School Leadership works. We will argue, for example, that there is evidence that Positive School Leadership is defined by its ability to create meaningful work, a transcendent work ethic, and moral relational communities. This is often the work not of a singular "leader" but of multiple synergistic leadership roles within a school. Such efforts, we see, produce an increase in positive work orientation in schools and the display of organizational citizenship behaviors, that is, positive actions that lie outside of formal role requirements.

Finally, at the far-right side of our model, we find the critical outcomes of Positive School Leadership. We begin at the individual level where we see an increase in psychological capital (e.g., sense of worth), human capital (e.g., sense of well-being), and organizational rewards (organizational recognition). We look also at a collective level, considering the development of social capital within the organization and between the organization and its relevant stakeholders. We close with organizational performance (e.g., goal achievement).

Throughout the model, we attend to contextual issues, the deepening development of trust, and reciprocity among the constructs. These two trust and context variables "stretch" across our model in the sense that they cannot easily be separated from what we know (or could imagine knowing) about any "chunk" that we have laid out—and are referred to (either in passing or in depth) in all of the leadership models that are listed in the Appendix. Because these two ideas are tightly bound up in our narrative, we wish to elaborate how we think about them, as we move into a narrative that is focused more specifically on leaders and leader–follower relationships.

Trust

We think of trust as both an input and an outcome variable that is in a continuous, dynamic relationship with all of the other elements of the Positive School Leadership framework. In other words, trust *mediates*, forming a firm connecting link with all other elements. Trust holds together positive, asset-focused organizations (Bryk & Schneider, 2002; Russell, 2001). Moreover, trust in leaders is viewed by many authors as a precondition for personal engagement: "If subordinates are to willingly change their attitudes, values, assumptions and commitments to bring them more closely in line with those of the organization, they must have trust in the integrity and credibility of their leader" (Simons, 1999, p. 90). Because trust in leadership becomes a "glue" binding members to the organization, it is also a precursor to both individual and group performance both in the private sector and in schools (Louis, 2007; Palanski & Yammarino, 2011; Tschannen-Moran & Gareis, 2015; Van Maele & Van Houtte, 2015).

Trust cuts across and through our entire model. It is both an antecedent and outcome step in the logic chain of Positive School Leadership. For example, trust is the major outcome of the leader–member exchange process involving the leader and those he or she supervises (Brower, Schoorman, & Tan, 2000). Trust serves in a mediating role allowing organizational action (an exchange between two people) to become a realized opportunity for engaged work, particularly where leaders and members are in close contact (Howell & Hall-Merenda, 1999). Organizational actions, such as the exchanges that bring mission to life, then reinforce and deepen trust between the supervisor and the worker. Trust cycles throughout the model, as shown in Figure 1.2, and appears as an outcome in one area before becoming the antecedent for the next link in the model (Dirks & Ferrin, 2002).

Definitions of trust ribbon through organizational science research articles. What is key to these definitions are their embedded concepts. For example, Palanski and Yammarino (2011, p. 721) tell us that the linchpin of trust is the "willingness to be vulnerable to another." Another highly related concept is the willingness to take risks, the willingness to trust that a leader "will behave in a way that is beneficial to the person" (Zhu, May, & Avolio, 2004, p. 19), and the belief that the leader "is (a) competent, (b) open, (c) concerned, and (d) reliable" (Simons, 1999, p. 93). Simons goes on to explain that the three factors of ability, benevolence, and integrity explain much of trustworthiness; that is, they are, depending on how one conceptualizes, necessary elements and/or antecedents of trust. If one element stands out in the research, it would be "behavioral integrity," "the perception of fit between words and actions, and the sense that the person's words can be relied on" (p. 95).

Trust enhances reflexivity by affecting "underlying processes: reflection and action" (De Jong & Elfring, 2010, p. 538). The Positive School Leadership chain then links to the empowerment of employees and enhances bonds between leaders and followers, both as individuals and as member of teams, which can ratchet up effort, cooperation and collaborations, and self-direction, leading to enhanced organizational performance (De Cremer & Knippenberg, 2005; De Jong & Elfring, 2010; Russell, 2001).

Context

Organizational and leadership theory have long recognized that a leader who is highly successful in one setting may fail in another. The person and the behaviors that "worked" in one place do not necessarily produce the same results in another setting. In other words, context matters. While embedded in the thinking of both leadership and organizational theorists, it demands further development. Cooper et al. (2005) argue that "it is important to remember that authentic and ethical behavior may be highly context-dependent" (p. 488), which corresponds to Griffin, Neal, and Parker's (2007) observation that "the nature of work roles cannot be divorced from the contexts in which they are enacted" (p. 328).

Unlike trust, context is not usually an outcome of leadership, nor is it always a cause of particular leadership behaviors. Rather, it is always there and is something to which leaders need to adjust. In other words, we, like the authors quoted above, consider context as a continuous moderator or boundary condition for leadership attributes and behaviors. Analysts routinely convey the importance of boundary conditions (or moderating variables) in processes designed to produce valued organizational outcomes (Cooper et al., 2005; Eisenbeiss, 2012; Park & Peterson, 2003) and typically define them as *conditions that help to account for inconsistent results*. They also proffer a variety of strategic lenses through which to examine context as a boundary condition.

This leads us, in some cases, to examine the intersection between personal and organizational conditions (Avey et al., 2011; Dirks & Ferrin, 2002), which can focus on the ways in which age, gender, race, or personality characteristics systematically interact with the setting. Thus, for example, in schools where teachers come from very different backgrounds, they may be more likely to form disconnected "tribes" than in schools where they are similar; Logan and Fischer-Wright (2006) evocatively refer to this phenomenon as based in collective "character armor." G. Chen et al. (2007) complicate this already-complex description by noting that group characteristics are also important: "Team interdependence is a critical boundary condition affecting the validity of theories and models" (p. 343). In addition, culture at all levels—national, industry, organization, unit, and team—make generalizations difficult (Cooper et al., 2005; Palanski & Yammarino, 2011), while organizational size and organizational type play a role across our model as well (Youssef & Luthans, 2007).

We could go on, but the takeaway message is clear: Context always matters. Moreover, context is so complex that we cannot realistically develop "laws" of Positive School Leadership that will be invariant between settings. There will always be exceptions based on situations or particular conditions. This limitation does not mean, however, that we should not search for important and general relationships that seem to hold across many different settings.

MOVING FORWARD

We have organized the remainder of this book around the elements of this model. Part I elaborates the elements of Figure 1.1, namely, the individual-level foundations, while Parts II and III focus on groups and organization-wide elements. Some chapters cover only one segment of the model, while others, particularly in Part II, cover more than one, demonstrating our understanding of the feedback loops among elements in more complex settings. In many cases, we rely primarily on research carried out in non-school settings, which requires us to draw on our extensive experience in schools and with school leaders at various levels to create the logical connections to educational settings. We end with reflections on the implications of our synthesized model of Positive School Leadership for the role of school leadership in shaping the development and lifelong learning of the many educators who seek to influence and improve schools from whatever formal position they occupy.

APPENDIX: LEADERSHIP MODELS
EMERGING FROM INITIAL SEARCH PROCESSES

Appreciative	Democratic	Principle-Centered	Team-Based
Altruistic	Developmental		Transcendental
		Relational	
Artful	Distributed		Transformational
		Self-Sacrificial	
Authentic	Ethical		Trustworthy
		Service-Focused	
Caring	Humble		Value-Based
		Socially Responsible	
Complex	Inspirational		Virtuous
Connoisseur	Integral	Spiritual	Worthy
Constructionist	Moral	Steward	
Creative	Participative	Strength-Based	

NOTES

1. See Cooper, Scandura, & Schriesheim, 2005, p. 480, and Dent, Higgins, & Wharff, 2005, p. 628, for similar calls for clarity about moral and ethical leadership frameworks, along with Starrett (1991) and Shapiro & Stefkovich (1997) for educational examples.

2. In this effort, we were influenced by the work of Fry (2003) and Dent et al. (2005) in striving to create a theory of spiritual leadership—a previously amorphous topic.

3. Note that both Morgan's and Bolman and Deal's books have been through subsequent editions. We cite the first edition of these bestselling books to demonstrate how difficult it has been to "change the conversation."

4. "This bipartisan measure reauthorizes the 50-year-old Elementary and Secondary Education Act (ESEA), the nation's national education law and longstanding commitment to equal opportunity for all students" (www.ed.gov.essa).

CHAPTER 2

Dimensions of Positive School Leadership

> Moral life rests upon foundations of individual virtue—and the individually virtuous person transforms others as well as the social environment. (B. M. Bass & Steidlmeier, 1999, p. 194)

> The communitarian paradigm . . . characterize[s] the good society as one that nourishes both social virtues and individual rights. (Etzioni, 1998, p. 4)

In today's "postmodern" and multicultural world, it sometimes seems old-fashioned to talk about morals and virtues. We may have mixed feelings because the words themselves cause a default to images of social and individual repression in the name of authoritative, religiously tinged political environments. Yet, when they are not part of the map and expectations of our social life together, we are faced, individually and collectively, with the sinking feeling that we are not safe. We question whether people who are motivated only by self-interest are putting us in harm's way. This chapter does not aspire to sort out all of the underlying philosophical and political debates about morals and virtues in leaders, which have been a subject of deep analysis from Plato to James McGregor Burns (1978). Instead, we limit our focus to what we know from organizational scholarship about virtues and morals as characteristics of leaders in contemporary organizations.

We raise the issue of values because schooling is fundamentally a process of moral as well as intellectual development. The goal of developing moral and virtuous adults has been articulated as an outcome for formal and informal education for centuries, as long as there have been schools. The ancient Greeks taught skills (reading, arithmetic) at home, while the contemplation of virtues was the purview of formal education. Howard Gardner (2012), who is closely associated with the idea of multiple intelligences, has written passionately about the role of educators in supporting students' understanding of "truth, beauty and goodness," while Darcia Narvaez (2008), one of the foremost empirical scholars of moral development in school settings, argues that "caring communities with high expectations and involved adults are more likely to raise morally engaged citizens" (p. 321). Narvaez goes on to argue for a focus on maintaining goodness and caring as part of a developmentally appropriate curriculum, a call that is evident in policy initiatives that support social and emotional learning. In summary, even when it feels uncomfortable to consider how we become moral leaders, we cannot ignore the role of schools, along with families and other social institutions, in ensuring the healthy development of student capacities to make wise choices using an ethical framework.

We assert that PSL's core dimensions define a foundation for Positive School Leadership. We argue here that understanding leader behaviors and their impact requires examining what forms and sustains them—the orienting individual dimensions/elements/constructs that define the architecture of Positive School Leadership. We undertake this assignment in the four broad dimensions that emerged from the grounded literature search described in the previous chapter: positive orientation, moral orientation, relational orientation, and spiritual stewardship orientation.

POSITIVE ORIENTATION

> Positivism is a recent strand in organizational theorizing, focusing on understanding the "best" of the human condition. (Fineman, 2006, p. 270)

> Positive psychology is focused on optimal human functioning. (Avey, Hughes, Norman, & Luthans, 2008, p. 111)

At the top of the list, we see that "a leader is guided by a disciplined framework that rallies the . . . states of confidence, hope, optimism, and resilience to achieve [a] positive performance impact" (W. L. Gardner & Schermerhorn, 2004, p. 273). Such values have a significant influence on organizations in areas ranging from trust to the nature of decisions (Russell, 2001), and organizations with virtuous leaders are better positioned to become virtuous organizations, or places in which most people act responsibly and ethically most of the time (T. A. Wright & Goodstein, 2007).

We begin by pointing out that a problem-solving approach to leadership "is more negative than positive. Leadership theories have been more concerned with what is wrong with organizations, teams, leaders and employees than what is right with them" (Luthans, 2002a, p. 703). This comment strikes a chord in the hearts and minds of educators who, in many countries, work in an environment where public opinion assumes that schools are failing. In contrast, a positive construct is defined by an asset-anchored approach to school leadership (Burrello, Beitz, & Mann, 2016; Owens & Hekman, 2012), an "essential humanism aligned with humanistic psychologies and philosophies" (Fineman, 2006, p. 273). The "focus is on what is best in people" (B. M. Bass & Steidlmeier, 1999, p. 188).

If we view a teacher or student as the cause of difficulty, the solution often becomes his or her removal. Positive School Leadership starts not by looking for the individuals and groups that are to blame for disappointments but by considering whether there are broader causes that create an unacceptable outcome. This perspective goes beyond the absence of valued states (Sandage & Hill, 2001) to consider whether and how the environment can be rearranged to help the student become more engaged or to provide the teacher with opportunities to learn that are not punitive. A positive orientation does not preclude individual consequences, but they are not the default choice.

In place of negativity and deficiencies in schools, a positive orientation is about "facilitating the good life and structuring talents" (Sandage & Hill, 2001, p. 241), about human "strength, resilience, and virtue" (p. 251), about strength-based strategies (Burrello et al., 2016) and "optimal human function" (Avey et al., 2008, p. 112). Remember that these, like the other virtues described below, are orientations and not specific behaviors, but they are felt over time and are described by others as their effects accumulate.

Positive School Leadership also incorporates the concept of positive psychological capital, which combines hope, resilience, optimism, and efficacy, and ties this bundle to the capacity to mobilize others (Luthans, Luthans, & Luthans, 2004). More recent investigations of positive psychological capital suggest that it is a malleable personal characteristic that can be developed rather than a fundamental personality characteristic (Avey et al., 2008; Luthans, Avey, & Patera, 2008). Whether scholars like the positive psychological capital bundle or prefer to focus on the separate elements, like hope (S. J. Peterson & Byron, 2008), is irrelevant to our main argument, which is that worthy leadership requires fusing "positive assumptions about human nature with moral rectitude" (Fineman, 2006, p. 272), the topic to which we now turn.

POSITIVE ORIENTATION: Asset-Based

MORAL ORIENTATION

Being a moral leader is more a creative art than science. Its hallmark is existential practice, where one engenders virtue in self, others and society through example and virtuous conduct. (B. M. Bass & Steidlmeier, 1999, p. 196)

School leadership is, by its nature and force a moral activity. (Greenfield, 2004, p. 174)

We focus in this section on the moral imagination of leaders, which we define as an ingrained reflex embedded in the ongoing consideration of what is right and wrong in one's relationships with others.[1] While philosophers (and dictionaries) may argue about definitions, we use the term *values* as synonymous with moral orientations. Both reflect broad and often-abstract core preferences for specific courses of action and provide "an internal reference for what is good, beneficial, important, useful, beautiful, desirable and constructive" (Wikipedia; see also Russell, 2001).

Values are normative and, at least in theory, emerge in adulthood as the enduring basis for organizing our lives (Russell, 2001, p. 81). They are tested and refined in personal relationships (Hood, 2003) as we mature. Schwartz (as cited in Lord & Brown, 2001) defines values as "desirable states, objects, goals, or behaviors transcending specific situations and applied as normative standards to judge and to choose among alternative modes of behavior" (p. 138). Positive school leaders are "first and foremost concerned with values and beliefs that provide humans with a moral compass regarding decisions about life and professional practice" (English & Ehrich, 2016, p. 1).

If the term *moral* makes contemporary educational leaders a bit nervous, the idea of "spiritual values" induces acute anxiety. In the United States, the association of that term with schools and school leadership eroded in the late 1950s as the legal demand to eliminate Christian references from U.S. public schools increased.[2] Beginning in the 1990s, however, the ideal of schools as places where nonsectarian/nonreligious spiritual values could develop began to emerge, with the argument that increasingly diverse schools were obligated to allow both students and adults to discuss issues that formed the basis for a more actionable set of values. While "values clarification" or "character education" programs in schools were sometimes superficial, poorly implemented, and controversial, there is evidence that they are important because they link individual choices to more inspiring values (Berkowitz & Bier, 2007).

Among the values that are believed to be *fundamentally human and transcendent* are goodness, truth, and beauty. We choose to use the term *spiritual values* in this book because it points to the importance of looking deeply, both inside oneself and in others. In an increasingly secular society, there is already a general awareness of the distinction between spiritual values and religious values, which tend to be more detailed, creedal, and narrow. Consistent with a theme woven through the dimensions of Positive School Leadership, spiritual values often occupy the moral high ground (Reave, 2005) and are contrasted with material values.

Moral orientations, as broadly and ambiguously defined above, have considerable influence over what happens in schools because, as Russell (2001) notes, they provide a basis for behavior and for others' perceptions of behavior. Positive formal and informal leaders are expected to "take ownership of, and therefore responsibility for, the end results of their moral actions and the actions of their followers" (Hannah, Lester, & Vogelgesang, 2005, p. 47). The obverse is also true: Followers observe the leader's behavior and import the perceived moral orientation into their view of the leader. One recent study, for example, showed that leaders' moral orientation toward an ethic of justice was associated with followers' perception of them as transactional leaders, while those whose moral orientation was based on an ethic of care were viewed as transformational (Simola, Barling, & Turner, 2010).

To be clear: For Positive School Leadership to be authentic, "it must incorporate a central core of moral values" (Cardona, 2000, p. 201) and a "moral foundation" (p. 206), but that foundation must match the needs of the organization and the needs of followers for a deeper set of values (which we have called spiritual values). Only when the underlying values are morally uplifting and part of relationships, can one claim that Positive School Leadership is ignited (B. M. Bass & Steidlmeier, 1999). Positive school leaders are "men and women who are true to him/herself, a person who is confident, hopeful, optimistic, transparent, resilient, and ethical" (Fineman, 2006, p. 273), someone whose "normative commitment to values transcends organizational imperatives" (Adler, Kwon, & Heckscher, 2008, p. 369). These are people who nurture their moral orientation in the cauldron of relationships. In a complex world, they assume that a robust moral orientation requires lifelong reflection, whether one is a school leader or a political activist (Tronto, 1994).

How do some leaders nurture a moral imagination? We have hints throughout the research that link a positive orientation with a moral orientation. B. M. Bass and Steidlmeier (1999) remind us that positive leaders "focus on the best in others—on harmony, charity, and good works," while others often "focus on the worst in others—on demonic plots, conspiracy, unreal dangers, and insecurities" (p. 188). Virtue-based leadership helps us see that positively anchored schools can be "a source for spiritual survival and must motivate [teachers] intrinsically through vision, hope, faith, and altruistic love" (Fry, 2003, p. 712), forgiveness (Thompson, Grahek, Phillips, & Fay, 2008), compassion and virtue (Luthans, 2002a), and justice and gratitude (Eisenbeiss, 2012; Thompson et al., 2008).

A moral imagination demands transcendence, which can be defined by four elements: a focus on the needs of others, altruism, a sense of calling, and humility. On one front, it shines the light on those who can lead beyond self-interests for the common good (Cardona, 2000; Harland et al., 2005). That is, leaders here "demonstrate a concern for followers' needs rather than their own self interest" (Conger, Kanungo, & Menon, 2000, p. 750). Eisenbeiss (2012) deepens this narrative when reporting that positive leadership "refer[s] to different aspects of human orientation by stressing the importance of leader altruism [and] leader respect for the rights and dignity of others" (p.

796), conditions that "are only possible through civic virtue" (B. M. Bass & Steidlmeier, 1999, p. 200). That leads, in and through one's work, to a pursuit of the right and the fair (Fry, 2003).

This requires forging a morally compelling vision (R. E. Quinn, Spreitzer, & Brown, 2000), a "transcendent vision of fulfillment, justice, and peace based upon the right ordering of relationships—the 'better future'" (B. M. Bass & Steidlmeier, 1999, p. 195). This, in turn, requires blending individual interest into an expansive view of a "common good that transcends a mere aggregation of individual goods" (B. M. Bass & Steidlmeier, 1999, p. 200), a sense of the "centrality of the community principle in the organization and experience of professional work" (Adler et al., 2008, p. 361), or what Reave (2005) calls "a sense of transcendent meaning surpassing both the individual and the situation" (p. 679).

Central to transcendence is humility, or "the ability to keep one's accomplishments and talents in perspective . . . which means not being self-focused" (Dennis & Bocarnea, 2005, p. 602). Others who reflect further on the importance of humility and "the character ethic" (Russell, 2001, p 77) to transcendence emphasize many of the points we have made, such as "making the needs and interests of others primary" (Cooper et al., 2005, p. 489), "humanity, altruism, trust, service, and empowerment" (Dennis & Bocarnea, 2005, p. 600), and forgiveness (Thompson et al., 2008). Zeroing in, we argue that humility is the ability to keep one's accomplishments and talents in perspective while focusing on the transcendent.

Thus, positive school leaders hold that all collective and individual goals are attainable only through the practice of civic virtue, through "moral maturity on the part of leaders and the moral uplifting of followers" (B. M. Bass & Steidlmeier, 1999, p. 192) and "the process of searching out moral excellence" (p. 211). Educational scholars tell us directly that leading schools "is a moral art" (Greenfield, 2004, p. 183), and that positive school leaders are more likely than others "to apply moral principles and virtues to the situation to make sense of what action to take" (May et al., 2003, p. 254). Civic virtue is a "sense of calling" [that] implies an integrative nexus of morality and health embedded within a cultural and political context" (Sandage & Hill, 2001, p. 252).

Finally, there is the potential for a sense of spirituality based on an inner conviction that humankind belongs to, but is not master of, the universe—in other words, collective humility (G. W. Fairholm, 1996). Russell (2001) and B. M. Bass and Steidlmeier (1999) capture this as an openness to the limits of humanness and materiality. Indeed, there is a sense that "the greater the value congruence the more individuals will experience transcendence through their work, and the organization's culture will underscore the global shift to post materialistic values [that] tend to be more idealistic and spiritual" (Fry, 2003, p. 703).

MORAL ORIENTATION:
VALUE-BASED, VIRTUE-BASED, TRANSCENDENT, SPIRITUAL

RELATIONAL ORIENTATION

Relational leadership is the fundamental starting point for leadership to flourish. (Burrello et al., 2016, p. 64)

The work of the leader consists of influencing, through his or her values and behavior, the motivations of the collaborator in order that the latter will seek to form with the former the richest possible partnership, i.e., a contribution partnership. In other words, the work of the leader consists in the creation of high value-added partnerships with his or her collaborators. (Cardona, 2000, p. 204)

A number of overlapping elements are embedded in the relational dimension of Positive School Leadership, ideas such as relationally grounded action, care, leadership as attention to means as ends, leadership in the service of the growth and development of teachers, and authentic leadership. As Thompson and colleagues (2008) remind us, leadership can be understood only with reference to relationships. It is "followers who confer leadership" (G. W. Fairholm, 1996, p. 14). And it is leaders who, in turn, "build leadership organizational capacity on a foundational capital" (Burrello et al., 2016, p. 67). Relational leading in schools requires:

A focus on achievement but an equal and more enlightened focus on doing and being a positive person who keeps individuals at the forefront of their goals and beliefs. If you lead with a focus on serving others, following the moral imperative of equity and excellence for all students while striving to be a relational leader, then good things will ensue. (Burrello et al., 2016, p. 90)

We find two core ideas in the concept of positive, growth-based leadership, which focuses on the idea that people and organizations that are not unfolding and becoming may be in the process of decaying or even dying.[3] A Positive School Leader comes to decisions through a path that emphasizes the needs of others, particularly their needs for personal growth (May et al., 2003; B. Smith, Montagno, & Kuzmenko, 2004). Emphasizing growth is based not only on employee skill development, but on a commitment to "develop employees to their fullest potential" and to "demonstrating genuine concern for others' career growth and development by providing support and mentoring" (Liden et al., 2008, p. 162). Most critically, positive leaders "instill in followers the self-confidence and desire to become servant leaders themselves" (p.

162), thus promoting the creation of Positive School Leadership throughout the school.

These days, leaders are urged to become coaches and mentors—but coaching and mentoring typically are poorly defined. The image is often of a sports coach, whose job is to ensure that each member will contribute to a winning game. In that sense, the "coaching for performance" model is focused on growth of a very narrow and goal-focused kind. As they move beyond their own self-interest or the attainment of specific collective goals, positive school leaders are expected to emphasize the development of others that is "intentional and generative . . . that actively promotes learning, socialization and identity transformation" (Mullen, 2012, p. 7; see also B. M. Bass & Steidlmeier, 1999; Owens & Hekman, 2012). Thus, positive school leaders focus on "continuous learning [and] development" (G. W. Fairholm, 1996, p. 15), and on the "betterment of workers" (Driscoll & McKee, 2007, p. 210). This commonly is considered to be the work of a mentor rather than a coach, but most leaders will need to focus on both generative and skill development. Both, to be effective, must be based in meaningful relationships.

This perspective is particularly important in education, where is it is typical to hear that "it is all about the students and their academic success." This near-exclusive focus on ends limits attention to the means (or those teachers who provide the means) as valuable in their own right. Positive school leaders do not fall into that camp (Burrello et al., 2016), but hold that "employees have intrinsic value above and beyond their connection to organizational productivity" (Driscoll & McKee, 2007, p. 207).

Lest one think that this is "nice-but-not-essential," the evidence from occupational studies of quality of work life in all occupations, from bus driver to Supreme Court justice, indicates that opportunities to grow and learn are central to people's satisfaction with and engagement in their jobs (Wanous & Lawler, 1972). Studies of teachers, in particular, show that opportunities for professional growth not only vary between schools, but are among the most important predictors of satisfaction and commitment (Louis, 1998; V. Wu & Short, 1996).

Positive school leaders realize that to move their schools and districts, they need to change themselves first, and that "organizational change begins with personal change" (R. E. Quinn et al., 2000, p. 158). Leaders who promote growth and values but do not demonstrate that they too have "skin in the game" are assessed as disengaged and inauthentic. In contrast:

> Leaders who continually strive for personal growth also demonstrate self-awareness. This involves a commitment to developing a keen insight about one's own motives, behavior, and impact on others, and a willingness to continuously look for even small developmental opportunities and feedback. Self-awareness is not simply attending to what works throughout the day. It also incorporates learning from painful "crash and burn" experiences. (Thompson et al., 2008, p. 369)

While there is a need for authenticity and being "true to self" (Leroy, Palanski, & Simons, 2012, p. 262), there also must be a commitment to "go beyond self interests" (B. M. Bass & Steidlmeier, 1999, p. 207), to "operate from the common good" (R. E. Quinn et al., 2000, p. 154). Positive school leaders need to foster the development of group relationships that also reflect common interests, as well as "recognizing and celebrating the achievement of others" (Fry, 2003, p. 709).

RELATIONAL ORIENTATION:
CARE-BASED, GROWTH-BASED, AUTHENTIC

SPIRITUAL STEWARDSHIP ORIENTATION

Earlier we introduced the ideas of transcendence and spirituality, two concepts often considered beyond the purview of leadership. Here we deepen those lines of analysis, noting their essential place in the Positive School Leadership algorithm. Spirituality is not about religion, but it does imply "a relationship with something intangible beyond the self. It is a source guide for personal values and meaning, a way of understanding self and the world as a means of personal and group integration" (G. W. Fairholm, 1996, p. 12). As noted above, leadership becomes a calling rather than a position or a career, a calling based on transcendent values (Dent et al., 2005; Markow & Klenk, 2005; Reave, 2005). These and other studies also find that there is not a contradiction between values and practices endorsed for spiritual success and those required for leadership success.

Spirituality links transcendent values to all aspects of leadership work (Reave, 2005). The altruistic components of leadership mean that "in assisting subordinates to grow . . . leaders attend to the affective and emotional needs of subordinates" (Liden et al., 2008, p. 163). It is about helping others to ascertain "correct principles and the application of techniques that enable self-governance" (G. W. Fairholm, 1996, p. 13). The organizational principles of Positive School Leadership rest on self-reflection and helping to make others self-reflective (Reave, 2005). G. W. Fairholm (1996) provides a skeletal model of spirit-grounded leadership "that embodies those values and practices proven effective" (p. 13). Model characteristics include:

- a carefully designed philosophy or vision embedded in culture;
- a value of personal and other forms of development (growth) to become one's best self;
- a commitment to serving others;
- a sense of interactive, mutual trust;
- an authentic concern for people and organizational goals;
- an environment that encourages openness, fairness, individuality and creativity;

- commitment to group unity, teamwork, and sharing;
- integrity in all interpersonal relationships;
- simplicity and flexibility of structure and systems;
- a process that emphasizes continuing evaluation of progress. (p. 13)

When we apply these principles to schools, they presume a moral underpinning to all conversations about the development of adults and students, where the goal is to promote self-governance. Spiritually anchored leadership is woven into the values and virtues of "compassion, patient tolerance, forgiveness, contentment, and sense of responsibility" (Fry, 2003, p. 705), and are anchored in humility and altruism (B. M. Bass & Steidlmeier, 1999, p. 207).

We learn from these observations that a renewed interest in a spiritual orientation in leadership is deeply intertwined with a focus on the individual spiritual growth of every person in the organization:

> The leaders' focus is to make the person served more competent to meet their own needs and be better equipped to serve the organization and society in general. The focus is to help followers become more autonomous, not more reliant on the leader. (Black, 2010, pp. 439–440)

Through all of this, we come to understand "that as development occurs there is a transcending of worldviews and a shift to higher levels of internal locus of control and human growth is achieved through the interplay of individual, community, and environment (Dent et al., 2005, p. 626). In other words, spirituality is about empowerment (English & Ehrich, 2016; Fridell, Newcom Belcher, & Messner, 2009), emphasizing the increasing ability of others to make virtuous choices. B. M. Bass and Steidlmeier (1999) remind us that "empowerment is more than broadening the scope of participation by followers. It is motivational and enabling, highlighting a new realization and transformation of the person" (p. 182).

The focus of research also is leading to a rethinking of management in terms of service and stewardship (Black, 2010). Leaders work to create a "social reality driven by concern for others, not just themselves" (R. E. Quinn et al., 2000, p. 159). They follow a "people first" philosophy (Reave, 2005). They labor to transform schools "so that humane practices and policies become an integral part of day-to-day functioning" (Driscoll & McKee, 2007, p. 207). Their actions are measured against the standard of well-being for others (Burrello et al., 2016). Overall, then, they change themselves, their teachers, and the environment in which work unfolds, including the overarching school vision (B. Smith et al., 2004).

Quinn and colleagues (2000) note that stewardship requires adjustments "away from self-interested behavior in trying to bring about a new social reality [and] works to build an emergent community that can learn, adapt, and grow" (p. 150). A stewardship orientation means, as we have touched on above, "to treat others with dignity and respect and to see them as ends not means" (Eisenbeiss, 2012, p. 795). As Owens and Hekman (2012) remind us, spiritual leadership demands transparency, especially concerning leaders' personal development process as they experience "work as a spiritual calling" (Reave, 2005, p. 658). Thus, "the surest way for a servant leader to succeed is to put others first" (Black, 2010, p. 439), and Positive school leaders ensure that all "stakeholders are conscious of . . . communitarian obligations" (Duignan, 2005, p. 2).

SPIRITUAL STEWARDSHIP ORIENTATION:
SPIRITUALLY GROUNDED, SERVICE-ANCHORED

CONCLUSION

Of course, we all want our school leaders to be "good people"—to be honest, trustworthy, and "nice," as well as capable. But our examination of research (and syntheses of that work) leads us to a more pointed conclusion. As B. M. Bass and Steidlmeier (1999) note, a positive leadership perspective carries us "to Kant's categorical imperative—never to deal with another person simply as a means to an end in his or her own self" (p. 210). Thus, consistent with all the positively centered views of leadership virtues reviewed above, Positive school leaders are keenly interested in elevating and empowering others in order to create individual and group growth.

When we entered this review, we were stunned by the challenge of making sense of the many authors who use different words or phrases in making the argument for the need for a virtue-based approach to leadership. We have chosen to reveal the complexity of the arguments underlying a virtue-based foundation for Positive School Leadership and to extract what we conclude are the four virtue-based dimensions that bind the wisdom detailed by others: a positive orientation, a moral orientation, a relational orientation, and a spiritual stewardship orientation.

We argue that the four orientations are theoretically sound and established in empirical work. We also argue that they have practical significance. They can be used to help leaders—both those in authoritative positions and those who rely on influence—to become more reflective about their work, to guide their decisions, and to consider how to rectify the small mistakes that challenge every person in a leadership role on a daily basis. We have focused above on school leader–teacher relationships, but the orientations are not limited to working with professional colleagues. As captured by Thompson and associates (2008), positive leadership demonstrates an acute awareness of and concern for five primary stakeholder groups: customers/clients (students and parents), team members (staff), the organization (the school and the district), shareholders (parents), and the community. Embedded is the principle of honoring and serving all people (Driscoll & McKee, 2007; Liden et al., 2008).

While educational leadership traditionally has had a fundamental ethical focus, much of the work on virtues and values that we use in this chapter comes from scholars who study the positive leadership practice in public administration and the corporate world. They too have a fundamental vision of the common good that "is served in the pursuit of . . . business objectives. Ethical leaders are also concerned about *the interests of multiple stakeholders,* including the *community and society*" (Treviño, Brown, & Hartman, 2003, p. 19, emphasis in original). We will return to the theme of the extended role of positive leadership at many points throughout the rest of this book.

NOTES

1. The concept of the moral imagination is derived from Edmund Burke's *Reflections on the Revolution in France*, as summarized and applied to leadership by Stephenson (2007).

2. This discourse did not, of course, disappear in countries where there is one or more state religions and/or public funding of religious schools.

3. This assumption is, of course, foundational to open systems theory, which recently has been applied to school leadership by Shaked & Schechter (in press).

CHAPTER 3

Principles of Positive School Leadership

A good leader inspires people to have confidence in the leader, a great leader inspires people to have confidence in themselves. (Anonymous)

Apart from values and ethics which I have tried to live by, the legacy I would like to leave behind is a very simple one—that I have always stood up for what I consider to be the right thing, and I have tried to be as fair and equitable as I could be. (Ratan Tata)

In the previous chapter, we examined four underlying *orienting dimensions* of positive leadership that emerged across a wide variety of authors: positive, moral, relational, and spiritual. Here we extend that work by creating a set of underlying *principles* to guide behavior that will ground our examination of leadership and its effects in the remaining chapters. *Again, our definitional work incorporates the attributes or characteristics from all leadership models that rest on positive axes* (Leroy et al., 2012; May et al., 2003). That is, "positive psychology, and now its application to the workplace . . . attempts to give a renewed emphasis to the importance of a positive approach" (Youssef & Luthans, 2007, p. 775).

We are committed to theorizing leadership as a moral and ethical endeavor. We note that "the principles can help educational leaders generate school cultures to assist students in steering a course in life away from intense individualistic and addictive practices, toward more communitarian and moral life choices" (Duignan, 2005, p. 11). In its details, no leadership theory is timeless or applicable in all situations, so we remind ourselves that these principles are affected by social and cultural contexts, type of organization, and the personal characteristics of leaders when they move into operation. Nevertheless, we conclude, based on our examination of the literature, that Positive School Leadership requires a firm foundation in nine guiding principles, each of which we articulate in this chapter. These are illustrated in Figure 3.1.

Figure 3.1. Nine Principles of Positive School Leadership

Principle	Defining Characteristics
Asset-Based	Is consistently focused on the assets that all stakeholders bring to the school.
Value-Centered	Clearly and regularly articulates enduring values that are the foundation of an enterprise committed to human development.
Virtue-Based	Consistently models value-based behaviors in ways that others would describe as virtuous.
Transcendent	Establishes a morally compelling vision that moves others to make commitments to the common good.
Relationally Grounded	Places the development of positive relationships with all stakeholders at the center of leadership work.
Means-Focused	Recognizes the importance of the daily tasks of school leadership as a foundation for positive transformation.
Growth-Based	Emphasizes the importance of personal growth and development for all members of the school.
Authentic	Requires self-awareness, transparency, balanced consideration, and self-regulated behavior.
Service-Grounded	Emphasizes the stewardship functions of leadership: conserving and nurturing the humanity of all those serving and served by the school.

ASSET-BASED

Positiveness is a recent strand in organizational theorizing, focusing on understanding the "best" of the human condition. (Fineman, 2006, p. 270)

Positive psychology is focused on optimal human functioning. (Avey et al., 2008, p. 112)

Positive leadership rallies confidence, hope, and optimism to support individual and group performance. "The efforts of leaders to build these assets has an important influence on organizations" (W. L. Gardner & Schermerhorn, 2004, p. 273; see also Russell, 2001). Many educators work in contexts where administrators, teachers, and students feel beleaguered by negative media coverage and pundits' efforts to frame vouchers and charter schools as necessary antidotes to school failure (T. S. Wilson, 2016). More positive and nuanced local assessments of the quality of public schools are occurring (Bali, 2016), but several decades of "bad news" and stories of "dropout factories" have left many educators dispirited. How can school leaders promote positivity without being Pollyannaish or unrealistic?

This question reinforces a point raised in the previous chapter: The approach to improvement in organizational settings often has been most attentive to the negative. Bryson (2010) argues that strategic planning emerged after World War II as a positive antidote to a focus on problems that need to be solved, and it has become an essential part of every educational leadership skill set. However, strategic planning usually begins with a "SWOT" analysis, where the emphasis is as much on identifying external threats and internal weaknesses as it is on opportunities and strengths. This ambiguity allows stakeholder groups and individuals many interpretations of the "future image" that can focus on warding off decline more than designing on new futures.

Luthans (2002a) notes that "we have been more concerned with what is wrong with organizations, teams, leaders, and employees than what is right with them" (p. 703). In contrast, an asset-based approach to school leadership extends beyond the absence of valued states (Sandage & Hill, 2001) to emphasize "an essential humanism aligned with humanistic psychologies and philosophies" (Fineman, 2006, p. 273). To focus on assets in a period of pessimism requires acknowledging external and internal constraints while concentrating on replacing images of negativity and deficiencies. In schools, this requires leaders at all levels to consider "facilitating the good life and structuring talents," while focusing on "human strength, resilience, and virtue" (Sandage & Hill, 2001, p. 241), and to emphasize strength-based approaches (Burrello et al., 2016) and "optimal human functioning" (Avey et al., 2008, p. 112).

Positive school leaders are "first and foremost concerned with values and beliefs that provide humans with a moral compass regarding decisions about life and professional practice" (English & Ehrich, 2016, p. 1). This tends to be relatively easy in school settings, since most educators choose their work because of its congruence with their personal values (Louis, 1998). Positive organizational leadership is also about developing "positive psychological capital" (Avey et al., 2008, p. 112), which exists at both the individual and group levels and engenders greater optimism about the future among all members of the group (Newman, Ucbasaran, Zhu, & Hirst, 2014; Wang, Sui, Luthans, Wang, & Wu, 2014). Positive School Leadership involves minimizing the application of power (B. M. Bass & Steidlmeier, 1999), while developing critical trusting relationships (Tschannen-Moran & Gareis, 2015). An asset-based approach focuses on "fusing positive assumptions about human nature with more rectitude" (Fineman, 2006, p. 272), thus reinforcing member understanding of "worthy leadership" (Thompson et al., 2008, p. 379) and providing a link to the positive value base of school leadership.

VALUE-CENTERED

To motivate followers, leaders must get in touch with their core values and communicate them to followers through vision and personal actions to create a sense of spiritual survival through calling and membership. (Fry, 2003, p. 693)

Values define positive organizational leadership and distinguish authentic leaders from those who rely on positional power but lack influence. There is ample evidence that leaders who are viewed as embodying important professional values have influence over what happens in schools (Furman & Shields, 2005; Gold, 2003; Møller et al., 2007; Russell, 2001). Many articles that focus on school leaders emphasize a few values (such as equity and social justice), but there is consensus that influential positive leaders use a wide array of "core beliefs—the underlying thoughts that stimulate human behavior" (Russell, 2001, p. 76)—to guide their own actions and influence those of others. Consistent with a theme that permeates the guiding principles of Positive School Leadership, spiritual values (e.g., integrity, honesty, humility) occupy the high ground (Reave, 2005). School leaders implicitly rely on these principles as they consider important decisions when they respond to external mandates (Larsen & Hunter, 2014) or are forced to make painful budget cuts during periods of fiscal austerity.

Why is this the case? Values are prescriptive and represent enduring standards that collectively form our lives (Reave, 2005). Many of these values are inherent in preparation programs that reflect the revised Professional Standards for Educational Leaders (National Policy Board for Educational Administration, 2015) that require struggling with issues of fairness and responsibility that go well beyond competencies to be checked off (Murphy, Louis, & Smylie, 2017). A review of any major textbook used in principal preparation programs will divulge a greater emphasis on values than one would find in management texts in other disciplines. Schools (and other service organizations) have at their core values-in-practice: Values-in-practice mature inside personal relationships and not compliance or reward-based exchange relationships (Hood, 2003). It is through personal relationships developed by Positive school leaders that values reverberate in an organizational context.

We cannot list all of the values that are important in education because there is no commonly accepted terminology. But we know values when we observe them as "desirable states, objects, goals, or behaviors transcending specific situations and applied as normative standards to judge and to choose among alternative models of behavior" (Schwartz, as cited in Lord & Brown, 2001, p. 138). When members see their leaders as value-based, they regard the leaders as authentic and as "moral agents who take ownership, and therefore responsibility for the end results of their moral actions and the actions of their followers" (Hannah et al., 2005, p. 47). For positive school leadership to be authentic, therefore, it must incorporate a central core of moral values or a "moral foundation" (Cardona, 2000, p. 206), and a personal accountability for living and modeling those values (Leithwood & Riehl, 2005, p. 22). Positive school leaders are "men and women who are . . . confident, hopeful, optimistic, resilient, and ethical" (Fineman, 2006, p. 273), and whose "normative commitment to values transcends organizational imperative" (Adler et al., 2008, p. 361). Thus, it is only when the underlying values are morally uplifting and guide difficult choices that we can claim that they are in play.

VIRTUE-BASED

The moral life rests upon foundations of individual virtue. The individually virtuous person transforms others as well as the social environment. (B. M. Bass & Steidlmeier, 1999, p. 194)

Philosophical accounts of virtue ethics suggest several areas of congruence between virtue and positive psychology, including the promotion of positive health and human flourishing (or "the good life"), a connection to healthy character and community well-being, the cultivation of human strength and resilience, a link to meaning in life, and a grounding in wisdom. (Sandage & Hill, 2001, p. 241)

In the previous section, we hinted that those who are working with the leader must accurately identify value-based leadership. If you ask yourself what values you hold, you are likely to mumble and describe your own or others' behavior. One of the reasons that we have a difficult time articulating our values is that we are likely to turn to something we have done that exemplifies an underlying principle that is important to us. The link between values and actions is important and is best captured by the idea of virtue-based leadership.

Virtues are what we see when there is consistent value-based action and behavior, and are an expression of underlying values (Hackett & Wang, 2012). However, the concept of virtue is poorly defined in modern usage. A quick review of dictionary definitions and contemporary writing finds both overlap and inconsistency, and so we rely on a synthesis definition that emphasizes virtue-based leadership as "a character trait that an individual acquires and maintains primarily through learning and continuous practice and is expressed through voluntary actions undertaken in context-relevant situations" (Hackett & Wang, 2012, p. 874).

Leadership scholars struggle with the ineffable relationship between values and virtues. B. M. Bass and Steidlmeier (1999) surface a core of virtue-based leadership when they remind us that positive "authentic transformational leaders focus on the best in others—on harmony, charity, and good works [while others often] focus on the worst in others—on demonic plots, conspiracies, real dangers, and insecurities" (p. 188). In other words, leaders express virtue by consistently nurturing the best in others while containing the less noble (Treviño & Brown, 2004). Eisenbeiss (2012) deepens the narrative when reporting that positive leadership "refer[s] to different aspects of humane orientation by stressing the importance of leader altruism and leader respect for the rights and dignity of others, conditions that are 'only possible through civic virtue'" (p. 796). Because schools have the responsibility for any society's most precious asset, children, the civic virtue construct prominently points to "an integrative nexus of morality and health embedded within a cultural and political context" (Sandage & Hill, 2001, p. 252).

Positively anchored schools can be "a source for spiritual survival and must motivate [members] intrinsically through vision, hope/faith, and altruistic love" (Fry, 2003, p. 717), forgiveness (Thompson et al., 2008), "compassion and virtue" (Luthans, 2002a, p. 698), and justice and gratitude (Eisenbeiss, 2012). In other words, when they act in a consistently virtuous manner, leaders elicit the best in others and contribute to positive school cultures (Chapter 8 will explore this further). It is the modeling of behavior in visible and contextually sensitive ways that allows others to see the embodiment of values in sensitive and nuanced ways. Virtue-based leadership is, therefore, not the opposite of unethical leadership but rather an advanced stage of moral development that moves beyond rules and expectations to acknowledge the complexity of morally grounded decisionmaking (Kohlberg & Hersh, 1977; Treviño & Brown, 2004) in ways that inspire others.

Even though the virtuous leadership literature is littered with inconsistencies, this perspective informs us directly that "school administration is a moral art" (Greenfield, 2004, p. 183), and that positive school leaders "are more likely than others to apply moral principles and virtues to the situation to make sense of what action to take" (May et al., 2003, p. 254). Integrity is a central aspect of positive school leadership (Palanski & Yammarino, 2009). So also is "making the needs and interests of others primary" (Cooper et al., 2005, p. 487). Humanity, altruism, trust, and service are powerful items in the virtue toolbox of Positive School Leaders. Hackett and Wang (2012), applying the writings of Aristotle and Confucius to modern leadership paradigms, would include courage and truthfulness, while many authors who write about virtues in school leadership would include empowerment of others (Leithwood & Riehl, 2005).

Underlying each virtue is the link between a character trait and its expression in action. Zeroing in, we learn, for example, that "humility . . . is not to be equated with poor self-esteem. . . . The servant leader sees humility as reflecting an accurate self-assessment and, therefore, '*maintains a relatively low self-focus.*'" We also learn that "altruism is helping others selflessly just for the sake of helping, which involves personal sacrifice, although there is no personal gain" (Dennis & Bocarnea, 2005, p. 602, emphasis added). However, action reveals virtues: Positive School Leadership holds that "all social as well as individual goals [are] only attainable through exercises of civic virtue" (B. M. Bass & Steidlmeier, 1999, p. 200), through "moral maturity" on the part of leaders and the "moral uplifting of followers" (p. 192).

TRANSCENDENT

Transcendence is a phenomenon or an experience that goes beyond the ordinary. We often associate the word with personal experiences that fill us with awe ("the transcendent experience of the Northern Lights . . ."), but it has more practical origins, as it is derived from a combination of the Latin prefix "trans" (beyond) and "scandare" (to climb). Here we focus on the grounded origins rather than the modern Kantian philosophical and religious connotations.

Transcendence is manifest in Positive School Leadership on four levels. On the first level, it is about leading beyond self-interest for the common good (Cardona, 2000) and demonstrating "a concern for followers' needs rather than [leaders'] own self interest" (Conger et al., 2000, p. 750). On the second level, transcendence is about forging a morally compelling vision (R. E. Quinn et al., 2000). Third, transcendence is about forging individual interest into a more expansive and collective vision associated with "a common interest of a community beyond the aggregate interests of individuals" (Adler et al., 2008, p. 200). Finally, leaders helping others to live into this experience manifest transcendence. In schools, it means supporting teachers to move beyond their own self-interests in ways that allow them to exceed beyond their individual goals (Cardona, 2000; Driscoll & McKee, 2007).

We have emphasized the practical and grounded consequences of transcendence, but for some there will be an associated sense of spirituality (Cardona, 2000). As defined in Chapter 2, a spiritual orientation is grounded in "a way of understanding self and the world and is a means of personal and group integration. It portrays leadership through calling and membership" (Dent et al., 2005, p. 642). Positive school leaders acknowledge that the majority of people drawn to become educators feel a sense of "calling" (Cook, 1918; Santoro, 2011).[1] This provides fertile ground for Positive School Leadership, because empirical work suggests that people who view their work as a calling have stronger motivation and psychological success (Hall & Chandler, 2005).

However, as Santoro (2011) points out, we know little about how teachers maintain their sense of higher purpose over the course of their careers. We suspect, however, that a key is being part of a moral community. "To the extent that professionals are piloted by ethical leaders, there is a greater likelihood that moral intelligence will be promoted in followers and that reciprocal trust will develop in relevant communities . . . confer(ring) legitimacy to agencies and actors serving the public good" (Sama & Shoaf, 2008, p. 42). This is particularly important for schools, where public support and trust provide both tangible and intangible resources.

RELATIONALLY GROUNDED

It is often *whom* leaders care about, and how they show that caring, that determines whether or not they will be seen as demonstrating worthy leadership. (Thompson et al., 2008, p. 375, emphasis in original)

Relational leadership is the fundamental starting point for leadership to flourish. It is the key to organizational success. (Burrello et al., 2016, p. 64)

The past several decades have seen a major shift in the way in which most leadership scholars (as well as those in leadership positions) look at their work. In a popular textbook, Bolman and Deal (2003) acknowledge the salience of a more structural approach to leadership that focuses on job design, efficiency, and policy, and that dominated organizational and leadership research through the 1970s. Then they quickly turn to the importance of approaches that emerged and largely supplanted the structural approach beginning with the human relations movement (see also Herman, 2002).

We argue, however, that the bestselling and most influential writers about leadership and organization pay insufficient attention to the nature of relationships, often describing them as necessary, but frosting on the cake of the real work of goal attainment, or as micro-strategies for managing employees.[2] McGregor's (1960) management Theory X points to the need for positive and negative rewards, while Theory Y emphasizes the salience of job satisfaction—but both leadership styles focus on how to organize people and tasks in order to get the work done. Similarly, Hersey and Blanchard's (1969) situational perspective on the people side of leadership relies on the assumption that relationships are important largely because "less mature" employees need coaching and supervision.

Positive psychology, in contrast, embeds deeper and more meaningful relationships in virtually every aspect of leadership, ranging from the design of work settings (Grant & Berg, 2012) to the capacity for organizational learning

(Gittell, 2012). Authentic, relationship-based leadership promotes employee trust, a sense of organizational justice, and a willingness to contribute voice to promoting the collective good; each of these is important in itself, and a precursor to collective performance. Connections nurtured by Positive school leaders are a manifestation of transcendent rather than command-and-control leadership.

The consequences of stronger principal–teacher relationships are apparent in many lines of work on school improvement. They include the accumulating evidence that professional relationships among teachers that focus on collective practice and joint responsibility for changing students' lives are strong predictors of student learning (Louis & Lee, 2016). They also contribute to understanding why networks among both administrators and teachers help to foster organizational learning (Daly, Liou, & Moolenaar, 2014; Daly, Moolenaar, Bolivar, & Burke, 2010; Leithwood & Azah, 2016).

Relationships between school administrators and teachers and staff are at the heart of Positive School Leadership, and there is increasing evidence that these promote a wide variety of ethically desirable outcomes, such as more equitable distribution of resources inside the school (Leithwood & Riehl, 2005; Louis, Murphy, & Smylie, 2016). As Thompson et al. (2008) remind us, leadership can be understood only with reference to relationships. It is followers who "confer leadership" (G. W. Fairholm, 1996, p. 14), and it is leaders who, in turn, "build leadership organizational capacity on a foundation of relational capital" (Burrello et al., 2016, p. 67). Burrello and his colleagues add that "relational leadership, in turn, is an activity not a personal trait" (p. 65).

FOCUSED ON MEANS AS WELL AS ENDS

> Such leaders value each employee and respect their right to be treated with dignity rather than just as a means to an organizational end. (Zhu et al., 2004, p. 23)

> Followers should not be mere means to self-satisfying ends . . . but should be treated as ends in themselves. (Bass & Steidlmeier, 1999, p. 185)

Positive school leaders are called to balance the value- /virtue-based transcendent work described above with the daily work of running a school. In the leadership literature, this often is disparaged as "management"—in contrast to "transformative leadership." Bass and Steidlmeier (1999) go further, distinguishing between leaders and managers as if they performed two distinct jobs, while John Kotter (2008), an exceptionally influential management writer, argues that managers are consumed with the status quo, while leaders have their eye on the future and what needs to change.

We disagree, and call on a solid base of empirical work that underscores the importance of all of the small actions that a leader takes that set a frame for a positive school culture and reflect the larger values and virtues outlined above. In this we follow the alternative (if less popular in management texts) path that argues that leadership and management are exceptionally difficult to distinguish in practice (Murphy, 1988). Smircich and Morgan (1982) articulated this perspective by arguing that leaders *create* organization by being makers of meaning within the formal structure. This occurs through human interaction—the grounded relationships described in the previous section—and not because an individual leader articulates a vision, hoping that it will inspire. Positive leaders who are "meaning makers" or "sensegivers" (Gioia & Chittipeddi, 1991) use "words and images, symbolic actions and gestures" (Smircich & Morgan, 1982, p. 263) to structure and shape the experience of others. "Big transformational work" (like strategic planning and visioning) is less often the site of this activity, which occurs more often in "small transformational work" that cements values and relationships through individual attention and articulation of values and has an impact on the significance that people see in their jobs (Piccolo & Colquitt, 2006, p. 334).

The daily nature of leadership work is a core of positive leadership. Although it sometimes appears varied and disjointed, transformational leadership grows from the settings and opportunities for influence that it creates (Maitlis & Christianson, 2014). People make sense of their work setting through observing actions and reactions, and eyes are always on the leaders. It is in this kind of work that leaders demonstrate "that employees have intrinsic values above and beyond their connection to organizational identity" (Driscoll & McKee, 2007, p. 207).

This principle of focusing on means tells us "that positive leadership is first and foremost about meeting and servicing the needs of others" (Driscoll & McKee, 2007, p. 208), "where teachers are developed for the sake of their well-being" (Burrello et al., 2016, p. 84). And consistent with a focus on assets, positive school leadership is also about "setting aside self-interest for the betterment of . . . followers" (Liden et al., 2008, p. 161), which means all members of the school. A sustained commitment to the professional ideal of putting the needs of others first requires that all leaders model it on a regular and visible basis.

GROWTH-BASED

Transcendental leaders are not so concerned about the collaborators' buying into their vision, as they are to reach out to their collaborators' needs and development. (Cardona, 2000, p. 205)

We find in this principle of Positive School Leadership a core idea that supplements the previous principles: Positive school leaders consistently attend to the adult school members' personal and collective needs for growth and development (Fridell et al., 2009; Liden et al., 2008; Louis, 1998; B. Smith et al., 2004). A focus on growth and development starts with a leader's "demonstrating genuine concern for others' career growth and development by providing support and mentoring," and also "instill[ing] in followers the self confidence and desire to become servant leaders themselves" (Liden et al., 2008, p. 162), thus promoting the creation and spread of positive leadership throughout the school.

There are significant implications of this focus for human growth and development that distinguish it from much of the writing about professional development in education. In most cases, professional development is seen as a means of increasing teacher skills in order to achieve learning goals. Teachers are the "tool" and professional development is the best way of honing that tool. The perspective taken here, in contrast, is that developing people is an end in itself. As Leithwood, Harris, and Hopkins (2008) note, this involves "providing individualised support and consideration, fostering intellectual stimulation, and modelling appropriate values and behaviours. These specific practices . . . are central to the ways in which successful leaders integrate the functional and the personal" (p. 30). At its core is a concern for individualized development programs for each teacher or other staff member of the school. As they move beyond their own self-interest, positive school leaders treat teachers as "individuals and provide coaching, mentoring, and growth opportunities" (B. M. Bass & Steidlmeier, 1999, p. 189; see also Black, 2010).

Like transcendence, growth-based leadership requires more than promoting professional learning opportunities. There is a spiritual basis to focusing on growth for all staff members of the school: "It means paying singular attention to the affective and emotional needs of others" (Liden et al., 2008, p. 163). "It is about modeling ethically-based principles and their application" (G. W. Fairholm, 1996, p. 13). The self-reflection of a Positive School Leader encourages others to be self-reflective (Reave, 2005). The relevance of this principle in schools is that it "compels a spiritual orientation that centres on moral conduct. It is a case of doing good while doing well" (G. W. Fairholm, 1996, p. 13). The enhanced capacities of people who are consistently growing and developing are assumed to result in sometimes unexpected but virtually always enriching outcomes for a school.

AUTHENTIC

Authentic leadership is defined in large part by the evidence of morality in the leadership influence process. (Hannah et al., 2005, p. 43)

The change agent is self-creating and self-transfiguring. (R. E. Quinn et al., 2000, p. 152)

Positive school leaders realize that to move forward their schools or districts, they need to change themselves first and that "organizational change begins with personal change" (R. E. Quinn et al., 2000, p. 158). When school leaders are not personally engaged in the change that they expect from others, their capacity to lead is diminished (Palmer & Louis, 2017). This observation points to the general principle that leaders should have a visible, personal stake in any important effort that is occurring. Indeed, "the reduction of personal integrity gaps is a foundation for change" (R. E. Quinn et al., 2000, p. 151).

Authentic behavior requires a leader to be "true to the self" (Leroy et al., 2012, p. 261), but this cannot occur without a solid foundation of self-awareness, or "a deep sense of self that provides knowledge about one's values, identity, emotions and motives/goals" (Pless & Maak, 2011, p. 7). Ryan and Deci (2003) propose three dimensions of authentic leadership in addition to self-awareness: relational transparency (always presenting one's authentic self), balanced processing (considering all available perspectives before reaching a decision), and self-regulation (based on an internal moral compass). Authentic leadership cannot be defined without observing actions and behavior. Zhu, May, and Avolio (2004) maintain that authenticity requires consistency between a leader's orientation and actions before it will have an impact on others.

At the same time, authenticity is also linked to transcendence: There is a commitment to "operate for the common good" (R. E. Quinn et al., 2000, p. 154), and to "take the interests of others seriously and to be forgetful of self alone" (B. M. Bass & Steidlmeier, 1999, p. 195). Paul Begley (2006) argues that authenticity in educational leadership is built not only on the foundation of self-knowledge, but also on the other principles articulated above, including the capacity for value- and virtue-based reasoning, transcendence, and a relational orientation.

SERVICE-GROUNDED

The art of serving includes a mission of responsibility to others. (Dennis & Bocarnea, 2005, p. 604)

Servant leaders are those who serve with a focus on the followers, whereby the followers are the primary concern and the organizational concerns are peripheral. The servant leader constructs are virtues, which are defined as the good moral quality in a person, or the general quality of goodness, or moral excellence. (p. 601)

The focus of much of the research reported above is on redefining leadership in terms of service and stewardship (Black, 2010), moving, as we noted above, beyond self-interest (B. M. Bass & Steidlmeier, 1999; Treviño et al., 2003). There is a significant literature that follows Greenleaf's (1977/1997) seminal work on servant leadership, but much of the positive leadership literature that is only loosely aligned with Greenleaf's model also incorporates the idea of service.

There is, for example, a line of empirical research on "public service motivation" that incorporates the importance of personal investment and a grounding in social justice and compassion (Bozeman & Su, 2015; Perry, 1996). Social psychologists emphasize the importance of leaders working to create a "social reality driven by concern for others, not just themselves" (R. E. Quinn et al., 2000, p. 159)—in other words, to create a strong collective commitment to service. Educational leaders work to transform schools "so that humane practice and policies become an integral part of day-to-day functioning" (Driscoll & McKee, 2007, p. 207). They elect "to take action with the well-being of others as their inspirations" (Burrello et al., 2016, p. 67).

Service-oriented leaders strive "to treat others with dignity and respect and to see them as ends" (Eisenbeiss, 2012, p. 795). Service also suggests that "for leaders the 'greater good' must be greater than themselves as well" (Reave, 2005, p. 678). In addition, as Owens and Hekman (2012) remind us, service-oriented leaders function in a transparent fashion, especially concerning "their own developmental processes" (p. 810). Servant leaders demonstrate trust (Simons, 1999) and practice "self-sacrifice on behalf of the group" (Knippenberg & De Cremer, 2008, p. 176). They gravitate away from the idea of work as a job to that of work as a calling (Black, 2010; Fry, 2003) that is spiritual (Reave, 2005), containing a "vision of life's purpose and meaning" (Fry, 2003, p. 706). Earlier we introduced the ideas of transcendence and spirituality. Here we deepen that line of analysis by linking spirituality and service. Spiritually anchored leadership is about the values and virtues we discussed earlier, for example, "compassion, patient tolerance, forgiveness, contentment, and a sense of responsibility" (Fry, 2003, p. 705). Moreover, as we reported in our analysis above, leadership grounded in spirituality "requires that leaders also go beyond their own self-interests" (B. M. Bass & Steidlmeier, 1999, p. 207). Finally, spirituality is about empowerment of others (English & Ehrich, 2016; Fridell et al., 2009).

SUMMARY

Articulating the principles underlying leadership, when examined over time, is a huge sandbox filled with attractive toys and tools, each of which has utility in some circumstances. Most strikingly, however, as we began to comb through this literature, was the relatively limited effort devoted to articulating a coherent sense of guiding principles—how do these toys and tools fit together? We do not argue that the list we have derived from our dive into a disparate set of authors will apply to all sectors in all cultures. Rather, our goal is narrower: to sort through what we have read using the lens of positive psychology and positive organizational studies, and to further narrow that filter based on what is known about life in schools.

We also acknowledge the obvious: The guiding principles we have described have porous boundaries. Virtues and values are distinct but overlapping; for example, it is difficult to talk about the principle of service without referring to the principle of relational grounding. Furthermore, as we have noted, in many cases the principles are revealed only by looking at associated behaviors. Nevertheless, we would argue that the threads that tie the nine principles together might be denser in some settings and on some occasions than in others.

Translating the principles into practice thus requires further grounding of their meaning in the context of how leaders enact the principles, which is the broad topic of the next part of the book.

In making this pivot toward action, we can be explicit about a fundamental paradox of Positive School Leadership: To improve "the bottom line" for students, leaders must be virtue-based and use the guiding principles to maintain a laser-like focus on the development of ethically grounded relationships among adults. Only then can they ensure the organizational conditions that will sustain high-quality and equitable achievement.

NOTES

1. Santoro (2011) documents that empirical basis, but the notion of teaching as a profession that has a "calling" has been controversial as it sometimes has been associated with anti-union and anti-scientific approaches (Capen, 1947; Williams, 1938).

2. Bolman and Deal (2010, 2011), particularly in their writing about educational leadership, have moved toward a synthesized position that focuses on values, ethics, and people as a core, with their four "frames" as strategic weapons.

PART II

POSITIVE LEADERSHIP IN ACTION

Relationships can be characterized as more versus less energizing for participants and ... the energy level of an entire work organization can be depicted with a network analysis of these relationships. By implication, the goal of any workplace should be to increase the density of energizing relationships while decreasing or eliminating those that de-energize.

—C. Peterson, Park, Hall, & Seligman, 2009, p. 168

There is a growing literature on positive interventions that suggests that what I am going to describe in a moment as the positive side of life—PERMA: positive emotion, engagement, relationships, meaning, and accomplishment—is actually buildable.

—Seligman, 2010, p. 231

The foundation of positive psychology begins with individuals and their dispositions, but quickly situates positive emotions in the context of relationships. Humans are inherently social, and the potential for connections with others to foster both great joy and despair is the stuff not just of psychological sciences but of the great art and literature of every culture.

As we explored the individual foundations for Positive School Leadership in the previous chapters, we saw that many prominent scholars presume that virtues, values, and principles provide a basis for healthy, positive relationships. However, the work of those scholars does not provide clear guidance for either theory or practices that could benefit both individuals and school communities. Furthermore, many popular leadership theories pay limited attention to relationships, largely due to simplified distinctions between "leadership" (focused on purpose) and "management" (getting the work done), and "transformational" work (focusing on shaping the organization for future needs) and "transactional" work (exchange relationships that contribute to today's needs). At this superficial level, what school leader will not choose to focus on becoming a transformational leader, delegating transactional management work to others?

Serious leadership scholars in both the private sector and education have long challenged a dichotomous perspective, arguing that transformational leadership demands serious attention to relationships (B. M. Bass, 1990; Leithwood & Steinbach, 1991). Nevertheless, investigations of the leader's role and its significance in developing relationships are somewhat limited in the educational leadership literature. In Part II, we explore what empirical research contributes to our understanding of how the virtues, values, and principles of Positive School Leadership can create a more vibrant life in educational settings.

Chapter 4 provides a brief overview of the relationship between leaders (people who exercise influence in schools) and other members, drawing primarily on "leader–member exchange (LMX) theory" and extrapolating it to school settings. We regard this as pivotal in our book because LMX research provides a rich basis for thinking about how relationships work in schools. In Chapter 5, we expand on this by examining how specific leader behaviors support the development of strong relationships with members of organizations, while enacting the principles that we outlined in Chapter 3. Chapter 5 allows us to situate the somewhat abstract nature of the positive leadership principles in the challenges that school leaders commonly face. Finally, in Chapter 6 we turn to one critical issue of outcomes: Positive school leaders who nurture relationships and member development need to be sensitive to cues that their work is taking hold. This chapter focuses on what they need to look for as they monitor their relationship-building work.

The goal of this part of the book is not to argue that managing relationships and developing solid, positive transactional connections is the only objective of school leaders. Rather, we lay the basis for an argument that relationship building is a critical foundation for the development of positive, vital, and engaged schools. In other words, relationships are the bedrock of every school's capacity for improvement.

CHAPTER 4

Positive Leader–Member Relationships
An Exchange Perspective

> It is the quality of the leader-follower relationship through which transformational leadership behaviors influence follower performance. (Wang, Law, Hackett, Wang, & Chen, 2005, p. 420)

> The subordinate's identification with this relationship has a significant influence on attitudes toward the organization. (Sluss & Ashforth, 2008, p. 810)

GETTING STARTED: WHY CARE ABOUT EXCHANGES?

Social exchange theory addresses the relationship between an employee and his or her supervisor. While this has been a focus of leadership theories since the early part of the 20th century, the development of a deeper theoretical and practical understanding of how leader–member relationships are established, are maintained, and function, emerged as a unique focus during the 1990s with the application of exchange theories to leadership practice. Exchange theory, which emerged full-blown in the 1960s, focused on applying economic ideas about transactional relationships to noneconomic situations by emphasizing that (1) every relationship between two actors is based on giving and receiving desired rewards, and (2) rewards can be both extrinsic (visible approval or a salary increase) or intrinsic (emotional investments that assume reciprocity in the relationship) (Emerson, 1976).

The importance of exchange theory in sociology was its contribution to the understanding of small-group relationships—such as families, community organizations, and work settings. This focus on work groups is particularly important for school leaders who, with few exceptions, work in settings that are small or modest in size. While the CEO of Ford Motor Company does not look at his landscape and try to figure out how to have a relationship with each of his 200,000 employees, principals of all but the largest high schools expect to know and have some kind of relationship with all of the people who work in the school. Thus, thinking about these relationships becomes a critical building block in considering Positive School Leadership.

Not surprisingly, leadership theorists quickly saw the potential for focusing on social relationships as an important unit of analysis in understanding why some work groups function better than others. Social exchange theory thus provides a major explanatory foundation for scholarship that has looked at leader–member exchanges:

> The exchange of favors creates "diffuse future obligations"—decreasing the likelihood of keeping an exact tally of favors and increasing the likelihood of engendering a trusting and mutually committed relationship. These favors . . . include both tangible resources such as monetary rewards, promotions, opportunities for training as well as intangible resources such as informal standing, goal alignment, encouragement and support. A positive exchange of resources results in generalized reciprocity. Generalized reciprocity . . . focuses interests on mutual goals rather than self-centered goals. (Sluss, Klimchak, & Holmes, 2008, p. 458)

In summary, generally *high-quality* exchange results when two parties take care of each other by exchanging and reciprocating favors over time.

The "ah-ha" for leadership theory was the fundamental assumption that leaders form unique relationships with each of the members of a group. A focus on understanding these particularistic relationships in order to gain insights into how members work with one another provided an alternative to the then-dominant (and often abstract) theories about "leadership style" (Ilies, Nahrgang, & Morgeson, 2007). By pointing to the human element of leadership, exchange theory pointed to the importance of every patterned transaction that occurs in a work setting:

> The LMX (leader–member exchange) is unique among leadership theories in that it focuses on dyadic relationships between leaders and followers and contends that leaders form different types of exchange relationships with their respective followers. (Liden et al., 2008, p. 163)

As it developed, the leader–member exchange framework has taken on both instrumental and value-laden dimensions. Because school leaders work in settings where employees tend to view their jobs—working with and supporting the development of children and youth—as value-laden, these values tend to take priority in day-to-day interactions. While leaders usually are motivated by a desire to enhance the performance of individuals and the group, positive organizational psychology provides a foundation for meaningful personal relationships that are based on shared values more on than extrinsic rewards (Sluss et al., 2008).

Readers of this chapter will not be surprised to see that many current and classic texts on school leadership reflect the features that define quality leader–member exchanges (Blumberg & Greenfield, 1986; Deal & Peterson, 1994; Sergiovanni, 1992, 1994). These and many other educational authors would agree that effective leader–follower relationships are defined as "the quality of the social exchange between leaders and followers, characterized by mutual trust, respect, and obligation" (G. Chen et al., 2007, p. 333). Ilies et al. (2007) note that the element of reciprocity is central to the continuing relevance of this focus because it points to the way in which leaders can create "a perceived obligation on the part of subordinates to reciprocate high-quality relationships . . . that are developed or negotiated over time through a series of exchanges" (p. 269). In other words, the actions of the leader create bonds that become part of the permanent fabric of a work group's life.

But leader–member exchange theories are about more than dyadic relationships, because leader behaviors, when visible, create links between individual and group responses to the demands of carrying out any task (Lord, Brown, & Freiberg, 1999, p. 169). These become particularly important in places like schools, where the work is exceptionally complex and involves both professional and praxis-based knowledge. In contrast to a simple leader-centric perspective, the culmination of dyadic relationships helps to shape the way in which all members work with one another to carry out a jointly agreed upon task. Thus, the development of strong dyadic exchanges has its greatest impact in organizations like schools, "in which cooperation, helping, and altruism are important for organization effectiveness" (Ilies et al., 2007, p. 270). In summary, it is the cumulative dyadic relationships of leaders and members—LMX—that form the basis for a leader's impact on group climate and cohesiveness (Cogliser & Schriesheim, 2000). Unfortunately, research using the leader–member exchange framework has been limited in education, so this chapter will rely almost exclusively on general organizational theory and empirical work.[1]

INTO THE WEEDS WITH LMX

Stating the importance of dyads does not explain the staying power of leader–member exchanges as a focus in leadership theory and research. Every work group is composed of many different types of relationships: employee to superior/leader, superior/leader to employee, and employee to employee (Walumbwa, Avolio, Gardner, et al., 2008; Walumbwa, Avolio, & Zhu, 2008;

Walumbwa, Cropanzano, & Hartnell, 2009; Walumbwa & Schaubroeck, 2009). Because, as we noted above, research consistently has suggested that the leader–subordinate relationship is particularly important in developing a wider group or organizational ethos, we start there.

Work relationships come in two varieties: "economic exchange relationships and social exchange relationships" (Walumbwa, Avolio, & Zhu, 2008, p. 801). We often emphasize the economic aspects of superior–subordinate relationships, although Chester Barnard (1938) emphatically stated in his early treatise on executive leadership that they were less important in understanding a leader's influence than most supposed. Walumbwa, Avolio, and Zhu (2008) also point out the limitations of economic exchange relationships, noting that they have a narrow potential for impact on employees. In contrast, "social exchanges involve implicit obligations that members of the social exchange feel compelled to reciprocate" (p. 801). Wang et al. (2005) go on to emphasize the importance of the social exchange in moving beyond the transactional economic model of "I will pay you for doing this for me." They point out:

> Followers are not passive "role recipients"; they may either reject, embrace, or renegotiate roles prescribed by their leaders. There is a reciprocal process in the dyadic exchanges between leader and follower, wherein each party brings to the relationship different kinds of resources for exchange. Role negotiation occurs over time, defining the quality and maturity of a leader–member exchange, and leaders develop relationships of varying quality with different followers over time. (p. 421)

In summary, while the role of leaders may be important, they do not control the outcomes of their efforts to establish relationships with those who work for them. Indeed, that is inherent in the phrase "leader–member exchange," which assumes that relationships are a two-way process.

Social exchange relationships have both formal and informal aspects (Sluss & Ashforth, 2008) that underscore the leader-to-member social exchange model. Both contribute to relational and organizational identification, or a sense of belonging:

> Relational identification (RI) may be a linchpin between the relational dimensions of work and organizational attitudes, squarely placing dyadic influences alongside other important antecedents of organizational attitudes such as micro-level individual differences (e.g., positive affectivity, conscientiousness) and macro-level organizational characteristics (e.g., structure, culture). (p. 808)

Leader–member exchange is a mediating variable between antecedents (such as leader values and virtues) and outcomes such as organizational commitment: "The key feature of social exchange theory is that the type of relationship is the most important proximal cause of behavior" (Walumbwa, Cropanzano, & Hartnell, 2009, p. 1106). In other words, leader–member exchange is associated with individual performance and collective outcomes (Bommer, Dierdorff, & Rubin, 2007). This occurs not because of simple instrumental or *quid pro quo* exchanges motivated by self-interest, but through the longer term development of strong dyadic social bonds (Wang et al., 2005, p. 430).

SUBORDINATE PERCEPTIONS

The willingness of followers to be influenced . . . is based upon trust in the leader. (Conger et al., 2000, p. 750)

In this section, we examine the ways in which subordinates respond to (and influence) leader–member exchange, as discussed above. We begin with a reminder: We are focusing on individual reactions to relationships with an individual leader. That is, within a given school, some may perceive a principal's actions as caring and visionary, while others regard them as flawed and deficient. We also know that followers scrutinize and assess leaders' actions within exchange relationships (Choi & Mai-Dalton, 1998; Ehrhart, 2004; D. M. Mayer, Kuenzi, Greenbaum, Bardes, & Salvador, 2009). Three sets of assessments are particularly relevant and closely linked to the principles of Positive School Leadership that we outlined in the previous chapter: trustworthiness, transparency, and fairness.

Trustworthiness

Trustworthiness is important because it expands what Chester Barnard (1938) called the "zone of indifference" or the willingness to assume that positive outcomes will result from accommodating to the actions and preferences of another person (De Jong & Elfring, 2010). In schools, for example, if a principal initiates an instructional conversation by asking a teacher to talk about some of the activities observed in the classroom, a trusting teacher will assume that the consequences will be helpful (or at least not negative). Many authors note that the connection between collegial or shared leadership and "the willingness of followers to be influenced . . . [is] based upon trust in the leader, an outcome of the self-determination associated with the sharing and delegation of control by leaders" (Zhu et al., 2004, p. 19).

Within the leader–follower exchange, leaders contribute significantly to follower trust, according to Conger et al. (2000), by "(1) identifying and articulating a vision; (2) setting an example for followers that is consistent with the values the leader espouses; and (3) promoting group cooperation and the acceptance of group goals" (p. 750). But these practices are not enough. In addition, the authors suggest that leaders "also build follower trust through a demonstrated concern for follower needs, risk taking, personal sacrifices, and unconventional expertise" (p. 750). There is here a strong link between employee perceptions and the positive leadership values of being asset-based, relationally grounded, but also transcendent.

Transparency

The second critical assessment by employees attends to transparency, a variable that also is linked to trust (Hannah et al., 2005). We are reminded consistently of the importance of transparency and trust in the public sector because nothing erodes public confidence in leadership and in government more quickly than revelations that important information has been withheld. In work settings, leaders who are seen as more transparent are more likely to elicit engagement (Vogelgesang, Leroy, & Avolio, 2013). Transparency is also a critical foundation for trust, according to Simons (1999), because it requires the follower to perceive the leader as honest or as possessing integrity as well as the "perception of honest self representation" (p. 94). This is where we again see a strong link between the values outlined in Chapter 3 and leader–member exchanges. Leaders must be seen as authentic (truthful and self-reflective) as well as virtue-based.

Fairness

The third assessment is a judgment about the fairness of the leader, which creates an organizational climate that members view as just (Ehrhart, 2004). The procedural justice climate created by a leader through individual exchanges is related to organizational performance. "When employees feel that they are being treated fairly, they reciprocate through the performance of organizational citizenship behaviors" (Hannah et al., 2005, p. 66), and when "leaders consistently display high levels of moral conduct, they set a positive ethical standard to be followed across the organization" (p. 71). This has practical implications for carrying out key leadership obligations that are often fraught with conflict, such as allocation of scarce resources or personnel evaluations. To give just one clear educational example, teachers who view the procedures and criteria used to assess them as fair tend to support teacher evaluations and use them for professional learning; those who see them as arbitrary or unfair do not (Tuytens & Devos, 2014; Vekeman, Devos, & Tuytens, 2015). Another study found strong associations between teachers' perceptions of their school as a just environment and their affective commitment to their school (Buluc & Gunes, 2014).

The Consequences for Principals and Teachers

As we have noted, few studies of leader–member exchanges involve schools. Nevertheless, from across studies in private- and public-sector work settings, we can extract some important ideas for principals. First, employees' perceptions of their individual engagement with and experience of leader–member exchanges have a profound impact on them. They become more committed, both to the individual leader and to the organization, which leads to greater effort (Liden et al., 2008; Walumbwa, Cropanzano, & Goldman, 2011). In particular, the effects of member assessments of their supervisors are based upon perceptions of leaders' "sensitivity to the environment [and] abilities, formulating and articulating an inspiring vision . . . and sensitivity to member needs" (Conger et al., 2000, p. 760). In schools, as we have argued elsewhere, authenticity in leadership also demands that leaders be responsive to the particular circumstances facing individual teachers (Louis & Lee, 2016): Sensitivity and responsiveness are situated in specific events and contexts rather than in generic leader behaviors. Teachers who feel a "high level of organizational support are likely to feel obligated to repay the organization" (Cullen, Parboteeah, & Victor, 2003, p. 131), which means that the commitment to the leader often generalizes to the organization as a whole. Sluss et al. (2008) note that "exchange-valued resources within the leader–member relationship [are] then attributed to exchanging valued resources with the organization" (p. 462). This means, in turn, that teacher commitment often results in emulating the positive leader behaviors exhibited by the principal (Hannah et al., 2005; Walumbwa, Cropanzano, et al., 2011; Walumbwa, Hartnell, et al., 2010; Walumbwa, Mayer, et al., 2011; Walumbwa, Peterson, Avolio, & Hartnell, 2010).

QUALITY AND TIMING IN LEADER–MEMBER EXCHANGES

Leaders do develop different quality relationships with members, and the extent to which their relationship with different subordinates is distinct increases over time. (Nahrgang, Morgeson, & Ilies, 2009, p. 260)

The older focus on leadership styles tended to assume that good leaders adopted a relatively uniform approach to working with all members of the work group. In real life, however, leaders do not possess a stock set of undifferentiated responses to all of the people with whom they interact, nor do those they interact with respond in precisely the same way. As Sternberg and Vroom (2002) point out, both individual preferences and particular situations affect leader–member exchanges.

Exchange theory's focus on dyads presumes that relationships are situational and personal. There is no consensus on the range of underlying social values that can be generated by "high-quality" leader–member exchange relationships. Wang et al. (2005, p. 422) explain that leader–member exchanges are powered by three variables, "mutual trust, respect, and obligation"—or in their words, "social exchange is moved to a high level" (p. 422) through the variables. Ilies et al. (2007) discuss "four distinct aspects of LMX: affect, loyalty, contribution, and professional respect" (p. 274), and Walumbwa et al. (2009) identify four dimensions of LMX: mutual affection, contribution to mutual goals, loyalty, and professional respect (p. 1112). Not only do each of these dimensions vary by leader—they also vary by the individual employee with whom the leader interacts. We all know this by reminding ourselves of the "bad leaders" we have observed, many of whom have a cadre of devoted followers (Kellerman, 2004).

But the development of solid dyadic relationships varies not only by individual, but also over time. Relationships are made, not born. A new principal coming into a school where a beloved former principal has retired has one job; a new principal entering a school that was led by an incompetent or abusive leader has a different task. Both, however, have to start at the beginning. Even established leaders confront inevitable turnover. One may have excellent social exchange relationships with an existing group, but when there is turnover, each fresh recruit (who enters with his or her own set of experiences with good or bad leadership) will enter into a leader–member exchange that is unique. Socialization is, by definition, social and develops through experience rather than the new employee orientation or handbook. Nahrgang et al. (2009) underscore the stages associated with the development of effective leader–member exchange interactions, demonstrating the leader's responsibility for initiating and maintaining quality relationships:

> The typical relationship begins with the *role-taking stage*, where the leader attempts to discover the relevant talents, motivations, and limits of the member. The leader discovers this by initiating a sent role to the member who receives the role and reacts. Through the feedback and behavior of the member, the leader evaluates the member and decides whether to initiate another sent role to the member. The relationship then progresses to the *role-making stage* where the nature of the relationship begins to be defined, and finally enters the *role routinization stage* where clear mutual understandings and expectations develop and the relationship stabilizes. (p. 257, emphasis added)

Attention to the temporal nature of leader–member exchanges highlights five practical conclusions that are of particular importance to school leaders. First, "leaders form different types of exchange with respective followers" (Liden et al., 2008, p. 163); a principal recognizes, for example, that a brand-new teacher requires a different kind of role-making signal than an experienced teacher-leader. Second, the earlier stages of the relationship carry more weight than the later stages (Nahrgang et al., 2009), an important feature to consider in schools with high teacher and/or principal turnover. Third, leader–member exchange relationships tend to remain stable once they are developed, meaning that establishing trust, respect, and mutual obligation through initial interactions is particularly important. Fourth, "leader and member's . . . ratings of LMX become more aligned" (p. 258) over time: A principal who can establish good relationships with a core group of teachers is likely (unless they represent a coalition in a conflict-filled school) to be able, over time, to extend this to teachers who may be more reluctant to interact frequently with their formal supervisors. Fifth, unlike many leadership narratives, leader–member exchange research is concerned with "how member characteristics affect leader perceptions of the members" (p. 258). As we have shown in our previous work, principals who see their teachers as professionally competent are likely to have stronger social bonds with their teachers (Louis & Murphy, 2017).

Additional Implications for Developing Relationships

How does a principal decide how to develop unique and situation-sensitive relationships with each of the staff members who work in the school? We have suggested above that experience and familiarity are important, but significant relationships also are based on a deeper understanding of the teacher member (or other staff) and are influenced by past experiences with that person:

> Leaders form differentiated exchanges with members based on the effort, resources, and support exchanged between the two parties. *Higher-quality leader–member relationships resemble social exchanges in that the exchange extends beyond what is specified in the formal job description.* (Nahrgang et al., 2009, p. 258, emphasis added)

Over time, relationships that initially were based on limited trust and reciprocity can deepen, as the parties' understanding of each other grows and they become more compassionate of each other. Wang et al. (2005) affirm this developmental approach to the development of extended relationships through leader–member exchange: "LMX is said to develop through three sequential stages, 'stranger,' 'acquaintance,' and 'partner,' each of which relies successively less on instrumental transactional exchange and more on social exchanges of a 'transformational' kind" (p. 423).

We must remember that this is not an abstract developmental theory, but the result of real people in real exchange settings. At the micro level, leader–member exchange can be thought about as an interactive response to leaders' actions: Leaders take action (the principal calls a meeting); followers read and interpret those actions within the immediate context ("her meetings are usually short and useful" versus "another wasted 45 minutes"); actions impact followers (the principal's passionate announcement of an important committee that needs volunteers); and followers respond (based on their reactions to all of the above). And the cycle is re-engaged as leaders respond to followers' responses: Where the principal sees many people stepping up, she will feel pleased and inclined to assume that the committee will go well; if arms need to be twisted, her impressions of both individuals and the group may be diminished and affect her later interactions with them. *Thus, a potentially transformational relationship is strengthened or eroded based on individual interpretations of smaller transactional events.*

Analysts also help us see the expressions of leader actions. To start, Walumbwa et al. (2009) inform us that "supervision can build high-quality LMX relationships by 'reaching out' to their reports, offering them respect, opportunity, and trust" (p. 1108). They also can "procure the necessary equipment, attempt to assign competent coworkers to teams, and allocate work schedules that afford enough time for successful completion of tasks" (Walumbwa, Cropanzano, et al., 2011, pp. 748–749). In other words, the principal who is disappointed that so few teachers volunteered for her important committee should make an effort to find out why and what she could do to alleviate discomfort or eliminate competing tasks, rather than simply settling into resentment or self-doubt. Even Positive school leaders may want to augment a value-based message with a classic transactional approach, including "appropriate rewards, human resource practices, and providing needed (as well as valued) resources [and] development opportunities" (Sluss et al., 2008, p. 458). Thus, the principal may need to rethink her request for volunteers, pointing to the benefits and possible rewards (being excused from lunch duty for meetings or being sent to an interesting professional development opportunity) that might be associated with a time-consuming/noncontracted task.

Above all, principals must keep in mind that every school leader's goal is to ensure that teachers do not see themselves as "working to rule" according to the district's teacher union agreement, but as high-functioning professionals with mutual obligations toward creating a productive school. We have been in many schools where teachers are more than willing to work outside of their required hours or job descriptions because their relationship with their principal encourages them to believe that they will be making a real difference.

So far we have emphasized the dyadic relationship between leaders and members. But work groups are composed of many individuals who also have relationships with one another. It has long been acknowledged that it is peer groups, often called the informal organization, that dominate the day-to-day life of any work group (P. M. Blau, 1955). We also have long known that strong ties within groups can have both positive and negative effects on leader–member exchange (P. M. Podsakoff, MacKenzie, & Ahearne, 1997; Seashore, 1954). Highly cohesive groups, for example, can be supportive of collective goals—or may play an oppositional role. In addition, groups that have stronger ties among the members are more likely to exhibit positive behaviors that support both the organization and individuals (Cogliser & Schriesheim, 2000). This is particularly true in schools, which vary widely in the degree to which teachers have strong personal and professional bonds. Some schools have robust professional communities, in which teachers rely on one another for both emotional and intellectual support in carrying out their work; in others, teachers work mostly alone even if they are polite and collegial.

A number of scholars whose work focuses on leader–member exchange emphasize the importance of taking the group context into account, and their results are particularly applicable to schools. Liden, Erdogan, Wayne, and Sparrowe (2006) report, in particular, that leaders who manage groups with high levels of task interdependence function best when they differentiate their exchanges with individual group members. But in schools, teachers' work is, at best, only modestly interdependent: Most of the time, teachers function individually in classrooms rather than with one another; coordination is important, but tends to take a backseat to the focus on the individual's relationships with students. Thus, according to Liden et al. (2006), "the advantages of strategically differentiating between group members appear to materialize only when the nature of tasks requires group members to work closely together" (p. 739). This should cause a sigh of relief for principals, who are responsible for relatively large numbers of groups (departments or grade-level teams) and teachers.

We also must remember that peer groups in complicated organizations like schools typically involve informal leaders—teachers whose expertise or influence is acknowledged as important by many of their colleagues (Anderson-Butcher & Ashton, 2004). Informal leaders emerge because they have established their own "systems" of leader–member exchange that make them trusted and attractive to others, and effective principals often acknowledge the importance of these teachers by investing additional leader–member exchange energy in ways that enhance the overall group effectiveness, cohesiveness, and energy. This does not reduce the importance of leader–member exchanges, but acknowledges that effective leaders—and perhaps principals in particular—need to understand not only the individual members who work in their setting, but also the informal organization.

ORGANIZATIONAL OUTCOMES OF LEADER–MEMBER EXCHANGES

The relationship with the individual's immediate supervisor is the most important factor in the individual's retention and performance. (Sluss & Ashforth, 2008, p. 810)

Leaders can profoundly influence subordinates' self concepts, and thereby influence follower behavior. (Lord et al., 1999, p. 167)

Given the analysis above, it is obvious that leader actions have an impact. We also have emphasized that employees "are not passive recipients of managerial care but have a role to play in the process" (Kroth & Keeler, 2009, p. 523). There is a clear developmental cycle that emerges from the organizational research. First, leader–member relationships lead to valued outcomes when they begin with a mutual understanding of the reciprocity inherent in the relationship (Nahrgang et al., 2009, p. 256). Second, Positive school leaders demonstrate both their expertise (Hannah et al., 2005) and their grounding in the values outlined in Chapter 3. A third stage of development is member satisfaction with the leader (Conger et al., 2000; Palanski & Yammarino, 2011), and members' commitment to realizing their "shared vision and the shared rewards that will accompany the outcomes of their mission" (Conger et al., 2000, p. 751). Fourth, members experience reinforced and deepened emotional connections with the leader (Avey et al., 2008; Fornes, Rocco, & Wollard, 2008), including "faith in and respect for the leader and emotional attachment to and identification with such a leader" (Choi & Mai-Dalton, 1998, p. 492). A final developmental outcome is affective organizational commitment that mediates the relationship between leader behavioral integrity and follower intrinsic motivation and work role performance. This cycle links dyadic relationships to the positive leadership principles that we outlined in the previous chapter, summarized in Figure 3.1.

Perhaps what is most important is the development of widespread reciprocity—a fundamental antecedent of the informal "psychological contract" that encourages both employee and leader engagement in creating an organization based in positive functioning (Bakker & Schaufeli, 2008; Coyle-Shapiro, 2002). Reciprocity underlies long-term relationships: Trust and commitment build as leaders (and peers) perform well. Nahrgang et al. (2009) go on to note that increasing trust creates a feedback cycle in which mutual obligations create associations and interpersonal commitments that are ever more positive.

CAN ANY LEADER DO THIS?

Nahrgang et al. (2009) argue that the leader's personal characteristics are in play in determining the quality of leader–member exchanges. In particular, they point to extraversion and agreeableness. Examining extraversion, they argue:

> Research finds that extraverts are more likely than introverts to seek social situations. Thus, extraverted leaders are more likely to start up conversations with their members in an attempt to get to know the members, and are also more likely to be assertive in initiating sent roles to the member in order to discover the member's talents, motivations, and limits. (p. 238)

Leaders who are more introverted (and we have known many) may find it necessary to learn how to play the role of an extrovert.

Turning to agreeableness, these scholars note:

> Agreeable individuals are described as good natured, trusting, and cooperative. Because trust is an important component of higher-quality leader–member relationships, even after little interaction, we would expect that agreeable leaders and members will place more trust in the relationship. . . . Likewise, agreeable members are more likely to accept the sent roles and be more helpful to their leader, which will increase the quality of the relationship. (p. 258)

We urge, however, that school leaders take such findings with some caution. Other studies, for example, suggest that people who are high on the extraversion and feeling scale (often associated with agreeableness) are also more likely to inaccurately remember exchanges that happened in the past (Frost, Sparrow, & Barry, 2006), which is obviously problematic for those attempting to develop trusting, in-depth relationships with others. Other scholars note that in the public sector, modest introversion and a tendency toward thoughtfulness tend to be associated with longer tenure, which may be important for principals who usually work to create improvements that require many years to come to fruition (Hanbury, Sapat, & Washington, 2004). Equally important is the finding that extraversion may be effective when working with passive groups, but is not effective when members have their own views and perspectives, as is normally true of professionals such as teachers (Grant, Gino, & Hofmann, 2011; Nobel, 2010). Indeed, Cain (2013) makes a strong argument that research overall suggests that in many settings introverts make better leaders. But there is an important lesson: Principals, whether introverts or extraverts, must recognize that if they want to develop solid, trusting relationships with teachers (and others), they need to get out of their offices, initiate exchanges, and do so in a positive manner. This leadership obligation may require more effort for some than for others.

Perhaps more important than personality characteristics are strategic behavioral commitments. In particular, paying attention to the need to empower others plays an important role, as does acting as a mediator between the quality of leader–member exchanges and enhanced commitment on the part of subordinates (Liden, Wayne, & Sparrowe, 2000). Even more critical, however, is the reminder that enactment of the leader values that we discussed in Chapter 2 in each and every change will be interpreted as behavior integrity. This, of course, has an important effect on how the member interprets, over time, the quality of the relationship (Palanski & Yammarino, 2011).

The goal of positive leaders who understand and make use of the principle-driven relational approach outlined in this chapter is to create strong bonds that inspire every member of the school community to be a committed high performer.

NOTE

1. There are several exceptions, some published in educational leadership journals, but most of the research appears in psychology or organizational journals that typically are not read by educational scholars (Erdogan, Kraimer, & Liden, 2004; Somech & Wenderow, 2006; Vancouver & Schmitt, 1991; Yariv, 2009).

CHAPTER 5

Positive Behavior and the Relational Basis for Organizing

The excellent leader is first a teacher of followers. (G. W. Fairholm, 1991, p. 78)

Positive organizational scholarship presents significant opportunities for bringing new meaning to classical organizational design as well as to theories of human resource management. (Gittell, 2003, p. 295)

The foundations covered in previous chapters—personal virtues, values, principles, and developmental relationships—are important because we expect them to result in observable behavior. Biographies of virtuous historical figures inspire us, but leaders whom we see and experience, either first- or secondhand, are more likely to influence us. Hannah, Woolfolk, and Lord (2009) point out that effective leadership is based on the capacity of individuals to develop and integrate personal qualities in ways that are reliably expressed as positive leadership, or "the activation of a set of cognitions, expectancies, goals and values, and self-regulatory plans that both enable and direct . . . behaviors" (p. 270). In other words, as is apparent from our discussion of leader–member exchange in Chapter 4, behaviors as others experience them determine whether leadership is actually in play.

Less well understood is what these influential leadership behaviors are, in large measure because of the diversity of positive leadership models and frameworks that, as we have noted, include the descriptors "authentic," "charismatic," "servant," and "spiritual," among others. In this chapter, we capture the behaviors that define or characterize what we know about positive organizational leadership behaviors and translate them from abstract or unfamiliar settings into the context of school leadership.

We begin with some notes to orient our storyline. First, while positive organizational leadership shares the language of other leadership theories and models, it focuses more pointedly on leadership as both a developmental process and a socially constructed reality. We have worked with many school leaders who are, in our view, personally upstanding, deeply motivated by the well-being of students and teachers, and ethical, but are seen by some members of their school community as inept or unsuccessful. Again, it is not who they are, but how others perceive them that matters.

Second, our starting point differs from many other traditional models of leadership because it focuses on principles for *action* rather than the *structures* within which action may occur. We tend to think of schools as bureaucracies, and the work of principals and district staff members as focused on producing particular results using "best practice." But several decades of striving toward best practice in schools—playing by "the rules"—have not produced significant changes in results, whether student achievement or teacher morale. We argue that it is time to think about leadership differently, to move beyond "instructional leadership" or "data-driven practices" to consider ways of thinking about positive school leadership that are not automatically constrained by current organizational structures.[1]

Third, positive leadership language exhibits a resounding penchant for possibilities for both individuals and groups. It is asset-based and uplifting. This is precisely what is needed in education, where the drumbeat of deficiency-based thinking has left many schools mired in low collective efficacy (Dumay, Boonen, & Van Damme, 2013). As Morieux and Tollman (2014) suggest, many organizations respond to external threats with either a "hard" (control structures) or a "soft" (more autonomy and individual training) approach. The architecture of Positive School Leadership provides an alternative by using a sharper lens to look at the patterns of leadership behaviors that honor and support the work of all members of the school community and create incubators for success.

BEHAVIORAL PERSPECTIVES: MORE WEEDS

The set of existing frameworks that capture specific behavioral recommendations for Positive School Leadership is almost limitless. For example, a review by Zhu and associates (2004) presents a list of "leadership dimensions such as initiating structure, consideration, communication, participative leadership," and empowering (p. 187). Witherspoon and Arnold (2010) talk of "healing, sustaining, guiding, and reconciling" (p. 224). Bright (2006) adds forgiveness. B. M. Bass and Steidlmeier (1999) describe positive leadership in terms of "articulating ideas and vision, providing inspirational motivation, stimulating intellectual creativity, and ensuring individual consideration within cooperative actions by the group" (pp. 203–204). Reave (2005), in turn, unpacks the core ideas as: inspirational motivation ("articulating a vision, providing a model, encouraging high standards, demonstrating determination and confidence, stimulating enthusiasm, building confidence, and providing encouragement" and individualized consideration "demonstrating patience, including others in decisions, and sharing sensitivity to feelings") (p. 662). Owens and Hekman (2012), in turn, provide three concepts or "categories" to define positive leadership: "(1) acknowledging personal limits, faults, and mistakes, (2) spotlighting followers' strengths, and (3) modeling teachability" (p. 794). And this list only begins to touch the surface of the head-scratching variety. In addition, the words provide very limited guidance for behavior.

What counts as a behavior and what is viewed as a virtue or a value is often imprecise. Cerit (2009), for example, presents positive organizational leadership as a cluster of attributes that includes some specific actions (follower development, emotional healing, and encouragement of follower autonomy) but also includes personal qualities that may be inferred only from patterns of behavior (humility and altruistic calling). Russell (2001) similarly provides a mixed list of attributes and behaviors associated with positive organizational leadership: vision, credibility, trust, service, modeling, pioneering, appreciation, and empowerment. Taylor, Martin, Hutchinson, and Jinks (2007) provide a comprehensive accounting of positive leadership behaviors, but also do not distinguish between principles (integrity, humility, servant-hood) and attributes of behavior that imply action (such as caring for others, empowering others, developing others, team building, and shared decisionmaking).

Other writers make a clearer distinction between principles and behavior. G. W. Fairholm (1991), for example, explains that "the central orientation of the new post-heroic leader is toward followers and a developer-leader model," but goes on to make these more concrete, pointing to artifacts such as "building a shared responsibility team, developing coworker skills, and building a common vision of the group's potential" (p. 60). Waldman, Ranier, House, and Puranam (2001) list the following key action orientations on the part of leaders: "articulating a vision and a sense of mission, showing determination, and communicating high performance expectations" (p. 135). Kouzes and Posner (1999, 2002) propose five key positively grounded leader behaviors: (1) challenging the process, (2) inspiring a shared vision, (3) enabling others to act, (4) modeling the way, and (5) encouraging the heart. Because schools are value-laden social institutions, we are particularly sensitive to observable behaviors that influence the *ethical behavior and climate* of the larger setting (Grojean, Resick, Dickson, & Smith, 2004).

We also know from the extensive body of research that the impact of school leaders on any "bottom line" is indirect (Leithwood, Louis, Anderson, & Wahlstrom, 2004), which is also true of other kinds of organizations (Detert, Treviño, Burris, & Andiappan, 2007). We also know that leaders make a difference in the organizations that they manage because they help develop member *commitment and motivation*. Finally, we paid more attention to models and empirical work that focus on *leading in complex settings,* based on our conviction that the work of schools is very complicated and this demands complex and varied leadership behaviors (Cerit, 2009; Leroy et al., 2012). Even with these screens, finding a way through this dizzying variety is no easy task.

We have synthesized six germane behaviors that we chose because there is empirical evidence of their impact on others in multiple settings; they are consistent with the foundations built in the previous chapters; and they can be observed either directly or through structures and routines that shape the behavior of others. These include: (1) supporting, (2) enabling, (3) modeling, (4) acting authentically, (5) establishing values, and (6) developing relationships.

SUPPORTING: A BEHAVIORAL FOUNDATION FOR EVERYTHING ELSE

> Support is a basic need. Effective leaders know that no matter where people work, they value support: it is a basic need of utmost importance. (Hensley & Burmeister, 2008, p. 127)

> The leader's primary role is to value and support human talent. (W. L. Gardner & Schermerhorn, 2004, p. 279)

Positive school leaders start their day by considering how they can develop the people who report to them (Detert et al., 2007; Graham, 1991). Indeed, there is a good deal of evidence that this may be the most important set of behaviors for any leader (W. L. Gardner & Schermerhorn, 2004; Reave, 2005). We know that "leaders can play a central role in helping employees realize their potential" (Liden et al., 2008, p. 172). One essential dimension here is an "increase in learning of some kind" (Rynes, Bartunek, Dutton, & Margolis, 2012, p. 518), helping others acquire more knowledge.

This will seem obvious to anyone who has examined the research on teacher motivation, which emphasizes the centrality of personal growth (Bogler & Somech, 2004; Louis, 1998). Teachers' dedication to their profession increases when they experience increased formal and informal development opportunities (McLaughlin & Talbert, 2006; T. M. Smith & Rowley, 2005; Youngs & King, 2002). There is, of course, a chicken-and-egg feature of these findings that is important for school leaders: Support for growth increases commitment—but commitment also increases the appetite for growth. In addition, the observation that sustained teacher development is critical begs the question of specificity: What can principals actually *do* to develop a supportive environment that increases vitality and energy in a school? We unpack leader support as consisting of four intersecting lines of action: supporting individual needs for growth, building a growth culture, sensemaking, and maintaining a balance of psychological safety and expectations.

Support Requires Knowing Individual Needs

Successful leaders are adept at developing the talents of the colleagues with whom they work (Cerit, 2009). This, analysts tell us, occurs when leaders have deep knowledge of the organization and its needs (Kropiewnicki & Shapiro, 2001; Morieux & Tollman, 2014), a "knowledge of each follower's unique characteristics and interests" (van Dierendonck & Patterson, 2014, p. 119), and a willingness "to provide opportunities for learning" (Cerit, 2009, p. 602).

In education, this contrasts with a "top-down," one-size-fits-all professional development strategy. In 1993, Judith Warren Little warned that the dominant training and skills coaching model of professional development in education was unsuited to the complexity of the demands emerging from within the profession and in policy. She, along with others, led significant efforts to revise the ideal standards for professional learning in education to emphasize the importance of reflection and smaller learning communities, which are recognized in the updated "standards for professional learning" (Learning Forward, 2011), but "best practice" skills training still dominates.

Research in other sectors emphasizes support for growth based on personalized relationships (Murphy, Beck, Crawford, & Hodges, 2001). This requires that leaders know persons well, "to read emotions well [and] to attune to the person" (Frost, 2003, p. 169). Alternatively, as Beck (1994) tells us, "administrators must possess the ability to understand persons and situations and the knowledge to use this understanding to engage in developmentally sound activities" (p. 107). Drilling down further, we discover that development is nurtured by "feedback that promotes continuous improvement" (Fornes et al., 2008, p. 349) and "guided mastery" (Luthans & Church, 2002, p. 62) that helps workers become adept at their tasks. Research in schools in a variety of settings supports this perspective, suggesting that teachers who receive frequent individualized formative feedback from school leaders have greater dedication and better practice (Canrinus, Helms-Lorenz, Beijaard, Buitink, & Hofman, 2012; S. M. Johnson, Kraft, & Papay, 2012; Louis, 1998).

Intentionality and the ability of leaders to "make explicit the step-by-step process of personal development" (Owens & Hekman, 2012, p. 802) are often important. As G. W. Fairholm (1991) captures it, "The technology of follower development asks the leader to be a teacher" (p. 78). This requires talent identification (Clifton & Harter, 2003), methods to "tap the intrinsic motives of followers" (G. W. Fairholm, 1991, p. 61), and "strengths development for each individual" (Clifton & Harter, 2003, p. 121). This strengths-based as opposed to deficiency-based approach to development is a consistent theme (Luthans & Avolio, 2003).

Personalized efforts to develop and nurture talent are so critical that they have been proposed by the global Boston Consulting Group as a bedrock of the "smart simplicity" approach to public-sector improvement (LaBresh, Watters, & Chandhoke, 2017). In many organizations (including schools), the structure guiding this work is bureaucratic: annual professional development plans. Our work in schools suggests that these plans rarely stimulate individualized consultation, but teachers are likely to point to periodic informal conversations that stimulate interest and reflection about where to go for learning opportunities (Wahlstrom & Louis, 2015). In other words, if the principal (or other school leader) knows a teacher well and is in a trusting relationship, there are many occasions to provide support for learning. Positive school leaders should consider how their current interactions with staff members might already be providing the needed encouragement for growth.

Support for Learning Requires Building the School's Culture

Beyond more personalization in development, support also focuses on the creation of a culture of learning (Murphy & Torre, 2014). This is a complex process, but requires the anchor of access to the physical and technical resources teachers need to do their work well (Harter, Schmidt, & Keyes, 2003; Kroth & Keeler, 2009; Liden et al., 2008; Walumbwa, Avolio, & Zhu, 2008). A second behavior concentrates on providing rewards and recognition for work. This goes beyond the individualized feedback discussed above and focuses on publicly communicating authentic respect and esteem (Cerit, 2009; Donaldson, 2001). The routinized practices of leaders that facilitate sharing positive affirmation of successful work contribute to a sense of overall commitment to the well-being of employees (Fehr & Gelfand, 2012).

Positive affirmation can be communicated both by overt expressions of trust and confidence in teachers' professional capacities (W. L. Gardner & Schermerhorn, 2004) and, at the same time, by expressing confidence that members will stretch themselves (R. E. Quinn et al., 2000). Creating a collective sense of efficacy in the school always incorporates a more general message of collective respect and affirmation (Donaldson, 2001; Walumbwa, Avolio, & Zhu, 2008), even in the face of challenges. For Positive School Leaders, an important element of this storyline is sensitivity to how teachers prefer to be recognized (Harter et al., 2002) and how the group responds to "calling out" individual performance. We easily can point to schools where highly effective teachers or teacher teams prefer to remain anonymous because they fear that "standing out" as individuals might diminish their collaborative relationships with peers, while in other schools there is joyful celebration of every success. Thus, creating a culture of support demands a delicate equilibrium between actions that nurture individuals and those that develop recognition of the school's broad talent pool. Louis and Murphy (2017) show that a principal's acknowledgment of the professional competence of the teaching staff as a whole is strongly associated with teachers' perceptions that the principal cares about their unique professional needs (see also G. W. Fairholm, 1991).

We emphasize that we are not arguing that affirming the positive is the same as avoiding all negative feedback. There is evidence that people and groups often can learn best by reflecting on "small errors"; in addition, many people seek authentic feedback in which nonpositive comments can serve positive functions (Kolb, 2014). Positive school leaders also must deal occasionally with serious issues of individual and group performance, but strategies and behaviors when negative feedback is required are beyond the scope of this chapter.

Support Requires Listening and "Sensemaking"

The idea of sensemaking, first introduced by Karl Weick (1979), provides a rich ground for positive organizational psychology (Lotto & Murphy, 1990). The world is complex and often confusing, and we navigate through it by using cues that have become shorthand tools for traveling through the usual paths. We "make sense" of road signs when we learn to drive, but become confused when we go to another country: Signs may look familiar but contain different information (kangaroo crossing), or there may be no signs where we expect them. That is when sensemaking—identifying the meaning of novel signs and figuring out a way of navigating to the desired destination—becomes important.

The same is true in schools. Most of the work is familiar and easily negotiated—until things change. What happens when there is a rapid increase in enrollment of a group of students from an unfamiliar cultural background? Or a new district or state mandate changes a basic curriculum focus (such as many recent initiatives to introduce social–emotional learning curricula)? This requires a positive leader's initiative to support members of the school community during a time when patterned familiar behavior and practices need to change.

When members of a school feel challenged by change, effective leaders provide support by learning to listen to the needs and concerns of those they manage, to hear voices of followers (Kelsey, 1981; May, Gilson, & Harter, 2004), and to focus especially on "developing followers by considering employees' input before making important decisions" (Walumbwa, Hartnell, et al., 2010, p. 520). However, they also challenge others to adapt by helping them to discern meaning out of confusing situations and by assisting them to find a new path that includes both themselves and others (Plowman et al., 2007). As one school librarian we worked with put it, "*When our principal came, she got us all on the same page . . . she really reaches out to encourage those of us who are not in the classroom, to support the classroom teachers in any way we can.*"

Support comes from identifying perceived barriers and allowing the emergence of new possibilities (Smircich & Morgan, 1982). This requires the co-construction of "shared narratives" that bring possibilities (or other ideas of support) to life (Bolino, Turnley, & Bloodgood, 2002, p. 515) and "leader storytelling which integrates a moral and spiritual component . . . so that organizational members feel connected to a larger community and a higher purpose" (Driscoll & McKee, 2007, p. 214). Support for sensemaking need not be long-winded. No one expects principals or other school leaders to become professional orators. Persistence in identifying positive opportunities and shorter stories about staying a course that engages all (or most) teachers in moving forward are, however, required.

The more challenging the circumstances, the more necessary leader sensemaking becomes. Teachers in low-income schools with ethnically/racially diverse populations express deep gratitude toward principals whom they see as having both a strong ethic of caring and a strong narrative of high expectations (Palmer & Louis, 2017; Wahlstrom & Louis, 2015). This is apparent in small practices, such as consistent reviewing of lesson plans with positive feedback and suggestions for trying something new. As a teacher from one school put it, "Our principal is really the kind of person that makes sure she does positive [feedback] first and then . . . she will offer her own suggestions . . . or she will also recommend a teacher to go and observe. She will help you find someone that can help you learn." These sensemaking behaviors are not epic, but they are focused on consistently negotiating the challenges of teaching while learning from small errors (May et al., 2004).

Support Requires Both Psychological Safety and Clear Expectations

Positive school leaders create a value-based sense of security in school settings that allows each teacher to feel that he or she belongs (Beck, 1994). Consistently calling attention to individual and collective talent affirms teachers' ability to negotiate the challenges of guiding the learning and development processes of vulnerable children and youth, and principals can boost efficacy "by affecting the way followers perceive the risks and challenges associated with their work setting" (Walumbwa, Avolio, & Zhu, 2008, p. 817).

Nevertheless, psychological safety also must be balanced with collective performance expectations. Principals and other school leaders are not just cheerleaders but also mentors and coaches (as we will discuss later). We argue, however, that Positive school leaders develop performance expectations in a cultural context, by positioning them in "an understanding of organizational culture, ensuring continuity of values and norms" (Grojean et al., 2004, p. 230). To foster collective expectations, they use what Morieux and Tollman (2014) call the shadow of the future, or helping people to understand the future consequences of continuing old behaviors, and helping them to "construct situations as opportunities rather than threats" (Frost, 2003, p. 82), thereby nurturing safe environments (Driscoll & McKee, 2007). In schools, this is often visible in the way in which principals (and district leaders) reframe policy mandates as a chance to extend and reinforce locally initiated goals that are linked to a commitment to student and family success (Louis & Robinson, 2012; Louis, Thomas, & Anderson, 2010).

Supporting—In Summary

Positive school leaders use the supportive base described above to help others develop their talents and acquire more knowledge (W. L. Gardner & Schermerhorn, 2004; Rynes et al., 2012). In other words, positive leaders "define their role in terms of coworker development" (G. W. Fairholm, 1991, p. 67), which is distinct from designing a program of group or individual professional development. Consideration of teachers' developmental needs allows principals to interact with and influence teachers to increase both their skills and their role as citizens of the school (Zhu et al., 2004), even at a time when some are inclined to withdraw or do not have the energy to make major changes.

Developing others means providing larger and smaller opportunities for individual development, but also developing group cultures that support reciprocal and semiautonomous learning (Smircich & Morgan, 1982). Providing support during challenging times requires an attitude of service to others (Cerit, 2009; De Pree, 1997; Greenleaf, 1977/1997), but also action. Leaders shape structures and policies by developing the capacity of others to meet new challenges (Takeuchi, Chen, & Lepak, 2009), "parlaying employees into the right places" (Owens & Hekman, 2012, p. 804), finding and providing "zones of proximal development" for growth. In other words, they engage in highly adaptive work (Heifetz, 1994) that focuses attention on creating a bridge between what was and what is emerging, for both individuals and the group as a whole.

ENABLING AND EMPOWERING: DEVELOPING STRONG PARTNERS

> The goal of empowerment is to create many leaders at all levels of the organization. (Russell, 2001, p. 76)

> Leaders are most effective when they can inspire others to engage in the responsibilities of leadership, rather than attempting to carry out all leadership responsibilities on their own. (Gittell & Douglass, 2012, p. 720)

Research suggests that "it is important to foster, enable, and encourage leaders throughout the organization and in other stakeholder relationships to behave like leaders" (Cameron, 2006, p. 143). G. W. Fairholm (1991) claims that enabling others to exercise leadership is perhaps the most significant element in positive organizational leadership. As a frequently quoted proverb of unknown origin proclaims, "Give a man a fish, and you feed him for a day. Teach a man to fish, and you feed him for a lifetime." We start with an examination of the related concepts of enabling and empowerment, which, like most of the ideas that we develop in this chapter, cover a wide range of interpretations.

Enabling

We think of enabling as consistent with our clarification of the role of support as development. As Yammarino, Salas, Serban, Shirreffs, and Shuffler (2012) argue, "Enabling leadership is a set of behaviors or actions taken to encourage the interaction of agents to increase coordination and interdependence between agents with relevant knowledge" (p. 392). This idea builds on the idea that "enabling others 'to act' fosters collaboration [and] serves to strengthen their subordinates" (Taylor et al., 2007, p. 412).

Using the fishing metaphor, enabling is not delegation but providing the conditions that allow people to perfect their capacity for fishing. When we apply the lens of organizational goals to enabling, we see that it has many facets. One goal is to free members from real or perceived constraints on positive actions (Conger et al., 2000), and one means is to involve followers in planning and decisionmaking (Russell, 2001). Enabling thus develops followers by sharing leadership and building collaborative work (Cerit, 2009; M. R. Fairholm & G. Fairholm, 2000).

Enabling can take many forms in schools, but it supplements the core idea of collective development articulated earlier. Positive school leaders provide the needed tools to teachers (and other professionals) so that they can do their job, and they also provide a framework for teamwork. Enabling thus incorporates the goal of learning from one another. Enabling voice boils down to a simple behavior with significant consequences: "When team members are able to speak up and get involved (voice), the likelihood that many of them will exercise leadership increases greatly" (Carson, Tesluk, & Marrone, 2007, p. 1223).

But school leaders can get "stuck" in their enabling role because they see themselves as hampered by larger organizational structures, union contracts governing roles and responsibilities, and limited budgets. Our image of educational bureaucracies becomes an iron cage that detracts from enabling and building assets. Positive school leaders think of rules as explicit norms of behavior, which makes them more pliable tools. Hoy and Sweetland (2001) give the example of "a general rule [for problem solving] that a professional judgment is encouraged and acceptable" (p. 298), and go on to point out that "enabling schools encourage trusting relations between teachers and between teachers and the principal; facilitate telling the truth and make it unnecessary, and likely dysfunctional, to spin the truth" (p. 314).

What underlying conditions enable individuals and groups to do their best? Carson et al. (2007) cite a long list of scholars who point to three critical conditions: shared purpose, social support, and voice. We have covered shared purpose and social support; here we turn to voice because it provides a link between enabling and empowering.

Empowerment Is Voice

Empowerment provides voice to followers (D. M. Mayer et al., 2009). Voice, in turn, enables them to act (Taylor et al., 2007), while also encouraging innovation (Park & Peterson, 2003). In addition, it represents a commitment by leaders to both speaking and (nonjudgmental) listening. Voice creates *opportunities* for influence, and the *capacity* to exercise influence is critical both for self-efficacy and for developing teams. Voice thus represents the behavior that underpins the *informal* side of empowerment. Empowerment also has a *formal* side, since it presumes that members have some rights and obligations to participate in decisions that affect them.

Because *power* is a word that has many connotations, it is important to be clear about how the positive leadership literature treats it. First, empowerment is not abdication or the unexamined handing over of decisionmaking to followers (Fry, 2003; Melrose, 2003; Russell, 2001). It occurs when "the leader shares stewardship responsibilities for actions with followers" (G. W. Fairholm, 1991, p. 75). The important modifier in Fairholm's definition is *stewardship* because it draws attention to the obligations of those who participate in decisionmaking and the design of work (Zhu et al., 2004). It is based not only on mutual obligations, but also on trusting that leaders will make decisions for the good of the whole, considering both the short and long run (Dennis & Bocarnea, 2005).

We cannot, however, ignore power. The practice and behavior of positive organizational leaders must acknowledge that empowerment is about "a process in which influence is shared among individuals who are hierarchical unequals" (Kim, 2002, p. 232). Every member of a school is aware of the inequality embedded in the bureaucratic structure—as well as the constraints on power that have been established through decades of state and federal activism in educational policy, union activity, and increases in specialized knowledge within subjects. As Aker-Hocevar and Touchson (1999, quoted in York-Barr & Duke, 2004) note, "The interdependence of structure, power and culture is corroborated by . . . teachers' stories over and over again, no matter what the situation—empowering or disempowering" (p. 273). The language of power in education is contested in ways that are quite different from, for example, the situation in entrepreneurial design firms or manufacturing organizations. In schools specifically, empowerment usually has a moral overtone and is a condition that "emphasizes that every person . . . is capable of making decisions and assuming responsibility and that the simple fact of personhood entitles each to act as a moral responsible agent" (Beck, 1994, p. 103).

York-Barr and Duke (2004) emphasize that power may be allocated to positions, but also must be awarded by peers. Empowerment is, thus, a process that focuses on individuals and their capacities as well as "teams as a whole" (G. Chen et al., 2007, p. 333). Positive school leaders, therefore, must behave in ways that are sensitive to the various interpretations of the kind of influence others expect to have, and must recognize that others may determine whether those who are formally empowered also will be influential.

Empowerment is undertaken to enhance organizational trust (M. R. Fairholm & G. Fairholm, 2000), but, particularly in professional settings, might not have that effect unless some trust is already present (Spreitzer, 2008). In schools where there has been tension between administrators and others, efforts to empower teachers can be interpreted as false and even demeaning (Louis, 2007; Mayrowetz, Smylie, Murphy, & Louis, 2007). However, even if building trust requires additional time, an important first step in empowering is to help people see where their efforts fit into the larger picture of work (Gittell & Douglass, 2012) and to convey "that they are part of each other and of the organization's greater purpose" (Ferris, 1988, p. 49, see also Zhu et al., 2004).

We close this discussion by noting that Positive school leaders continually must attend to the need to balance the enabling, voice, and empowerment of individuals—particularly those teachers who are already influential leaders among their peers—with the empowering of teams or teachers as a whole (G. Chen et al., 2007). At the root, both enabling and empowering are experiences by individuals who feel listened to and taken into consideration. The work of schools, however, requires more. Empowerment is about enabling colleagues (G. W. Fairholm, 1996; Fry, 2003), which requires every influential person or group to lead by example (Taylor et al., 2007). In schools, this is about "leaders providing teachers a sense of control and influence over their work" (Stockard & Lehman, 2004, p. 754), and influence "in developing and implementing organizational strategies" (Beck, 1994, p. 81). Positive school leaders do not operate from a power framework, but enable and empower by attending to involvement and shared responsibility (Senge, 1977). Empowerment is about "creat[ing] followers who are capable of independent self-direction" (G. W. Fairholm, 1991, p. 8) and also about building social capacity (Bolino et al., 2002) and a sense of ownership of decisions that have consequences (Kropiewnicki & Shapiro, 2001; Taylor et al., 2007). In summary, it is not about changing formal structures but about changing social relationships inside the school (Murphy, 2016b).

MODELING: ILLUMINATING THE BEHAVIORAL PATH

Leaders who model the way create standards of excellence and then set an example for others. One way that people learn is by observing the behavior of others and the consequences of it. Observed behaviors that have desired consequences become part of an individual's repertoire, and later become translated into actual behavior in the appropriate situation. This is referred to as modeling. (Grojean et al., 2004, p. 228)

So far, we have reported that positive organizational leaders are known for supporting and enabling followers. Here we add that they also model the way followers should understand and carry out their work (Avolio & Gardner, 2005; Ferris, 1988). Adults learn in many ways, and one of them is by watching closely what others are doing, and then "striving to duplicate the values and behaviors of models deemed credible and attractive" (D. M. Mayer et al., 2009, p. 3). Leaders model by "manifesting . . . inner convictions in outer behavior" (Reave, 2005, p. 663), and many writers claim that this is the primary way that they influence the behavior of others (Avolio & Gardner, 2005; Palanski & Yammarino, 2011; Walumbwa, Peterson, et al., 2010).

While this covers a good deal of ground, key issues for school leaders parallel those raised in other sectors:

1. Modeling by providing a clear message about one's own character and conduct (Reave, 2005), which includes moral capacities (Lennick & Kiel, 2007), and "creating the self as an example of someone who can be trusted, relied upon, and admired" (Reave, 2005, p. 663)
2. Modeling positive traits and states such as confidence, hope, optimism, and resiliency (Luthans & Avolio, 2003) and self-determination (Avolio & Gardner, 2005)
3. Modeling to influence organizational culture (Owens & Hekman, 2012)

School leaders who wish to develop others recognize that *what they do* is more important than *what they say*. They do not tell others what to believe or how to lead, but "establish and maintain cultural values through social learning, whereby employees observe, initiate, and internalize leaders' values" (Fehr & Gelfand, 2012, p. 675). Seeing is believing: When teachers observe leadership that they admire, they internalize and emulate it (Cerit, 2009; Leithwood & Riehl, 2005; D. M. Mayer et al., 2009; Neal, 1999; Palanski & Yammarino, 2011).

Thus, a fundamental premise is that in order to effectively model, school leaders must be visible rather than laboring in their offices (Treviño,

Hartman, & Brown, 2000). When principals are in the hall, it is often the small actions that are most noticed: How did a principal treat a student who was running in the hall or who was late to class? Was that treatment respectful? Condescending? Authoritative? Empathetic? If the principal was respectful and empathetic (although firm), other adults as well as students will notice it, and if these behaviors are practiced regularly, others will come to understand that they are what is expected. Modeling is not a one-way process but, as we discussed in Chapter 4, occurs in the context of meaningful relationships. To model, a principal must first engage deeply with others in the work of the school and be attentive to the social context. (See Figures 1.1 and 1.2.)

This is where instructional leadership and leadership for data-based decisionmaking and instructional improvement become important. Modeling instructional leadership may involve (in a few cases) demonstrating the leader's pedagogic expertise. More important, especially in most secondary schools, is the modeling of insightful, situation-specific questions. Asking thoughtful questions about what is happening in a classroom requires reflection and suggests to the recipient of the (nonjudgmental) question that asking questions about what is happening and why is as important as covering the textbook (Reitzug, West, & Angel, 2008; Spillane, Hallett, & Diamond, 2003). Such conversations also set expectations about instructional quality and thoughtfulness, which establish the principal as a transformational leader (Leithwood, Jantzi, & Steinbach, 1999). Modeling is important if teachers are expected to become data users: As Cosner (2011) and Datnow and Hubbard (2016) point out, the principal's communication about and participation in data use may be critical to teachers' engagement in this task.

Principals also need to rely on others. They are rarely the only people in the school who are behaving in ways that are consistent with shared values and ideals, and they can use the positive modeling of other individuals or teams to reinforce "the way we do things around here." Principals who learn from observing others—a teacher who is particularly effective in working with students on the edge of a meltdown or parent liaisons who effectively diffuse difficult situations—can expand their own leadership toolkit, while acknowledging the professionalism and service focus of those around them (Eisenbeiss, 2012). As Doh (2003) points out, effective leaders have a "teachable frame of mind" (p. 64), and that includes explicit modeling of learning from others.

M. E. Brown and Treviño (2006) emphasize that leaders must establish themselves as credible before they can begin to influence others through their own behavior. In other words, principals who are new to a school should not expect their behavior to have immediate consequences, no matter how experienced they are. New leaders establish credibility over the long haul by pointing out what they are learning from others.

Modeling, Mentoring, and Coaching

Kouzes and Posner (2002) argue that "any skill can be strengthened, honed, and enhanced if we have the motivation and desire, the practice and feedback, the role models and coaching, and the support and recognition." In other words, they mention coaching in the same breath as modeling and mentoring. However, they are distinct (Scandura, 1992).

In our view, modeling relies on a person's power to observe leadership behaviors, while coaching evokes a stronger hand through targeted questions or nonjudgmental feedback designed to improve another's capacities (Knight, 2009; D. M. Mayer et al., 2009). In contrast, mentoring usually refers to the establishment of a longer term, trusted, nurturing relationship in which an older/ wiser person has a younger person's developmental interests at heart (Brockbank & McGill, 2012; Garvey, Stokes, & Megginson, 2014; T. Thomas, Thomas, & Firestone, 2015) and may involve more explicit teaching. Of course, there is a fine line: A principal may think that he or she is modeling, but someone else in the school may ask, "Why did you do it that way?" and the principal immediately may be propelled into an explanation that is more directive. We make this distinction because in most circumstances Positive school leaders also will coach and mentor, particularly when they are working to enhance individual capacities (in other words, mentoring specific individuals).

Modeling, coaching, and mentoring share one important characteristic: They cannot be imposed. Principals, using their authority, often can tell someone what to do. However, if the same person chooses to pay attention to a principal's best leadership efforts, or persistently seeks feedback, the principal's ability to influence beyond mere compliance will increase. In other words, it doesn't matter very much what it is called, as long as the principal is viewed as a trusted, wise, and more ethical model.

Connecting Modeling to Previous Chapters

We have seen that positive leaders emphasize ethical and moral action (Hannah et al., 2005; B. Smith et al., 2004). This value basis allows them to be role models and to influence the ethical conduct of their followers (Murphy & Beck, 1995). Ultimately, effective and ethically based leadership behaviors can have an impact on the ethical climate of organizations by influencing the underlying values and attitudes of others (Grojean et al., 2004; Luthans & Youssef, 2007). As Russell (2001) tells us, "Modeling is an important means for establishing [organizational] values" (p. 78). Positive school leaders clearly frame moral dilemmas, transparently respond to them, and thus become ethical role models. In summary, leaders who model the way create standards of excellence and then set an example for others to follow.

Leader role modeling also increases followers' sense of optimism. "Because optimism can be acquired through modeling . . . one way leaders can influence their followers' optimism is to increase follower identification with the leader by modeling" (Avolio, Gardner, Walumbwa, Luthans, & May, 2004, p. 814). We also discover that "approaches of modeling teachability are important for fostering intrinsically engaged employees" (Owens & Hekman, 2012, p. 807) and the "commitment of followers" (G. W. Fairholm, 1991, p. 63). Last, we note links between positive leader role modeling and follower self-efficacy and well-being (Ilies, Morgeson, & Nahrgang, 2005). And, all of these outcomes may spread contagiously among followers (Emmons, 2003).

ACTING AUTHENTICALLY: BEING CONSISTENT AND TRUE

Behavioral integrity . . . is the perceived degree of congruence between the values expressed by words and those expressed through action. It is the perceived level of match or mismatch between the espoused and the enacted. (Simons, 1999, p. 91)

Similarly, behavioral integrity has been demonstrated to drive follower performance and organizational citizenship behaviors through perceived trust in and satisfaction with the leader, and follower affected organizational commitment. (Leroy et al., 2012, p. 256)

Of course, to be viewed as a model, coach, or mentor, a leader also must be seen as genuine or authentic. We explicitly pointed to the importance of authentic behavior in Chapter 2, where we noted that authenticity was a foundation for a strong relationship orientation. Authenticity means being "true to the self, and one's core values in particular, and resistant to social or situational pressures to compromise one's values" (W. L. Gardner et al., 2005, p. 350), and is about "discovery and expressing oneself . . . finding the design of one's own life" (Zhu et al., 2004, p. 19).

However, by this definition alone, not all authentic people could be positive leaders: One could be authentically true to a self or on a path that others viewed as erratic or wrongheaded. So, we must add more substance to this definition in order to include it in our list of Positive School Leadership behaviors. More specifically, positive leaders will have their words line up with their actions, which, in turn, are guided by the values that we described in Chapter 2. Positive School Leadership is about what Walumbwa, Avolio, Gardner, et al. (2008) emphasize as resistance to the temptations provided by "external threats, inducements, or social expectations and rewards" (p. 93). In other words, both values and principle-driven behaviors are visible to others in times when there might be an easier or softer way.

The idea of authenticity appears to encompass most leader virtues, including "self awareness, positive self-regulation, positive psychological capabilities, and positive self development" (W. L. Gardner & Schermerhorn, 2004, p. 272). Begley (2001, 2006) argues, however, that *behaving authentically* is the most critical component of ethical school leadership. Not surprisingly, a number of analysts have worked to provide a way through this thicket by clarifying the elements of behaviors that support authenticity, which we synthesize below.

The first stage is internal, emphasizing *self-awareness* or knowing where one stands on important beliefs (W. L. Gardner et al., 2005; Reave, 2005). According to Avolio and Gardner (2005), an authentic self-awareness has behavioral dimensions, which include being true to oneself rather than conforming to outside expectations; acting on conviction rather than a desire for status, honors, or personal benefits; and basing one's actions on personal values and convictions. For school leaders, as we have argued in Chapter 2, this moral stance is particularly important because education is an inherently value-based endeavor. However, this initial work is internal.

Stage 2 moves into behavior, engaging a leader's *observable morals* to address and adjudicate issues that are characterized by competing values (Luthans & Avolio, 2003). Indeed, adding an explicit moral perspective to decisionmaking "has been consistently identified as a primary mechanism whereby authentic leaders influence and develop followers" (Avolio & Gardner, 2005, p. 325). Schools, for example, often are faced with dilemmas about how to allocate scarce resources to valued programs, groups, or goals, or how to balance the need for caring with the equally pressing need for standards, which make the capacity to engage in complex moral reasoning particularly critical (Duignan, 2012). Positive school leaders need to be very explicit (authentic) about placing values and ethics at the center of these decisions (Duignan & Bhindi, 1997).

Stage 3 is about *transparent sharing*, or making values and positions explicit (Leroy et al., 2012). Morally grounded but difficult decisions will be more powerful when one can explain them using value-infused language and being clear about difficult trade-offs. Even those who disagree are more likely to attribute positive ethical leadership under those conditions.

Stage 4 is about being transparently *accountable to oneself and others*. Much of accountability in education focuses on student test scores, but positive school leaders have a different benchmark in mind. Richard Elmore (2005) argues that "as schools become more coherent and effective as organizations . . . the work of school leaders becomes defined as the explicit reinforcement of organizational values. . . . The alignment of individual values with collective expectations . . . results in internal accountability (pp. 135–136). Teachers want to know that they are part of a value-centered organization and that they are "accountable to a standard of relationship that is far beyond the structures of simple economic activity" (Ferch & Mitchell, 2001, p. 76). Elmore (2005) goes on to emphasize that these collective standards can develop only in settings where values are openly discussed.

Stage 5 returns to the internal work of Positive School Leaders: developing a *personal, value-based leadership theory* that grows as they become increasingly experienced. Leithwood and Steinbach (1995) studied decisionmaking among educational leaders and found that experts (those able to solve complicated problems well) were more likely to incorporate the needs of others, vision, and values into their thinking. When faced with more difficult, ill-structured problems, they were more likely to search their own leadership value system than to rely on "research" or information. Leithwood and Steinbach (1995) also found that experts were more likely to be seen by teachers as transformational leaders, which aligns with Leroy et al.'s (2012) observation that "leaders who remain true to the self in their behaviors . . . will be perceived as . . . delivering on promises and aligning words and deeds" (p. 258).

Authenticity encourages integrity in others, and as "followers continue to act with high behavioral integrity when representing the team, so too might they also display high behavioral integrity when acting as individuals" (Palanski & Yammarino, 2011, p. 768). We also know that authenticity leads to other intermediate outcomes, such as trust in leaders and organizational commitment (Avolio, Gardner, et al., 2004; Leroy et al., 2012; Palanski & Yammarino, 2011).

ESTABLISHING VALUES: ACTIONS SPEAK LOUDER THAN WORDS

> Leaders are the focal point for the development of work-related values. (Lord & Brown, 2001, p. 142)

> If people do not hear about values from the top, it is not clear to employees that values are important. (Treviño et al., 2000, p. 135)

We elaborated on the importance of personal values for Positive school leaders in Chapter 3, noting that they serve as a foundation for a sense of purpose and for establishing a basis for positive behaviors in others (Lord & Brown, 2001). Here we expand on that to show how leadership behaviors can contribute to a value-driven school environment beyond behaving authentically.

Principals and other leaders are not the only source of values, but they "play a vital role in shaping follower values" (G. W. Fairholm, 1991, p. 63), which then shapes everyone's interpretations of the work of the school. The leader's task is to help elicit core values and to make them vital and visible (Russell, 2001), and to make explicit what Cameron (2006) refers to as an "abundance value system" (p. 140). Values provide a glue that holds individual virtues together (G. W. Fairholm, 1991) and offers grounding for followers (Atkins & Parker, 2011; Leroy et al., 2012). These tasks—determining/shaping core values, keeping them vibrant, and ensuring that they bind people together—are critical in schools where the daily work is rarely easy and often ambiguous, and where feedback on performance is rarely immediate.

Values and Routines

Susan Rosenholtz (1985) argued that schools benefit from a "tight coupling" of values, norms, and behaviors at the managerial level. Principals bring values to life through daily action rather than mission statements. Routine behaviors (such as how students are greeted at the beginning of the day) allow all members to experience values as the blueprints or foundations for action that can be brought into play when larger issues (designing solutions for major problems, or resolving incidental conflicts) arise (Russell, 2001). In other words, translating values into behaviors that others regularly see, means that they are extrapolated to new situations with "a strong sense of determination to act in value-consistent ways" (Atkins & Parker, 2011, p. 533).

In addition to ensuring that the routine actions of a school leader are value-driven, keeping values vibrant requires attention to language. We have emphasized that Positive school leaders are not expected to become public orators, but they must be able to articulate "a coherent value pattern within a particular culture" (Lord & Brown, 2001, p. 139) and make values public and vivid by explicitly pointing to actions of others that mirror critical values. Again, consistency and reliability are the key: "Communication about values without the action to match is probably worse than doing nothing at all" (Treviño et al., 2000, p. 136).

School leaders invariably design and model a variety of practices within the school to enhance values. Teachers notice, for example, when we build values into regular rewards and recognitions because these are noticeable signs of what is valued (Grojean et al., 2004). The visible and more subtle ways of recognizing teachers and students are part of managing meaning, where "the saliency of organizational values is underscored through the use of . . . language, rituals, and other forms of symbolic discourse" (Smircich & Morgan, 1982, p. 269). These include "encouraging the formation of traditions that foster and inculcate the core-value vision" (G. W. Fairholm, 1991, p. 76). School traditions matter, and Positive school leaders regularly examine them to ensure that the values they convey are consistent with those that are most important. Is the chess team celebrated along with the football team? Are teachers, nonprofessional staff, and students recognized for the positive contributions they make to the school community? (Murphy, 2016b). As leaders establish new traditions (or discontinue some), "they transparently convey their values to followers, and encourage them to do likewise. . . . Followers come to know what the leader values and stands for" (Avolio, Gardner, et al., 2004, p. 811).

In summary, we expand on the importance of value-based leadership outlined in Chapter 3, noting that "it is not enough to be an ethical person. An executive leader must also find ways to focus the organization's attention on values" (Treviño et al., 2000, p. 128). Nothing does this better than routines.

Values and Vision

One important task for leaders is to develop a strategic vision that vitalizes group potential (G. W. Fairholm, 1991; Murphy, 2016b). Most of us think of vision as it is described in the dictionary, "something seen in a dream, trance, or ecstasy; especially: a supernatural appearance that conveys a revelation" (Merriam-Webster online), and therefore we rarely associate it with behavior. But the dictionary also provides another way to think about vision, as "something seen" (Merriam-Webster online), which implies a more solid experience. This is our view: Vision carries values—or values come to life through vision (G. W. Fairholm, 1991; Fry, 2003). R. E. Quinn and colleagues (2000) add that "not just any vision will do, but a vision for the common good" (p. 153), even if it has no personal benefit (W. L. Gardner et al., 2005).

Much of the writing on leadership asserts a connection between vision and the behavior of members. Visions are expected to foster "development of cooperation, trust, mutual caring, and a commitment to team and organizational effectiveness" (Fry, 2003, p. 710). They direct people "to feel motivated to achieve excellence in their own lives and the life of their organization" (Ferris, 1988, p. 48) and provide a "'moral compass' to guide . . . through unpredictable territory" (Glynn & Jamerson, 2006, p. 168).

Positive school leaders need to consider how to create the link between vision and behavior through their own actions. Authentic storytelling that includes examples from real life seems to be an especially powerful way for leaders to make visions concrete (Driscoll & McKee, 2007). It may be particularly essential where the vision ("every child college ready") may inspire but have few concrete behavioral implications for kindergarten teachers or bus drivers who want to see their part in it. Translating a clear vision into stories that demonstrate desired actions motivates followers. Vision also works its magic when it provides strong images that show congruence between the participants' and the leader's beliefs and values, participants' trust in the leader, the extent to which participants were intellectually stimulated and inspired by the leader, and the extent to which participants saw the leader as charismatic (Kirkpatrick & Locke, 1996).

DEVELOPING RELATIONSHIPS: BEHAVIORAL STRATEGIES

Finally, authentic leaders can foster follower well-being through the development of high quality relationships. (Ilies et al., 2005, p. 387)

> Great managers appear to be very good at creating opportunities for people at work to get to know one another. (Harter et al., 2003, p. 213)

We argued in Chapter 4 that research establishes relationships as the most basic building block for Positive School Leadership, so it is not surprising that this is the final element in our exploration of leader behaviors. Before we delve into specifics, three points merit attention. First, "currently many organizations are held together not by meaningful caring relationships but by bureaucratic systems" (Kaczmarski & Cooperrider, 1997, p. 251)—as Glynn and Jamerson (2006) put it: "There seems to be an overemphasis on asocial conceptions of leadership" (p. 158). This is problematic in school settings, whose effectiveness in goals achievement is dependent on relationships—among students, within classrooms (Murphy 2016b), and between teachers and administrators (Louis et al., 2016; Neal, 1999; Smylie, Murphy, & Louis, 2016). Second, there are antecedents to relational leadership that we made explicit in our discussion of authenticity. Third, our relational framework assumes that density of relationships adds critical social capital that permits rapid on-the-spot adaptation and learning in schools (Gittell & Douglass, 2012; Penuel, Riel, Krause, & Frank, 2009).

Relationship-Fostering Behaviors

Researchers have produced a robust picture of the leader behaviors needed to bring relationships to life and make them grow. We summarize those that are helpful in considering how Positive School Leader behaviors contribute to structures, routines, forums, culture, and designs in the service of vital relationship development.

Effective relational leaders:

- Minimize control routines and emphasize trust (R. E. Quinn et al., 2000, p. 153)
- Are good at reading opportunities for people to work to get to know one another (Harter et al., 2003, p. 219)
- Encourage dense networks that are integrated across levels and functions, and provide rewards for relational rather than solo performance (Atkins & Parker, 2011, p. 538)
- Are aware of the needs of those around them and assist others in meeting those needs (L. Bass, 2012, p. 83)
- Nurture community involvement (Liden et al., 2008, p. 162), develop a "web of inclusion" (Kaczmarski & Cooperrider, 1997, p. 255), and reach out to disenfranchised or discontented members (L. Bass, 2012, p. 84)

- Work side-by-side with those they manage, resulting in stronger connections between them (Gittell, 2003, pp. 290–291)
- Consistently show caring and consideration (Reave, 2005, p. 675); encourage a caring atmosphere (Solomon, Schaps, Watson, & Battistich, 1992, p. 50)
- Develop organizational structures that make relationships more accessible (Gittell & Douglass, 2012, p. 727); facilitate rewarding co-worker relations (W. L. Gardner et al., 2005, p. 368)
- Encourage shared rituals [and] routines, particularly those that celebrate relationships (Noblit et al., 1995, p. 685)
- Develop listening skills (Ferris, 1988, p. 45), which includes paying attention to other's values (Frost, 2003)

The cumulative storyline shows a deep relationship between leaders and employees, and among employees. We also see the development of structures that facilitate both informal (e.g., conversations) and formal (e.g., routines) behaviors that allow these deep relationships to take root and grow (Murphy et al., 2001).

The Impacts of Relationship-Fostering Behavior

Relationships build social capital and strengthen ties within the larger team or teams. As Avolio, Gardner, et al. (2004) point out, the consequent "heightened levels of personal and social identification mean the reciprocation of good deeds . . . and willingness to cooperate with the leader for the benefit of the organization. As a result, followers feel more comfortable and empowered to do activities required" (p. 810). Strengthened relational coordination helps workers in their sensemaking and fosters the development of interpersonal trust (W. L. Gardner et al., 2005; R. C. Mayer, Davis, & Schoorman, 1995). Denser relational networks increase retention (Avey et al., 2008, Reave, 2005), trust (Dirks & Ferrin, 2002), a focus on improving the collective work, and improved performance (Gittell, 2003; Wang et al., 2005). Positive emotions become an additional support for more vital and productive schools (Emmons, 2003; Frost, 2003).

POSITIVE SCHOOL LEADER BEHAVIORS: A CATALYTIC STRATEGY FOR IMPROVEMENT

Leadership theories are "based on the general assumption that leaders influence performance at some macro level through their impact on individuals and groups who contribute to the accomplishment of broader organizational goals" (Ilies et al., 2007, p. 269). This view treats leadership behavior as a kind of magic wand. Starting with dyads, on the other hand, M. E. Brown and Treviño (2006) point to the link between the building block of leader–member exchanges and collective social learning that determines the broader ethical climate of the organization. We have seen that principle-centered leadership is relationship-based and authentic. Leaders who exhibit the range of behaviors we have identified "are likely sources of guidance because of their attractiveness and credibility as role models" (p. 597), and thus influence not only the direct leader–member relationship but the way in which all members treat one another.

Because we know that Positive school leaders are in reciprocal relationships with others, we easily can assume that when leaders meet members' needs for "sense of belonging, of integrity . . . and of identity" (Sluss & Ashforth, 2008, p. 809), members' responses will reinforce future ethical, value-centered, and asset-based behavior on the part of the leader. Thus, we will see a virtuous cycle in which leaders elicit the best in others, "which in turn, are critical determinants of social and organizational processes" (Lord et al., 1999, p. 170).

This is good news for Positive school leaders because it provides a basis for counteracting increasing levels of teacher burnout, particularly for those who are dealing with mounting poverty and stress in the lives of the children they teach and the encroachments of assessment into classroom work. We know that trust is an antidote to teacher burnout (Van Maele & Van Houtte, 2015), and the positive behaviors outlined in this chapter provide principals with a set of conceptual tools for how to build that trust (along with other school assets) most fully. Leaders who seek to support teachers and prevent emotional exhaustion do not need to turn to complicated external interventions: The building blocks for creating a resilient organization are at the micro level, one interaction at a time.

Effective positive leader behaviors encourage followers to begin "to place collective needs over short-term personal gratification" (Wang et al., 2005, p. 422), which can be a powerful reinforcement for working to strengthen and collaborate across a whole school, promoting what often is referred to as "collective responsibility" (J. H. Wu, Hoy, & Tarter, 2013). This is particularly important in schools, where the daily challenges are so complex and variable that they cannot be covered in any job description. A single study of teachers' organizational citizenship behavior in schools shows that it is strongly linked both to principal actions and to the general school climate (DiPaola & Tschannen-Moran, 2014).

Most critically, we learn that Positive School Leadership influences student learning in large measure because of the consistent and reliable relationship between leader–member exchanges and empowerment, individual and collective growth, and job identification and performance (Leithwood et al., 2004; Liden et al., 2008; Sluss et al., 2008; Walumbwa et al., 2009; Walumbwa,

Mayer, et al., 2011). The outcomes noted above become more robust as positive leader behaviors strengthen and deepen relationships. And in schools, high-quality relationships are particularly helpful in assimilating new teachers to the organization because all members take responsibility for teaching newcomers the nature of the deepening "psychological contract."

We have seen that, in essence, social exchange theory proposes that individuals who receive valued rewards from positive leaders, particularly those that are virtue- and principle-based, are motivated to reciprocate with contributions of similar value. In schools, these "extra efforts" may induce the principal to increase his or her perception of a teacher's professionalism and provide additional "rewards" that give that teacher additional learning opportunities (Liden et al., 2008). Translated across many teachers, this relationship-driven outcome may lead to increased capacity for organizational learning and improvement (Louis & Murphy, 2017). It is also connected to the tendency of employees to grant their leaders more latitude in acting as a bank of "idiosyncratic credits" (Hannah et al., 2005), which allow leaders to make an occasional mistake without sacrificing all of the goodwill that has been built up. All of these latter points attend to employee reciprocation in "ways that are consistent with a leader's behaviors [and] values" (Ilies et al., 2007, p. 274), competencies (Choi & Mai-Dalton, 1998), expectations (Walumbwa, Cropanzano, & Goldman, 2011, Walumbwa, Mayer, et al., 2011), and moral decisions (Hannah et al., 2005).

NOTE

1. Of course, this does not mean that we think that instructional leadership or data use is unimportant, but only that they are strategies tied to the specific structures of schooling and are not foundational. We will discuss this in more detail later in this chapter.

CHAPTER 6

Taking the Organizational Temperature

A Focus on Individual Well-Being

There are three key ways in which . . . leaders motivate followers: by increasing follower self-efficacy, by facilitating followers' social identification with their group, and by linking work values to follower values. (Bono & Judge, 2003, p. 555)

Research suggests that identification and self-efficacy mediates the effects of transformational leadership on outcomes. (Walumbwa, Avolio, & Zhu, 2008, p. 801)

The quotes above hint at the complex ways in which leader behavior affects others in the organization. As we traveled through the empirical work on this topic, we found that authors identified many different outcomes. The leader impacts on individuals that come up most frequently include *positive emotions* (well-being, meaningfulness, optimism), *positive psychological states* (psychological capital, psychological empowerment, self-efficacy, identification), and *positive orientations to work* (motivation, commitment, job satisfaction, self-concordance). *These three individual responses to leadership are important because they point to the immediate indicators that leaders can use to determine how well things are going.*

Assessing group and organizational performance, which we turn to in Part III, usually requires either more observation or more reliable data, but if a school leader stops to talk to a teacher at the coffeemaker, the leader usually can determine whether that teacher is in a state of well-being. Assuming that they have established a transparent and open relationship, a few quick exchanges may suffice for the leader to see whether a previously high level of motivation has slipped, or whether self-doubts about job performance are creeping in.

Chapter 5, which dealt with how positive leaders can develop such relationships, assumes that leaders can develop proficiency in "reading" the conditions of others. However, to become expert at reading individuals and monitoring the ongoing state of the school, leaders have to have some clarity about what they are looking for. That is the focus of this chapter.

POSITIVE EMOTIONS

> Emotions are intricately intertwined in theories of leadership and lie at the core of many leadership mechanisms such as inspiring followers, building and sustaining interpersonal relationships, and investing in follower outcomes such as satisfaction, performance and citizenship behaviors. (L. M. Little, Gooty, & Williams, 2016, p. 85)

> The leadership literature on charisma, transformational leadership, leader–member exchange, and other theories have the potential to shed light on how rhetorical techniques and other leadership techniques influence emotional labor, emotional contagion, moods, and overall morale. (R. H. Humphrey, Burch, & Adams, 2016, p. 1022)

> Positive emotions positively impact followers' work attitudes, which in turn elicit desirable follower work behaviors. (Avolio, Gardner, et al., 2004, p. 813)

Our emphasis has been on what Positive school leaders do rather than how they feel, which is not surprising given the evidence that principal behaviors have more of an impact on teachers than "style" or personality (Kirby, Paradise, & King, 1992). In considering positive leadership, however, we cannot ignore the importance of emotions. Emotions are contagious, and it is always possible for any group member to behave in ways that influence the emotional states of others. Leaders, like others, are influenced by the positive and negative emotions of the group (Connelly, Gaddis, & Helton-Fauth, 2013; Ilies et al., 2005). The topic of teacher emotions has received considerable scrutiny in recent years, culminating in Leithwood and Beatty's (2007) observation that principals cannot be effective without attending to the affective state of teachers:

> We argue that teacher emotions . . . are a potent and largely untapped resource, which educational leaders need to understand better if they are to be directly and intentionally helpful . . . in the shared task of improving student learning. (p. 2)[1]

Our attention, in line with Leithwood and Beatty, will be on how leaders influence other members because "leaders who understand these fluctuations in emotions and how individuals regulate emotions are more capable of managing these processes across the organization" (R. H. Humphrey et al., 2016). This is important because leaders have an outsized influence. As one study notes, "Leader moods travel through the work group via contagion" (Gooty, Connelly, Griffith, & Gupta, 2010, p. 989). Unfortunately, as Berkovich and Eyal (2015) point out, we know relatively little about how school leaders affect the emotions of others, and the methods used in studies of school leaders and emotions are often relatively weak. Many of the same issues pervade research in other sectors as well (Gooty et al., 2010).

How a school leader should "read" an emotional situation in order to effect a desirable outcome goes beyond "respond positively." Instead, a principal needs to know that, although positive is often better, in some cases individuals and groups may be buoyed by an incisive analysis that "something is not going well"—when accompanied by a thoughtful and constructive problem-solving response (Stephens & Carmeli, 2016). Zembylas (2010), another scholar who regularly has investigated emotions in schools, proposes that leaders must be prepared to provide emotional support around an "ethic of discomfort" that is an inevitable component of a complex and difficult job.

Much of the writing on emotions in the workplace has focused on leaders' "emotional intelligence" or EI (Goleman, 2000), which proved controversial and is still viewed as scientifically suspicious "folderol" because of inconsistent findings about its impact (Daus & Ashkanasy, 2005; Føllesdal & Hagtvet, 2013; Walter, Cole, & Humphrey, 2011). While the jury is out on how we should measure and assess EI, the main message—that a leader's capacity to identify and manage emotions in a positive way is a key aspect of leadership—rarely is questioned.

There is a great deal of variability in how leaders "manage" their own and others' emotions. The management of feelings may be particularly important in school settings, which are sites in which all work is emotionally charged because of the high level of responsibility for nurturing future generations (Day & Hong, 2016; Wyness & Lang, 2016). How teachers and others express their emotions may vary, however, including "surface acting," or superficial expression of emotions because they are expected, and "deep acting" (Hochschild, 1983), as well as "natural emotional labor," which is associated with people who identify strongly with their work roles (Ashforth & Humphrey, 1993). The more invested teachers are in their professional competence and their students, the more likely it is that they will experience small failures with intensity (Hargreaves, 2000).

L. M. Little et al. (2016) show that leaders have four basic strategies for dealing with emotions. Two are positively associated with followers' perception of the leader: *modifying the situation* (removing some feature that creates negative emotions or adding one that may make the situation more positive) and *creating cognitive change*, which involves helping the follower to see the situation in a more favorable light. The remaining two have a negative impact on leader–member relationships: *distracting through attentional deployment*, drawing attention away from emotionally negative situations through humor or other behaviors, and *modulating the emotional response* by encouraging the follower to suppress his or her reactions. Other scholars distinguish the impacts on other members depending on whether they are nuanced in their use of strategies and responses and adjust them depending on the person, the situation, and the history of their relationship (W. L. Gardner et al., 2005).

To understand the implications for school leaders, we first must situate these possible responses in today's schools, which are increasingly professionalized, employing teachers with higher credentials. In addition, the role of school leaders (not always the principal) in many countries has changed to incorporate more engagement with instruction and teacher development. Finally, there is consistent pressure for innovation and reform, both from central governments and from communities. The condition of schools is, thus, more fluid, more interactive, and more dynamic than it was in the past—and the level of activity creates both energy and stress. This dynamism creates an environment that is ripe for heightened emotions (Kelchtermans, 2005; O'Connor, 2008; Oplatka, 2007; van Veen & Sleegers, 2009). Thus, while teachers are ultimately responsible for their own emotional work and bear the brunt of the responsibility for helping students to manage their emotions, school leaders increasingly must hone their capacities to "read the signals" in order to support all staff in creating an effective school climate and culture.

POSITIVE PSYCHOLOGICAL STATES: SELF-CONCEPT

Authentic leadership is positively related to followers' social identification with the collective. (Avolio, Gardner, et al., 2004, p. 808)

We found that employee perceptions of a supportive, high-quality relationship between themselves and their leaders were related to the energy needed for employees to engage in creative tasks and for creativity to emerge. (Atwater & Carmeli, 2009, p. 271)

Emotions can be permanent, but are often fleeting. Psychological states, or self-concept, on the other hand, develop over time but are, on a day-to-day or weekly basis, rather stable, because (according to most early psychologists) they are central to maintaining psychological well-being (S. Epstein, 1973). As we will observe below, self-concept is linked to important "motivational behavioral outcomes" (Stajkovic & Luthans, 1998, p. 240) and self-awareness (Ilies et al., 2005). Among educators, the moral identity aspect of self-concept is especially significant (Aquino & Reed, 2002). Because theories of self-concept are so broad, we will not explore them in detail, but will focus on four prominent elements in recent research about positive organizational leadership: self-efficacy, identification, psychological empowerment, and psychological capital.

Self-Efficacy

Self-efficacy (Bandura, 1988) is one of the best-known psychological constructs to penetrate organizational leadership. In 1998, Stajkovic and Luthans argued that self-efficacy may be a better predictor of work-related performance than other personality-based predictors, and Luthans and Church (2002) later went on to claim that "self efficacy is *the most pervasive and important* of the psychological mechanisms for positivity" (p. 59, emphasis added). Walumbwa, Avolio, and Zhu (2008) also make expansive claims for the significance of self-efficacy, arguing that it encompasses all of a person's self-concept that can be activated in the work setting.

The idea of self-efficacy is firmly rooted in social learning theory. In other words, individuals don't "invent" their efficacy, but learn through feedback and interactions with others in specific contexts. As Wood and Bandura (1989) put it, "Neither self-efficacy nor social environments are fixed entities" (p. 374). And this implies that self-efficacy is in constant development. It is the dynamic nature of self-efficacy that is important for positive leaders, whether in schools or other settings, because we know that leaders can influence it.

Although there are many definitions of self-efficacy, there is also a great deal of commonality. Walumbwa, Avolio, and Zhu's (2008) definition is representative: "Self-efficacy is the belief that one can execute the behavior required to cope with potentially challenging situations" (p. 803). It is operationalized as "belief in one's capacity . . . in terms of challenging self-set goals, self-selection into difficult tasks, self-motivation, generous effort investment and mobilization toward task mastery and goal accomplishment, and perseverance when faced with obstacles" (Luthans & Youssef, 2007, p. 328). Lurking in the background is the knowledge that self-efficacy is always contextualized: The same person may have a strong sense of self-efficacy in his or her role as a parent, but a weak self-efficacy in adapting to new technologies in the workplace.

Positive theorists claim that developing self-efficacy in work settings requires "both positive psychological capabilities and a highly developed organizational context" (W. L. Gardner & Schermerhorn, 2004, p. 271), that it "can be developed and managed" (Luthans & Church, 2002, p. 60), and that "organizational support is an integral mediating mechanism" (Sluss et al., 2008, p. 458). In summary, while school leaders can influence it, the development of self-efficacy in individuals requires authentic relationships such as those described in Chapter 4, and is dependent on the behaviors described in Chapter 5, but poses additional leadership obligations beyond those already discussed.

More concretely, Positive school leaders "may provide programs designed to enhance employees' self efficacy" (Stajkovic & Luthans, 1998, p. 255) and, in particular, draw on training and development work to strengthen any needed skills. School leaders do this directly through professional development and the encouragement of learning in teams, but also indirectly by "enhancing their beliefs as to what they can do with the skills they already have" (p. 255). Principals also may call into play their skills in storytelling and sensemaking (see Chapter 5), helping members of the school community to understand the full range of resources and opportunities that they may have within the school to carry out tasks that initially appear daunting. School leaders influence teacher self-efficacy by ensuring that teachers "have the best tools and/or resources to do their work" (Walumbwa, Avolio, & Zhu, 2008, p. 801) and by "demonstrating care and empathetic attention" (Frost, 2003, p. 5). Walumbwa, Hartnell, et al. (2010) go on to point to the link between support and self-efficacy, by "assist[ing] them in attaining their career goals" (p. 519), which may include enhanced responsibilities and even teacher leadership positions.

Even Positive School Leaders, however, have limited power to shape the evolution of individual school members' self-efficacy. Researchers call attention to the importance of unresolved complexity: When the working environment for some individual teachers feels multifaceted and chaotic, the leader's ability to shift an eroding sense of self-efficacy may be diminished (Stajkovic & Luthans, 1998). In addition, Lord et al. (1999) note that all aspects of self-concept, including self-efficacy, are defined in terms of relationships to others, with the relationship with the school leader being only one of many that a teacher will have in a school. Self-efficacy is dependent on the reflected self, or the self as seen through the eyes of others, which includes students and colleagues.

We also learn that self-efficacy in schools has to do with the tools available to undertake tasks, "a belief in the efficacy of the means available to them [leaders] to be successful" (Walumbwa, Cropanzano, & Goldman, 2011, p. 748)—more concretely, no school leader can always control whether textbooks arrive on time or substitutes are available for lunch duty. Finally, we see that self-efficacy is consistently related to individual work performance (Luthans & Avolio, 2003; Stajkovic & Luthans, 1998), but a school leader's ability to directly affect any single individual's sense of efficacy is mediated by a variety of other factors. For example, a teacher's perception that the district is unfair in some critical way (such as how teacher evaluations are prescribed) may impede the school leader's ability to positively affect that teacher's self-efficacy (Cole & Latham, 1997; Lind, Kanfer, & Earley, 1990; Truxillo, Bauer, & Sanchez, 2001). Thus, school leaders must have their senses attuned not only to their own personal behavior, but to the larger context in which they are acting. We will return to this important point in Chapter 8, where we look at the role of leaders in "sensemaking" to develop organizational cohesiveness.

Psychological Empowerment

Some argue that empowerment is a distinctive dimension of positive self-concept, incorporating *self-efficacy* and three additional dimensions: (1) a *sense of meaning*, or the correspondence of the value of work and individual values; (2) *self-determination*, or the ability to make choices about how to do the work, and (3) *impact*, or the perception that individual actions will affect the larger group (Spreitzer, 1995; K. W. Thomas & Velthouse, 1990). These three indirect indicators of an individual's sense of empowerment can be applied to understanding the underlying significance of informal interchanges with others and to take note of possible areas for celebration or concern.

Organizational studies have used psychological empowerment to study motivation, engagement, and satisfaction with work, as well as with individual performance (Spreitzer, Kizilos, & Nason, 1997). As Liden et al. (2000) put it:

> Individuals tend to be appreciative of organizations that provide opportunities for decision latitude, challenge, and responsibility, as well as for the feelings of meaning, impact, self-determination, and mastery that result from these conditions. They are likely to reciprocate by being more committed to the organization, that is, their identification, attachment, and loyalty to the organization will increase. (p. 410)

There is a history of examining teacher empowerment in education, but little consensus about definitions and measurement (Keiser & Shen, 2000). Many authors view teacher empowerment through the lens of power and authority, looking primarily at teachers' involvement in decisionmaking (Rice & Schneider, 1994; White, 1992; Zembylas & Papanastasiou, 2005). Others, like Short (1994), use multidimensional definitions of teacher empowerment, some of which are consistent with K. W. Thomas and Velthouse (1990)—teacher impact, autonomy (self-determination), and self-efficacy—but others that are not: teacher status, involvement in decisionmaking, and opportunities for professional development (Short, 1994). Still others seem to conceptualize teacher empowerment as distributed leadership, where the primary indicator is teachers' perception of influence in multiple domains (Harris, Leithwood, Day, Sammons, & Hopkins, 2007; Marks & Louis, 1999; Spillane et al., 2003). The lack of distinction between psychological empowerment and distributed leadership is not limited to studies of schools, but appears in other areas, such as community psychology (Zimmerman, 1995).

Perhaps not surprising, given the lack of conceptual consensus, are the inconsistent links between psychological empowerment and leadership. Some (Zhang & Bartol, 2010) have found a strong association, but others (Avolio, Zhu, Koh, & Bhatia, 2004) determined that the relationship was weak. One study found a connection between psychological empowerment and teachers' trust in their principal (Moye, Henkin, & Egley, 2005), but more ambiguity is suggested by other studies showing that teacher psychological empowerment is most important because it mediates how teachers respond to efforts to exercise leadership (A.N. Lee & Nie, 2017; Shapira-Lishchinsky & Tsemach, 2014). This ambiguity is seen outside of educational research where psychological empowerment is treated as an independent factor that either constrains or enhances the ability of positive leaders to foster motivation, job satisfaction, or other personal responses to work (Avolio, Zhu, Koh, Bhatia, 2004). Finally, most scholars connect psychological empowerment not only to leader relationships and behaviors but to the larger work environment, which includes the characteristics of the organization, the job, and relationships with peers (Dust, Resick, & Mawritz, 2014; Houghton & Yoho, 2005; Liden et al., 2000).

Virtually all of the studies of psychological empowerment have been survey-based, and there is limited understanding of the dynamics that might account for these disparate findings. Thus, while the idea of psychological empowerment is intriguing and cannot be ignored by principals, more work needs to be done to unpack the complexity of the relationship between leadership, psychological empowerment, and individual work experiences.

Identification

A sense of pride in belonging to a group or organization is a critical feature of many people's identity (Avolio, Gardner, et al., 2004). Furthermore, we know that members who have positive perceptions of the leader of their team or organization are more likely to report a sense of identification (Riggio, Zhu, Reina, & Maroosis, 2010). Research suggests that identification is distinct from other positive work-related attitudes and that there is robust evidence that it plays an important role in the performance of individuals (Murphy, 2005; Riketta, 2005).

The scholarly literature proposes a variety of definitions of organizational identification but they have much in common: a feeling of openness or belonging (Beck, 1994; Mayeroff, 1971; Walumbwa, Mayer, et al., 2011) and inclusion (Murphy, 2016a; Sluss & Ashforth, 2008). It also is commonly seen as a product of reciprocal leader–member identification (Avolio, Gardner, et al., 2004) and as a catalyst for other organizational outcomes (Rauner, 2000; Walumbwa, Avolio, Gardner, et al., 2008), including job satisfaction and commitment, which we will discuss later in this chapter (Sluss & Ashforth, 2008; Walumbwa, Avolio, & Zhu, 2008; Walumbwa, Avolio, Gardner, et al., 2008).

Identification links to increased satisfaction with relationships in the work setting (Owens & Hekman, 2012). As Rauner (2000) reminds us, "From membership in a supportive social network, individuals derive a sense of stability, predictability, control, and the sense that others will help in the event of need" (p. 74). In schools, teachers' relational satisfaction is obtained most easily by a sense of connection with students (Frymier & Houser, 2000; Murphy, 2014) and other teachers (Kruse, Louis, & Bryk, 1995), both of which are directly connected to their professional identity and self-concept (Canrinus et al., 2012). But school leaders also have a significant role to play in creating a dynamic sense of an individual teacher's identification with the school and its goals.

First, of course, Positive school leaders have individual relationships with members, and individual relationships are strongly predictive of organizational identification (Carmeli, Atwater, & Levi, 2011; Epitropaki & Martin, 2005). This occurs, according to Sluss et al. (2008), because stronger relationships entail a sense of positive support from leaders. Another recent study concluded that leader–member relationships are so critical to organizational identification that leaders should devote significantly more resources to developing skills in this area and to monitoring both leader–member relationships and organizational identification (Loi, Chan, & Lam, 2014). We note that most administrator licensure programs include limited attention to this, so professional development and coaching may be needed over time.

Principals also can affect identification through routine daily practices and positive interactions, as well as by inspiration. Zhu, Sosik, Riggio, and Yang (2012), for example, found that both transformational and active transactional leadership were associated with organizational identification, where transformational behaviors included intellectual stimulation, value focus, and vision, while active transactional behaviors included individual goal setting and rewarding desired performance. In other words, all sorts of individualized and general positive behaviors were important (Zhu et al., 2012). This association between principal–teacher relationships and identification is apparent in schools: Teachers who see their principals as providing individualized support are more likely to have strong positive relationships with peers (Louis et al., 2016), and those relationships promote a sense of identification with the school. We also know that principals who are viewed by teachers as positive leaders are more likely to express commitment to the school's goals (Ross & Gray, 2006).

Across a variety of studies, a clear logic emerges. Teachers who believe that their school leaders are interpersonally effective are more likely to be satisfied, more likely to express commitment to their profession, and more likely to identify with others in their school (Bogler & Somech, 2004; Louis, 1998; Price, 2011; Wahlstrom & Louis, 2008). The opposite is also true: Teachers who leave a school but stay in the profession are likely to point to weak identification with and confidence in the school's leadership as a primary cause for their decision (K. M. Brown & Wynn, 2009; Grissom, 2011).

Psychological Capital

The importance of human capital has a fundamental position in economic approaches to productivity, in both organizations (microeconomics) and global economic development (macroeconomics) because human capital affects the

collective resources available to a group. The underlying idea of available resources is also applicable to the way we think about individuals.

In popular parlance, social capital refers to the resources each of us has because of whom we know. Psychological capital, in contrast, consists of a cluster
of personal resources that each individual can draw on to enhance his or her
well-being and effectiveness. First introduced to economics and other social
sciences in the 1990s, it was picked up by positive psychologists and quickly
incorporated into leadership studies (Luthans et al., 2004; Luthans, Youssef,
& Avolio, 2007). Many studies of psychological capital agree that it includes
four distinct positive orientations—optimism, hope, confidence (self-efficacy,
again) and resilience—that are so intertwined that it is difficult to distinguish
among them in adults in nontherapeutic settings.

While the lines of research on psychological capital and leadership are
relatively new, results are surprisingly consistent. First, studies uniformly
conclude that leaders can influence psychological capital (Alok, 2014; Arnold
& Connelly, 2013; McMurray, Pirola-Merlo, Sarros, & Islam, 2010; L. Woolley, Caza, & Levy, 2010). In addition, many find that psychological capital
is sensitive to other features of the organizational context. In other words, a
teacher's psychological capital cannot be explained only by his or her relationship with the principal, but also is influenced by factors such as perceptions of organizational trust (Clapp-Smith, Vogelgesang, & Avey, 2009), peer
relationships (Luthans, Norman, Avolio, & Avey, 2008), and a service-focused
climate (Walumbwa, Peterson, et al., 2010). It is important to note, however,
that all of these organizational factors also can be influenced by leaders, and
we will explore this in greater detail in Chapter 7. Finally, all studies point
to strong associations between psychological capital and desirable individual
work-related outcomes (Luthans, Vogelgesang, & Lester, 2006; S. J. Peterson,
Luthans, Avolio, Walumbwa, & Zhang, 2011).

POSITIVE ORIENTATIONS TO WORK: JOB CRAFTING AND MEANING

> Meaningfulness can be seen as a feeling that one is receiving a re-
> turn on investments of one's self in a currency of physical, cognitive,
> or emotional energy. People experienced such meaningfulness
> . . . as though they made a difference and were not taken for
> granted. They felt able to give to others and to the work itself in
> their roles and also able to receive. (Kahn, 1990, p. 703)

> Research shows that employees are more motivated to expend
> effort when they recognize that their actions can benefit others.
> (Grant, 2008, p. 110)

> Job crafting focuses on the process by which employees change elements of their jobs and relationships with others to redefine the meaning of their work and the social environment at work. (Van Wingerden, Derks, & Bakker, 2017, p. 54)

In Chapter 5, we examined the behaviors that define PSL. In this chapter, we have, so far, extended this to examine how leaders affect the way in which people experience personal enrichment as a consequence of leader actions. Based on the empirical evidence, there is a critical additional task for Positive School Leaders: creating meaningful work. Here we attend to how leaders do this, using the framework of job crafting.

Meaning and Job Crafting

The important contribution of leaders is premised in the understanding that jobs are more than position descriptions and constantly are being reinterpreted through changing interpretations of the tasks and relationships that constitute the work itself, which is referred to as job crafting. As Wrzesniewski and Dutton (2001) point out, people's agency in designing their jobs can change the meaning of work (G. Chen et al., 2007) as well as people's ideas about what is required or optional, and, thus, can be either good or bad for the organization. While we are aware that both employees and employers are job crafters, our focus here is on the work of school leaders, work that sets the context for other school members' job crafting.

Based on their review of the literature, Berg, Dutton, and Wrzesniewski (2013) argue that some elements of job crafting are theoretically grounded, tested in practice, and supported by research. These include changing relationships, changing tasks, changing perceptions, and creating a better person–job fit (which could range from altering resources to changing people's job categories).[2] In other words, they cover almost every aspect of a principal's responsibilities in supporting other adults in the school. Thus, the value of the job-crafting model is not its novelty, but its laser-like concentration on the dimensions of work that create meaning and the agency that staff have in organizing and carrying out the work.

Job crafting is tied to the idea of empowerment, which was discussed earlier in this chapter. We note that autonomy (a key element of empowerment), in conjunction with sustained investment of effort, is central to our causal narrative of job crafting and meaningfulness (Giardini & Frese, 2008). Avey et al. (2008) add ownership, while Bond, Flaxman, and Bunce (2008) refer to psychological flexibility as well as levels of job control as factors that promote innovation and reduce burnout.

The Relational Base of Job Crafting

The leader's role in job crafting starts, as we noted in Chapters 4 and 5, with relationships. For example:

> A school principal might reframe what it means to have relationships with teachers to be about getting to know their individual work preferences and interests. . . . Approaching relationships in this way may change the nature and content of interactions with teachers by compelling the principal to ask more questions . . . which may produce more high-quality connections with teachers and thus enhance the meaningfulness the principal and the teachers derive from their relationships. (Berg et al., 2013, p. 90)

But what is the point of school leaders taking on the responsibility for helping teachers to be reflective about their own job crafting? As Kahn (1990) notes, meaningfulness covers a good deal of conceptual and empirical space. We start by traversing that space to explore the attributes of the landscape and go on to show how a leader's approach to job crafting can make the terrain a more fertile ground for member growth.

One core aspect of meaningfulness is *job-related resources* provided by leaders (Schaufeli & Bakker, 2004). As we note above, this may have a big impact on person–job fit if it means access to the copy machine in the school office or a space that is needed for an art teacher's project. However, establishing the social conditions that encourage positive individual reflection on how daily work is carried out has deeper ties with job crafting (Wrzesniewski & Dutton, 2001). Socially situated reflection creates meaning (Lave & Wenger, 1991), which, in turn, causes people to reflect more deeply on how to carry out their work. For example, when people see that their contributions are valued, the significance of the work increases (Grant, 2008). When recognized, a teacher may work even harder to elaborate a new approach to using technology instruction or refining challenging content.

Leaders who combine a focus on increasing psychological capital (which increases engagement) while at the same time "increasing challenging job demands, increasing structural job resources, and decreasing hindering job demands . . . may satisfy basic psychological needs for belonging, competence, and autonomy" (Van Wingerden et al., 2017, p. 66) and thus set the stage for active job crafting.

Job Crafting Below the Radar

Job-crafting support rarely requires visible interventions. For example, many studies, as noted previously, point to the importance of employee autonomy as an element of meaningfulness (e.g., Detert et al., 2007), where autonomy may be best expressed as confidence in teachers' professional competence (Louis & Murphy, 2017). Thus, a Positive School Leader's job-crafting intervention may be as subtle as reminding a teacher of the freedom to tinker with instructional practices and the curriculum. F. Lee, Caza, Edmonson, and Thomke (2003) yoke opportunity to learn and meaningfulness, maintaining that "a continuous . . . process of assessment, search, interpretation, and integration" (p. 196) makes job tasks more purposeful. Thus, a Positive School Leader's focus on professional opportunities is particularly important for teachers as well as other professionals (Louis, 1998).

A job-crafting perspective, however, requires leaders to pay attention to the emergence of individual adaptations when people start to take on new work that they report as meaningful. These instances point to agency in developing "job enrichment, work role fit, and employee experience[s] at work," which provide meaning (May et al., 2004, p. 14). Mayrowetz et al. (2007) argue that many school improvement interventions can be viewed through the lens of job design and job crafting, which requires principals to pay a great deal of attention to how teachers make sense of new tasks. McAllister and Bigley (2002) add that reinforcing teacher agency through signaling demonstrates that innovations and adaptations are valued by organizations. Leaders also must attend to opportunities to indirectly reinforce *task significance* (the extent to which a job provides regular opportunities to improve the welfare of others) and *perceived social impact* (the extent to which members feel that their own actions improve the welfare of others) (Grant, 2008). Murphy (2015) points out that this requires some attention to student experiences, since teachers typically measure their work by its impact on young people.

Job Crafting and Boundaries

Any effort to engage in more visible leader-initiated job crafting must be subjected to additional levels of scrutiny. One issue is that the zealous pursuit of increasing the meaningfulness of work can end up as overwhelming. An ethic of care has to balance the effort to design meaningful work (McAllister & Bigley, 2002). Liedkta (1999) defines organizational care as "growth enhancing . . . in that it moves [members] towards the use and development of their full capabilities," but is conditioned by individuals' "context of their self-defined needs and aspirations and in service to the larger community of care" (p. 13). Social support promotes teachers' sense of psychological safety and allows them to take risks (Edmondson, 1999; Kahn, 1990; May et al., 2004).

Leaders also must attend to the psychological boundaries around teachers' jobs (Kahn, 1990). If boundaries are too weak, the job becomes impossible because the teachers believe that they can never do enough, but rigid boundaries reduce teachers' freedom to act. Both extremes inhibit successful job crafting and reduce meaningfulness. Thus, an important component of principal caring involves recognizing when a teacher's perception of boundaries has become too extreme and explicitly discussing "right sizing" the work (Murphy, 2006). Luthans and Youssef (2007) note that "individuals exhibit upward spirals, contagious effects, and individual organizational exchanges," suggesting that the personal negotiation of boundaries is an ongoing process in leader–member exchanges.

We remind school leaders that there are important reasons to take on the complicated responsibility of paying attention to job crafting among school staff, although the work that we have described above cannot be reduced to simple lists. Job crafting is deeply connected to teachers' (and others') sense of meaningfulness, and meaningfulness leads to increased job commitment and higher motivation.

LEADING THE SCHOOL BY TAKING
THE TEMPERATURE OF INDIVIDUALS

There is consistent evidence that the leader behaviors that we reviewed in Chapter 5 are associated with positive emotions, positive psychological states, and positive orientations to work. School leaders who wish to ensure that they are taking the temperature of the school staff must be attentive to these, even if there is no need for further action. But in order to have access to critically important information about how well the school is functioning, leaders must have established a groundwork based in interpersonal trust, a belief in the fairness of the leader and peers, and authenticity—in other words, the guiding principles outlined in Part I.

In taking the school's psychological temperature, leaders also need to pay attention to themselves. Bakker and Xanthopoulou (2013), for example, showed that teachers saw principals who developed their own self-efficacy and resilience as more charismatic and effective. Another positive leadership scholar notes that this requires unrelenting courage: Leaders who wish to foster change must first "walk naked into the land of uncertainty" (R. E. Quinn, 2010, p. 3) and face their own journey of identity development. According to Hall (2004), unless principals understand their own self-concept—as an individual and a member of the school community—they will have difficulty shaping and promoting positive self-concept in others, as well as finding the balanced boundaries that allow them to engage in leadership job crafting.

Unfortunately, there is no checklist of actions that Positive school leaders should take to routinize the monitoring of their own or others' psychological well-being. As Salovey and Mayer (1990) point out, positive attention to the

Figure 6.1. Positive School Leadership: The Foundations

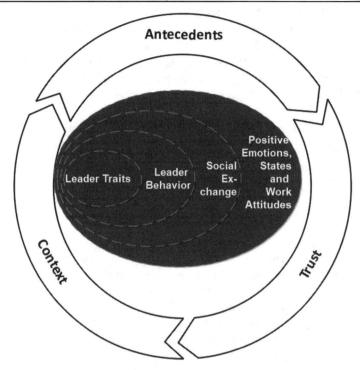

emotional temperature of an organization requires imagination as well as predispositions and skills.

It is also critical to emphasize that taking the temperature of the organization by monitoring the well-being of individuals does not imply that a Positive School Leader is responsible for either solving every problem or celebrating all of the information collected. The purpose of consistent sensitivity to individuals is not always to intervene but to use the knowledge gained to consider next steps to improve relationships in the school as a whole and, as Berkovich and Eyal (2015) point out, contribute to the reframing of emerging negative emotions in a more positive light.

At this point, we have laid out a line of argument that connects the fundamental assumptions of positive psychology (Chapter 2) through the guiding principles for positive leadership (Chapter 3) to the fundamental role of relationships to positive organizing (Chapter 4), which feeds into leader behaviors (Chapter 5) and, in this chapter, the individual outcomes that positive leaders need to keep in mind as the context for change. These, we have argued, form the essential foundation for any collective improvement. A visual summary of our synthesis is shown in Figure 6.1.

Our major point is that a wealth of both theoretical and empirical research suggests that Positive school leaders lay the foundation for significant impact by focusing on how they can affect the experiences of others. The prosocial behavior that defines and is linked to meaningfulness is significantly related to reward equity and recognition of desirable behavior, which are leader actions (as described in Chapter 5) "that seem to be responsible for employees experiencing higher job satisfaction and performing prosocial behaviors to benefit the organization" (McNeely & Meglino, 1994, p. 842). We thus argue that the understanding leaders gain from observing, understanding, and supporting individual members will determine the course of positive collective improvement. We turn, therefore, to the next part of the book, in which we will look at the broader impact of positive leadership.

NOTES

1. We do not attempt to summarize either Andy Hargreaves's (1998, 2000, 2005) extensive work on teacher emotions or Leithwood and Beatty's (2007) discussion of their implications for school leadership. Our approach is more sharply concentrated on leader–follower relationships and behaviors.

2. They also point to one trademarked intervention that was tested on a limited number of people, the Job Crafting Exercise. We choose not to include it here.

PART III

THE EFFECTS OF POSITIVE SCHOOL LEADERSHIP

When the best leaders' work is done, the people say "we did it ourselves."

—Lao Tzu

The single biggest way to impact an organization is to focus on leadership development. There is almost no limit to the potential of an organization that recruits good people, raises them up as leaders and continually develops them.

—-Maxwell, 2001, p. 185

The above quotes capture the heart of the next phase of our research-based story about Positive School Leadership. Personal virtues, behaviors, relationships, and influence are at its heart, but in order for leadership to be successful, there also must be some evidence of valued outcomes that, as Lao Tzu suggests, can be seen by others. However, many leaders make the mistake of presuming that they have the ultimate responsibility for finding the next big problem and, in addition, the answer. In contrast, both Lao Tzu and the popular leadership writer John Maxwell agree that the key to those outcomes is through developing others.

In this part of the book, we build our argument about the power of Positive School Leadership in three steps. As we move into the discussion of the visible outcomes of leadership, we find a stronger base of research carried out in school settings than we found in the topics discussed in the previous six chapters. Chapter 7 looks at the evidence about how positive leaders can help develop teams that have the energy and motivation to go beyond the minimal requirements of their jobs and to support one another. Leaders do this through the relationships they have established, which help to shape an emotional environment in which team members see themselves as more powerful and engaged.

However, schools (and other organizations) are more than good teams. As educational research consistently has pointed out, for example, there is a great deal of variability within any school in teachers' experience of being part of a strong professional team (Voelkel & Chrispeels, 2017). Chapter 8 goes further, therefore, to examine how leaders create productive organizational environments in which teams work together to achieve purposes on which they all agree. In schools, much of this research has focused on the limited goal of student achievement (which is only one of many development objectives supported by schools), but research from other sectors examines leadership impacts in other areas, suggesting new paths for positive school leaders.

Finally, in Chapter 9, we draw attention to the larger role of schools and positive school leadership, providing a strong argument for the importance of social impacts on local communities and on the prospects for sustained, productive civic development.

CHAPTER 7

Positive Leaders, Teams, and Meaningful Work

INTRODUCTION

The goal is to have productive leadership dynamics firmly embedded throughout the organization through delegation, empowerment, and shared leadership so that turnover has little chance of derailing the good work done by invested individuals. (Printy, 2014, p. 301)

By means of social identification . . . , followers come to view their individual efforts and work roles as contributing to a larger collective cause. This perspective enhances the personal meaningfulness and importance of their work. (Wang et al., 2005, p. 421)

Positive organizational research has, until relatively recently, focused either on the leader (personal characteristics and behavior) or on dyadic relationships, such as those covered in previous chapters. However, in larger organizations, including schools, much of the work is performed within departments or teams. Moreover, teams are not just committees, but can be the true life force in many organizations, particularly those that are concerned with knowledge. A. W. Woolley, Aggarwal, and Malone (2015) put it succinctly: "An organization's overall ability to learn productively—that is, to improve its outcomes through better knowledge and insight . . . depends on the ability of its teams to learn" (p. 153).

Even when there is considerable individual autonomy in carrying out the "core work" (as is the case in schools and other professional organizations), teams are essential to coordinate and create cohesiveness. Secondary schools have department structures; grade-level teams coordinate the work of elementary schools; and middle schools sometimes combine team and department structures. Hospitals have both permanent teams (orthopedics and general surgery) and cross-functional teams that carry out much of the work (anesthesiologists work with nurses and surgeons). For many people, the relationships developed within teams are central to their job satisfaction. *New York Times* columnist David Brooks (2017) puts it this way:

> Thick institutions have a physical location . . . where members meet on a regular basis . . . there's an intimacy and an identity borne out of common love. Think of a bunch of teachers watching a student shine on stage or a bunch of engineers adoring the same elegant solution. (p. A19)

What Brooks points to is the bonds that develop within a team that create a sense of collective responsibility for the outcomes of joint tasks.

Much has been written about leadership within work teams (Kozlowski & Bell, 2013), but there has been less focus on teams in positive psychology and positive leadership. One of the first edited books dealing with positive organizational theory (Cameron, Dutton, & Quinn, 2003) had only one page with a reference to teams; the voluminous *Oxford Handbook of Positive Organizational Scholarship* includes only three pages that mention teams (Cameron & Spreitzer, 2012). In addition, the accumulating research pays limited attention to the way in which an "external leader" (such as a principal) may influence teams, but continues to focus on leadership *within* teams. Similarly, although there has been extensive attention to how leadership is distributed within schools (G. Johnson, Dempster, & Wheeley, 2016; Leithwood, Mascall, & Strauss, 2009), fewer connect this with the way in which teams or departments carry out their work (Halverson & Clifford, 2013; Klar, Huggins, Hammonds, & Buskey, 2016; Leithwood, 2016).

We argue, however, that positive leaders cannot ignore teams and their work in schools. Every school we know has "equity teams," "professional learning communities," or "data teams" in addition to departments and grade teams. As Printy (2014) points out, principals need to know how to think about their role in relation to these groups.

One consequence of these "gaps" in research is that we will push beyond the boundaries of what is known to venture into areas in which positive school leaders (and those who prepare positive school leaders) may wish to consider how strengthening teams could contribute to the work of the school. However, we will hold close to the general topics that we explored in the previous chapter, focusing on how leaders can influence the emotional work of teams, the development of teams' self-concept, and the meaning attached to teamwork. We also note that eminent team-leadership scholar Richard Hackman (2003) warns that a phenomenon that appears clear at the level of the individual can become very murky when multiple people become involved and contexts differ.

We begin with a simple definition of teams as "interdependent collections of individuals who share responsibility for specific outcomes for their organizations" (Sundstrom, De Meuse, & Futrell, 1990, p. 120). In schools, this could cover almost any collection of people who take responsibility for a task related to the work of the school. However, teams are not all the same: Leaders of professional organizations whose members have broad responsibilities and a depth of expertise typically will have a range of teams to manage. Some are enduring while others are temporary and project-based; some are engaged in regular, interdependent, face-to-face collaboration while others coordinate irregularly or even virtually. In schools, these range from permanent departments and interdisciplinary child study teams to temporary book study groups that provide a basis for schoolwide professional learning. Furthermore, every principal knows that there are informal groups that have a deep influence on school practice—a "team" of two or three teachers that are working on interdisciplinary curriculum or another group that is dedicated to service learning. Given this complexity, positive leadership that focuses on creating meaning that motivates individual teams and holds the many teams together around a shared purpose becomes extremely important. As Weick's (1993) seminal work suggests, without clear, positive, trusted leadership, the ability of both individuals and teams to "make sense" of their joint work collapses.

We will review briefly what we know about how leaders influence teams' emotions, collective self-concept, and sense of meaningfulness in their joint work. We then move on to a central positive leadership function—thinking about the design of teams and how variability among them affects what they do.

EMOTIONS

Recent empirical studies in psychological and organizational behavior have established the veracity of collective emotions, the mechanisms that contribute to their development, and their effects on important organizational outcomes. (Sanchez-Burks & Huy, 2009, p. 25)

Team members, rather than experiencing the sense of belonging and support they were led to expect, described a real sense of isolation, disconnection and alienation. . . . Reported experiences included resignation and sadness. (Parris & Vickers, 2005, p. 293)

We know that emotions are contagious within groups and that within any organization not all groups react to positive or negative events in the same way. We also know that one of the ways in which Positive School Leadership may fumble is by focusing only on positive feelings and emotions, and paying less attention to emerging negative sentiments that may spread rapidly within a group that interacts frequently.

Enthusiasm about teams in the popular organizational literature emphasizes the benefits to performance and happiness in their work. In education, this excitement has focused on introducing "professional learning communities" which, according to DuFour (2004), are intended to ensure systematic, timely, and directive intervention to support student achievement. Thus, the rhetoric focuses on cohesiveness, "team players," and spirit.

However, the reality is that teams also can be places that produce alienation and disengagement (Parris & Vickers, 2005). Sometimes there can be a sense of purposelessness that increases member distance from the objectives suggested by leaders. One doctoral student recently commented that colleagues in his school colloquially referred to professional learning communities as DaMIT—district-mandated instructional talk—meetings. A recent comment submitted to the EdWeek blog suggests a similar confusion:

> While my school district says it is committed to professional learning communities, I am not sure what they mean by it. We have lots of meetings, but I don't think things are getting better.[1]

The more diverse the membership of the committee, particularly if it is composed of people who don't know one another well, the more likely it is that the results will be disappointing (Mannix & Neale, 2005), a response that often was noted in earlier studies of school-site councils (Leithwood & Menzies, 1998).

However, leaders may have a lot to do with whether the results of developing collaborative teams touch the positive emotions of their members rather than eliciting disappointment. This was noted in early experimental studies (Lippitt, 1939) and continues to be a topic of discussion. Some argue that leaders' own emotions can humanize them in the eyes of group members (Lurie, 2004), but the impact also may depend on how well the group members get along and on their motivations for participating in the group (Van Kleef et al., 2009).

In other words, a positive leader needs to understand the group as well as the individual members in it. This, however, presents Positive school leaders with an apparently impossible task: How can principals intervene in the emotional life of all of the groups that exist in a school? The answer is that in most cases they probably cannot (Rapp, Gilson, Mathieu, & Ruddy, 2016). Sometimes they are members of the group and regularly attend its meetings, in which case they can take on a coaching role if negative emotions begin to emerge. In other cases, they must develop indirect influence through interactions with formal or informal leaders within the group.

Positive school leaders at all levels can, however, hone their capacities to focus on "the emotional aperture" (Sanchez-Burks & Huy, 2009) that provides insight into the emotions of groups. Developing this capacity demands looking not at the reactions of individuals, but at the composition of reactions in a group. Is one person smiling, while others are stony-faced? Is there emotional distance for a few, but engagement of many? While the previous chapter encouraged school leaders to pay attention to the emotional valences of individuals, Sanchez-Burks and Huy (2009) point out that deep study of groups is not necessary: "Quick automatic assessment of the emotions that occur both within and between groups might provide critical information for effective coordination of relational and task resources" (p. 26). They go on to emphasize that monitoring the emotions of teams may not be part of the daily routine of leaders, but becomes essential in times of turbulence or change when emotions—both negative and positive—tend to run high. Leaders also will be influential because they are instrumental in the design and maintenance of team structures, a topic that we turn to later in this chapter.

COLLECTIVE SELF-CONCEPT:
TEAM CLIMATE AND MENTAL MODELS

Our results suggest that in order for teams to be highly effective, they must be autonomous and their members must experience potency, meaningfulness, and impact. (Kirkman & Rosen, 1999, p. 70)

Effective teamwork mental models in [self-managing work teams] include: (1) psychological ownership of team processes and outcomes; (2) a need for continuous learning; and (3) a need for heedful interrelating. . . . These mental models flourish when organizational supports back up their existence. (Druskat & Pescosolido, 2002, p. 283)

Research on teams rarely uses the word *self-concept* but more often refers to related terms such as *team climate* or *mental models* (Z. Chen, Zhu, & Zhou, 2015; Druskat & Pescosolido, 2002; Edú-Valsania, Moriano, & Molero, 2016; Zaccaro, Rittman, & Marks, 2002). Positive school leaders can, however, draw on strong conceptualizations underlying these alternative terms that have been validated in a large number of cross-national studies and work sectors (Hülsheger, Anderson, & Salgado, 2009). Existing teams or departments will develop their own ways of working that may persist even when there is turnover (Printy, 2014), and, like individuals, each team may have its own unique social ties, bonding rituals, and ways of distributing the team's work. In schools, some will focus on administrative minutia (ordering supplies and allocating responsibilities for parent conferences), while others will eagerly attack problems of curricular cohesion and pedagogy over a beer on Friday after school (McLaughlin & Talbert, 2001).

Positive leaders tune in to these differences because uniqueness can be both a strength (creating "thick" internal relationships within the team) and a weakness (posing obstacles to collaboration between teams with different norms and practices). While there are no quick nostrums for "fixing" weak teams, seeing differences between teams can help diagnose areas where leadership may make a difference. Some of the dimensions that Positive school leaders can look for, without engaging in heavy diagnostic activities, include:

1. *Team vision:* "The extent to which the vision has a value [to] individuals in the group and thus engenders their commitment to group goals. Sharedness to the extent to which the vision gains widespread acceptance by individuals" (Anderson & West, 1998, p. 240)
2. *Psychological safety:* "Involvement in decision-making [that] is motivated and reinforced, occurring in an environment which is perceived as interpersonally non-threatening . . . where all members of a work group feel able to propose new ideas and problem solutions in a non-judgmental climate" (p. 240)
3. *Task orientation:* "Emphasis on individual and team accountability . . . reflecting upon work methods and team performance; intra-team advice; feedback and cooperation; mutual monitoring; . . . exploration of opposing opinions; constructive controversy" (p. 240)
4. *Support for innovation:* "The expectation, approval and practical support of attempts to introduce new and improved ways of doing things in the work environment" (West, 1990, p. 38)
5. *Ownership:* the sense, within the team, that its members have an understanding of and influence on the organization, and that they have some accountability for organizational performance (Druskat & Pescosolido, 2002; Wagner, Parker, & Christiansen, 2003),

Another point buttresses these elements of unit climate or self-concept. There is evidence that Positive school leaders can affect them in two ways, through more effective human resource practices in designing teams (Hon, Bloom, & Crant, 2011) and through a positive leadership style (Z. Chen et al., 2015). The latter authors point to specific leader behaviors that work to increase group motivation and service orientation:

Practices such as showing interpersonal acceptance, remaining authentic and humble in the presence of followers, offering task and psychological flexibility, and expressing trust help managers motivate their followers to achieve better service performance. (p. 520)

In schools, leaders also are exhorted to promote organizational learning, knowledge sharing, and professional development, largely through collective, job-embedded learning experiences (Mizell, Hord, Killion, & Hirsh, 2011), but there is increasing evidence that leaders' efforts to do so require the presence of "thick" teams (Brooks, 2017), with a stronger self-concept and group identification (Edú-Valsania et al., 2016; Louis & Lee, 2016). In addition, this also requires that leaders establish supportive and caring relationships with the teams, because these create the optimal circumstances for the development of trust and open communication (Boies, Fiset, & Gill, 2015). Even productive "self-managing" school teams may require effective leadership from the principal. As one study notes:

> At first pass, it appears paradoxical that a self-managing work team would require a leader. However, those studying these teams agree that the actions of the leader to whom a team reports, known as the external team leader, can make or break the team's success. (Druskat & Wheeler, 2003, p. 435)

Druskat and Wheeler go on to report that the biggest tension for the external leaders they studied was to maintain a good balance between trusting and empowering their teams, and intervening when teams experienced troubles. The most successful leaders erred on the positive side, building trust and empowerment:

> The superior [external leaders], who were trying to cultivate the sense of ownership required for team self-management and successful performance, replied with comments such as: "It's not what I think, it's what *they* think." (emphasis in original, p. 452)

This finding is affirmed in at least one study of principals (Louis & Murphy, 2017), which found, like other studies (Schaubroeck, Lam, & Peng, 2011), that leaders needed to express both cognitive trust (in the team's professional capacities) and affective trust (caring for the well-being of members) in order to be influential.

Let us be clear: Positive school leaders cannot pretend to coach and monitor all school teams on a regular basis. On the other hand, they also cannot afford to wait until a key team falls apart or becomes embroiled in dysfunctional sniping with another team. There is only one realistic solution to managing a large number of teams, which is to check in regularly and informally with team leaders or, as Druskat and Wheeler (2003) put it, "scout for information inside their own teams" (p. 449). For this to occur efficiently, there must be sufficient trust between a principal and any school teams that honest conversations about issues of effectiveness will occur while the problems are still anticipated or emergent.

MEANINGFUL WORK

> If it can be shown that meaningful work enhances quality and pro-
> ductivity, then the moral case for meaningful work is buttressed by
> a practical case. And such a case, as we shall see, can be made.
> (Bowie, 1998, p. 1088)

> Team members collectively develop and share the meaningful-
> ness of their tasks. Thus, team members have direct effects on
> the experiences of meaningfulness of other members. (Kirkman &
> Rosen, 1999, p. 59)

A thick line of research in the 1950s and 1960s on industrial work teams suggests that they are more productive when they are "self-managing" and have
the responsibility for meaningful tasks (Cummings, 1978). While professional work may look quite different from manufacturing, this finding quickly
infused the emerging excitement about the role of teams in other settings.
Starting from a very different perspective, Bowie (1998) integrates Kantian
perspectives on meaningfulness with research on good leadership practices,
and concludes that the development of teams and work groups is a central
leadership responsibility.

The reasons are not difficult to find. If they are not oversold, teams provide significant opportunities for affiliation, which is both psychologically and
socially important (Putnam, 1995). Because well-designed and empowered
teams create interdependence among the members, they become sites for joint
problem identification and solving, which provides additional meaning and
satisfaction (Kirkman & Rosen, 1999). This occurs, of course, because individuals within the teams are motivated to contribute:

> Team member proactivity reflects the extent to which an individual engages in
> self-starting, future-directed behavior to change a team's situation or the way
> the team works. For example, a nurse might suggest a new roster to improve the
> way his or her team works or might put forward a better way of communicating
> among team members. Behaving proactively in relation to one's team is particu-
> larly important when teams are self-managing, as are autonomous work groups
> and many types of project teams. (Griffin et al., 2007, p. 332)

Another aspect of working in teams is particularly important in schools:
providing teachers with a broader view of "the work" of nurturing student
development than can be seen by any single teacher working in his or her own
classroom with a particular set of students. Richard Hackman and Greg Oldham, who are pioneers in the design of work, point out that when the individual's view is expanded through confronting common issues, meaningfulness

increases (Oldham & Hackman, 2010). For example, when both social workers and teachers are involved in child study teams/student support teams, the perspectives of both contribute to addressing the issues presented by a student (Anderson-Butcher & Ashton, 2004), which provides each with satisfaction and deepened understanding.

External leaders—principals who are not members of a team—have a significant impact on the degree to which members view teamwork as significant. First, meaningful teams are empowered teams, but effective empowerment typically requires coaching from leaders (Carson et al., 2007; Druskat & Wheeler, 2003). Second, as we also have argued above, positive leaders are critical in helping teams interpret what is happening outside the team that may affect the meaningfulness that they attach to their work. This is particularly important in public professional settings, like schools, where media, shifting policies, and other events may heighten a sense of uncertainty.

There is some irony here, however, because active coaching and sense-making work with teams under conditions of high uncertainty may have a negative impact on team members' satisfaction with the leader, even as it increases ratings of leader effectiveness and team effectiveness (Morgeson, 2005). Thus, a warning to principals that is straight from Machiavelli: Sometimes it is important to be assertive in guiding your school teams, even if it means that you will be less well loved.

Finally, in the case of formal teams, positive leaders bear responsibility for initial design decisions, and design is central to meaningfulness. We turn next to this topic.

DESIGNING AND DEVELOPING TEAMS

Team leadership encompasses a wide variety of activities—it can mean everything from deciding to form a team in the first place, to composing the team, to exhorting members to exert more effort. . . . Leadership functions can be fulfilled by a designated leader with formal authority, but also by team members themselves, or by external coaches with no formal authority over the team. . . . Team leadership is almost invariably shared leadership. (Wageman & Fisher, 2014, pp. 455–456)

Responsibility for deciding when teams should be used to perform work does rest mainly with those who create them because teams are remarkably passive and accepting even when given work that is inappropriate for performance by a team, when the design of the team's task is flawed, or when contextual supports for teamwork are unavailable or inadequate. (Oldham & Hackman, 2010, p. 474)

Leaders' engagement in decisions about how to organize teams is, according to Hackman (2002), one of the most critical tasks of any leader. But what kind of teams? Wageman and Fisher (2014) use empirical studies to identify distinct types, where the differences among them are based on implicit control, or who determines the work processes and goals. The differentiation among types is critical in schools, which employ professionals who bring their own ideas about goals and processes and perform most of their work with minimal supervision and irregularly measured "productivity indicators" (student test results, etc.) (Hallinger, Heck, & Murphy, 2014; Murphy, Hallinger, & Heck, 2013). In other words, principals have limited capacity to exert tight control over individual teachers and most teacher teams. Furthermore, unless it is clear that formal leaders have more expertise than others on the team, attempts to control either process or outcomes are likely to be unsuccessful (Wageman & Fisher, 2014). In other words, as implied throughout this chapter, positive leader influence over teams is often a matter of influence, through developing relationships and providing support, rather than of control.

Nevertheless, positive school leaders can be very influential at the design stage of team formation, and there are models of team design that are particularly relevant (Sundstrom et al., 1990). In descending order of the opportunities for direct leader control, these are:

1. *Semi-autonomous teams,* which are designed to meet goals or use processes established outside the team (and sometimes outside the organization) and which include close contact with the formal leader. In schools, these would include departments, child study teams, and others over which principal influence is often direct (through hiring, allocation of resources, feedback on outcomes, etc.).

2. *Self-regulating teams,* which are initiated by the formal leader to carry out significant work but are not directed by the formal external leader. They typically have an internal leadership structure and are largely self-managing. In schools, examples might include teacher data teams, some professional learning communities, and curriculum review committees.

3. *Self-organizing teams,* which are a response to a particular need and often are composed of volunteers who have a particular interest in "solving" a presenting problem or issue, such as investigating restorative justice approaches to discipline or developing an embedded professional learning focus for the school. A self-organizing team may become recognized and more formal if it is successful.

When the need for a new team arises (or when an existing team is functioning poorly), positive leaders turn first to the design question: "What type of team is this/should this be?" (A. W. Woolley et al., 2015). The above descriptions of types of teams focus primarily on the *team structure*. Thinking about additional underlying organizational design questions also will help (Galbraith, 2002). These include *strategy* (overall goals and objectives), *processes* (how information and activities should flow within the team and to others), *rewards* (what motivations are there for authentic participation), and *people* (what special skills are needed). If these are not carefully considered, teams can be set up to fail—for example, by being given tasks that they can't accomplish, direction that is unclear, time frames that are cumbersome, or weak connections to others who eventually may need to be engaged. In other words, *design conditions determine how likely teams are to be successful* (Wageman, 2001; A. W. Woolley et al., 2015).

In addition to thinking about design (or redesign if teams get into trouble), positive leaders need to remember the importance of support and development. Yet, in 2001, a review article noted, "We know surprisingly little about how leaders . . . manage effective teams. Previous leadership theories have tended to focus on how leaders influence collections of subordinates, without attending to how leadership promoted team processes" (Zaccaro et al., 2002, p. 452). Developing effective teams can be quite problematic in schools where team functioning has been limited to self-regulating functional groups with limited responsibilities. People are not born knowing how to work well in teams, and when teachers are placed in teams without any development, they may experience the frustrations mentioned earlier in this chapter. Parris and Vickers (2005) quote one dissatisfied team member, who said, "They pay lip service to it [support]. . . . There's no real support. It's whatever's the flavour of the day" (p. 292–293)." It is also critical to remember that in team development, one size does not fit all (Shuffler, DiazGranados, & Salas, 2011). Those authors distinguish between team building (focusing on strengthening interpersonal relations and group processes) and team training (instruction designed to build and ensure team competencies related to the task), and they conclude that determining which is appropriate will depend on the issues facing the team.

The role of the external leader—in schools, the principal—may be particularly important in the early stages of a new team's work, when the leader informally reminds members of the purpose and meaning of their work (Beck & Murphy, 1998). Weick (1993) calls this "sensemaking," and Zacarro et al. (2002) point out that this is particularly important if it provides cues suggesting how the team's environment (school or district) links to its work. Since many teachers view their time out of the classroom as less important than active instruction, affirmation of the meaning of the work may be essential to developing commitment to the team.

In schools, coaching has become an often-used solution to almost every development issue. Without leaping on a coaching bandwagon, in many cases leaders may need to provide new teams with some preparation for how to carry out teamwork, given the type of team. Teachers who are used to semiautonomous teams (goals/processes provided from outside) may be uncomfortable developing their own—in other cases, members who thought they had complete autonomy may be discomfited by the need to include others in their decisionmaking. A leader can help teachers to understand what kind of a team they can become and what role they can play in improving the school.

A combination of good design and good positive leader coaching contributes to creating high-functioning empowered teams (Murphy, 2005; Wageman, 2001). While there is some evidence that external facilitators are needed to function (Rapp et al., 2016), other studies point to reinforcing opportunities and skills related to reflective practice (Foldy & Buckley, 2010), which may benefit from external coaching but could be carried out by a school leader with experience in fostering reflection (Murphy, Smylie, Mayrowetz, & Louis, 2009).

Before leaving the topic of team design and development, we must address the gnarly issue of diversity, a topic that has salience to Positive school leaders because of the rapid changes in school and community demographics, coupled with a predominantly White and female teaching profession. When organizations appoint teams, often leaders intentionally promote diversity in team membership. The assumption is that giving people with different perspectives (whether gender, race, professional training, or something else) voice in groups will foster creativity in outcomes—and possibly their legitimacy (Mannix & Neale, 2005). Diversity imposed by design also may backfire, however, unless prior work has created psychological safety and affirmative identity (Foldy, Rivard, & Buckley, 2009). As the latter authors note, "Power inequities drive dynamics in racially diverse teams, often leading to conflict, withdrawal, or assimilation—all of which can impede team learning" (p. 25). Racial diversity is only one of many factors in teams that contribute to unexamined (and therefore uncontrolled) power differences in diverse teams (Ingrid & Edmondson, 2006). Other researchers conclude that designing teams based on superficial/ visible differences (race, gender, age) tends to have negative effects on group functioning (Mannix & Neale, 2005). In contrast, forming teams through affinity and self-selection can become a structural form of exclusion that makes the teams function well but does not necessarily drive creative solutions.

Overall, Mannix and Neale (2005) conclude that teams with underlying diversity in opinions, education, or background "are more often positively related to performance—for example by facilitating creativity or group problem solving—*but only when the group process is carefully controlled*" (p. 32, emphasis added). Carefully controlling team processes is rarely possible in schools, and optimistic perspectives on easy ways of making teams more diverse, more effective, and more equitable will require considerably more attention to issues of team and organizational development, which are beyond the scope of a book focusing on positive leadership.

What can a Positive School Leader do, given this perplexing set of findings? Perhaps the best insight is to adapt Tolstoy's aphorism: All successful teams are similar, but every unsuccessful team has its own roots in weak design, limited or irrelevant development, and unexamined power differentials. Checking in without controlling is important to providing support and coaching before a team falls apart, as is an investigation whenever a team is clearly in trouble.

NEXT STEPS

This chapter sets out an argument for why Positive school leaders need to pay explicit attention to working with teams. Teams can be an enormous asset to any organization because they are sites for affiliation and the development of commitment. They also present many opportunities for dissatisfaction and negativity. Positive school leaders need to attend to teams, using all of the relationships that they have developed (along with a sixth sense) because simply paying attention may shift group emotions, mental models/self-concept, and a sense of meaningfulness. It is usually easy to lift up a successful team because its members are eager to tell their story; it is equally easy to ignore the ones that are functioning at a lower level if they are not sources of resistance or visible pain. Thus, a regular "scan" of team functioning is as important as the check-ins with individuals, and it needs to be accomplished without the leader's appearing to exert direct control, in order to safeguard the authority allocated to self-regulating and semiautonomous teams. In addition, Positive school leaders are aware that each building or district will vary in which teams are central to maintaining the forward movement—even if they have the same names or position in the formal organization chart.

The research base for documenting the major dimensions to which Positive school leaders should attend is reasonably well established but, in both in-school and nonschool settings, there is very little basis for a "what works" summary. One of the reasons, as Hackman (1998) points out, is that every team is different—and that means that some are extremely effective while others actually make things worse. We know, in fact, more about what makes them work poorly than what leaders can do to ensure that they are performing well. Thus, it is perhaps appropriate to end with Hackman's summary of the "mistakes managers make" as they do their best to establish high-functioning teams.

1. Using a team for work that is better done by individuals (this is particularly important in schools, where teachers prioritize their work in the classroom)
2. Calling a unit a team, but continuing to manage the members as individuals (which may be seen as leader favoritism)

3. "Falling off the authority balance beam" (which happens in design through lack of clarity about the team's and principal's roles)
4. Dismantling existing structures and teams (including informal learning communities) to make way for new ones whose purpose is unclear
5. Specifying challenging team goals but skimping on support

The obverse of each of these mistakes is equally apparent, but it may be easier for a Positive School Leader to remember that an important part of the job is to pay attention to avoiding errors so that, with deep humility, they can take steps to correct as quickly as possible those that do occur. If handled carefully, this attentiveness will reinforce the well-being of individual team members, the team, and others who are not on the team.

NOTE

1. Retrieved from blogs.edweek.org/edweek/learning_forwards_pd_watch/2015/05/ what_is_an_authentic_professional_learning_community.html.

CHAPTER 8

Positive Leadership and the Organization

> Many of the normal everyday practices and events of organizational life serve to influence the values of the people within those organizations. Without attention to the organizational structures and processes, the types of role modeling and other leader influences, and the socialization process in general, these effects will be haphazard, with unknown eventual organizational outcomes. (Grojean et al., 2004, p. 237)

> Job performance is a multi-dimensional construct which indicates how well employees perform their tasks, the initiative they take and the resourcefulness they show in solving problems. Furthermore, it indicates the extent to which they complete tasks, the way they utilise their available resources and the time and energy they spend on their tasks. (Rothmann & Coetzer, 2003, p. 68)

Until recently, organization induced theories presumed that individual preferences and benefits motivated people to work hard. In education, this contributed to the view of schools as "egg cartons," with teachers valuing autonomy and quasi-isolation, where they could practice their craft as they wished (J. W. Little, 1990). Unfortunately, relying on individual motivation and incentives, with limited attention to structures and leadership, often results in mediocre organizational and collective outcomes: Some individuals perform brilliantly, while others struggle and fail (Barnard, 1938; Leithwood & Steinbach, 1991; H. A. Simon, 1972). At worst, leaders who make an effort to maximize individual incentive systems may inadvertently stimulate competitive cultures that may undermine long-range success. An individual-incentives model has "consistently malfunctioned" in public-sector settings, according to James Bowman's (2010) extensive review of performance incentives, where it tends to deflect attention away from service and toward numbers-based productivity (p. 70).

However, in Chapter 6 we argued that positive organizational scholarship disrupts the assumption that a focus on individual motivation and commitment is the most effective means to create productive work settings. We showed that strong leader–member relationships also could create a positive affect toward co-workers and documented the way in which leader–member relationships create a sense of personal empowerment and efficacy. In Chapter 7, we went on to explore the role of strong teams as an essential building block in which relationships support the conditions and incentives that allow individuals to move beyond a singular focus on their self-interest.

In schools, we know that engagement in professional communities can lead to an increased sense of collective responsibility for student learning (Bryk, Camburn, & Louis, 1999; V. E. Lee & Smith, 1996). We also have shown that positive leadership increases effort in collaborative work settings, a state that "involves maintaining . . . motivation to exert effort toward team goal accomplishment, even when one is experiencing setbacks or when others are taking it easy" (De Jong & Elfring, 2010, p. 538). Also on the list of benefits that accrue from being in flourishing and supportive organizations are work-related "positive expectations" (p. 538), along with respect and trust for others (Edmondson, 1999), skill variety, task significance, personal identification with the work, and perceived feedback about performance (Liden et al., 2000) within a fair evaluative structure (Rich, Lepine, & Crawford, 2010). These findings from the organizational literature correspond to what we have long known about teachers' work (Louis, 1998; Rosenholtz, 1985; Tschannen-Moran, 2014). Finally, we discerned a set of states that help to define how members feel: competent, motivated, optimistic, honest, capable, confident, adaptable, reflective, and persistent (De Jong & Elfring, 2010; Griffin et al., 2007; S. E. Humphrey, Nahrgang, & Morgeson, 2007; Owens & Hekman, 2012; Palanski & Yammarino, 2011; Rich et al., 2010).

This chapter argues that that although these findings are impressive, neither positive individuals nor stronger teams are enough. Without a deeper organizational identity, individuals continue to pursue their own ends, and teams also can become a source of friction and conflict where different groups vie for position and their own interests. Thus, we look further, to the lines of research pointing to organizational outcomes.

Except in the smallest settings, leadership effects on the school as a whole are largely indirect, mediated through leaders' relationships with individuals and teams (Louis, Leithwood, Wahlstrom et al., 2010). The finding that leaders do not, in most circumstances, have a direct impact on (for example) achievement or productivity is affirmed in studies from other organizational sectors (Schein, 2010). Nevertheless, existing empirical research points to three ways in which positive leadership has an organization-wide impact: on organizational climate, culture, and productivity.

We emphasize that the distinctions between these three categories are rarely clear and the best minds differ on how to think about them. Our visual depiction of the relationship among climate, culture, and productivity (Figure 8.3) therefore suggests that they overlap and reinforce one another, and that causal relationships are neither well established nor necessarily linear. Organizational climate, for example, sometimes is seen as an underpinning of organizational culture (Glisson & Hemmelgarn, 1998), and at other times as a consequence of a strong, positive culture (Sarros, Cooper, & Santora, 2008; Schein, 2010), while a third recent review concludes that they are mutually reinforcing and equally important ideas (Schneider, Ehrhart, & Macey, 2013). There is, in addition, no consensus about whether culture or climate is an outcome or a cause of organizational productivity—or simply an additional factor that mediates the relationship between leadership behaviors and productivity. The absence of simple or conclusive answers will require some patience on the part of this chapter's readers.

POSITIVE LEADERSHIP AND ORGANIZATIONAL CLIMATE

Job satisfaction would seem to be a particularly relevant outcome to assess in productivity research. (Youssef & Luthans, 2007, p. 783)

At a general level, employees who are highly engaged in their work roles not only focus their physical effort on the pursuit of role-related goals, but are also cognitively vigilant and emotionally connected to the endeavor. (Rich, Lepine, & Crawford, 2010, p. 619)

Numerous analysts have pointed out the negative consequences of the impersonal, alienated, "shopping mall," organizational climate often found in large public schools. (Ingersoll, 2001, p. 527)

A strong and consistent line of research associates positive leadership with *organizational climate*, generally considered as an important but relatively temporary sense of how people consciously "feel" about their work setting (Denison, 1996; Schneider et al., 2013). In educational research, organizational climate often is viewed as a reflection of overall organizational health (Hoy & Hannum, 1997; Hoy, Tarter, & Kottkamp, 1991). Because perceptions and feelings can be affected by people and events, organizational climate is a relatively easier target for positive leaders' efforts to improve the quality of members' work life.

Unfortunately, although there is a long line of research on organizational climate beginning in the 1970s, there is limited consensus about its underlying dimensions or ways of measuring them (Hoy, Smith, & Sweetland, 2002). According to Schneider et al. (2013), "Early measures . . . had between 6 and

10 dimensions, but the dimensions chosen for study seemed to cover a variety of territories that emerged from a variety of researchers" (p. 365). They go on to point out that recent research simply has accepted the idea that climate indicators may vary between studies, depending on their context and purpose.

An examination of highly cited empirical articles suggests that among the many dimensions are affiliation, sense of belonging, fairness, trust, autonomy, support, engaging work, relationships with supervisors, and goal/focus—each of which can be defined and measured very differently. For some, positive leadership is part of organizational climate (Hoy & Hannum, 1997), but others regard it as exogenous (Dickson, Smith, Grojean, & Ehrhart, 2001). Increasingly, research is focused less on the general concept of organizational climate and more on specific types of climate, such as service climate, ethical climate, or safety climate (Schneider et al., 2013). Faced with this ambiguous scholarly disorganization, we focus on those dimensions that are consistent with the literature on organizational climate *and* are studied in the context of positive leadership.

In Chapter 6, we reviewed the consequences of positive leadership behaviors for individual member's job satisfaction, commitment, and perceptions of being treated fairly. There is a clear path leading from positive relationships between individuals to organizational or communal flourishing. In other words, positive leaders have an impact on organizational outcomes because they shape individual experiences, but when most or all members of the organization feel similarly, we can begin to talk about organizational climate and overall organizational performance. In this section, we explore what empirical research tells us about these organizational outcomes.

Job Satisfaction: A Collective Sense of Meaningful Work

Job satisfaction, as a core concept in organizational studies, is both an individual perception and a property of larger groups, particularly when it occurs because of positive leaders' attention to work design and human resources behaviors (S. E. Humphrey et al., 2007; Shipton, West, Parkes, Dawson, & Patterson, 2006). In other words, there is a distinctive difference between organizations, including schools, where almost everyone is satisfied with their work and ones in which there is a constant litany of complaints. Many studies suggest that job satisfaction is a distinctive element of climate, but is strongly associated with other measures of climate, such as those discussed below (Fassina, Jones, & Uggerslev, 2008; Harter et al., 2003; Kirkman & Shapiro, 2001).

There is also consensus that the link between positive leadership and overall organizational performance is traceable through job satisfaction (Luthans & Youssef, 2007; Pratt & Ashforth, 2003). An analysis of nearly 8,000 business units by Harter et al. (2002) shows, for example, a very strong relationship between job satisfaction and organizational performance: "Across companies, the difference between business units above the median and those below the median was more than one half of a standard deviation on composite performance" (p. 274). There is also a "significant relationship between unit-level employee satisfaction (positive) and unit-level customer satisfaction" (Koys, 2001, p. 105).

Commitment: Enthusiasm About "the Work"

Commitment is one of the climate indicators that is on virtually every scholar's list because it involves a sense that all members are working hard for a common goal. Links between positive leadership and employee commitment have been recognized for some time (P. M. Podsakoff, MacKenzie, & Bommer, 1996), and efforts to link positive leadership practices to high-performance work cultures, which include high employee commitment, are increasing. Ethical leadership (Demirtas & Akdogan, 2015; Hassan, Wright, & Yukl, 2014), transformational leadership (Boehm, Dwertmann, Bruch, & Shamir, 2015; Robertson & Barling, 2013), servant leadership (Goh & Zhen-Jie, 2014; E. M. Hunter et al., 2013; Liden, Wayne, Liao, & Meuser, 2014), and authentic leadership (Hallinger & Heck, 2011; Hsieh & Wang, 2015) are all associated with measures of employee commitment.

A variety of studies suggest that systemic positive leadership practices are related to organizational performance largely because "they help to positively affect employees and inspire them to contribute to important organizational outcomes" (Huang, Ahlstrom, Lee, Chen, & Hsieh, 2016, p. 300). They also are linked to overall employee well-being, which is then associated with organizational commitment and lower turnover (Harter et al., 2003), as well as increased organizational performance (Boerner, Eisenbeiss, & Griesser, 2007; Jacobs & Washington, 2003; Nasomboon, 2014; Steyrer, Schiffinger, & Lang, 2008).

Retention: "This Is Where We Want to Be"

Consistent with the previously mentioned lack of agreement about organizational climate, absenteeism, turnover, and intention to leave are considered by some scholars as simply other indicators of commitment (G. J. Blau & Boal, 1987), but in education they often are seen as indicators of climate or even consequences of a poor climate (Ingersoll, 2001). We assume that both absenteeism and turnover will have reverberating consequences for others in the work setting.

Absenteeism and turnover have long been recognized as particularly costly in terms of organizational productivity (Mowday, Porter, & Steers, 1982; Ybema, van der Meer, & Leijten, 2016), and are an indirect measure of organizational performance (Sun, Aryee, & Law, 2007). A number of studies demonstrate a direct relationship between positive leadership and employee absenteeism (Kim, 2002) and turnover (Cameron, 2003; Nahrgang et al., 2009). Stockard and Lehman (2004) demonstrate that these outcomes also are connected to job satisfaction, where "worker satisfaction is the primary influence on workers' retention" (p. 762). Positive leadership to reduce them focuses on "mutual investment" or reciprocity as a strategy rather than simply offering additional individual inducements (Shaw, Dineen, Fang, & Vellella, 2009).

Retention is a particular issue for professional settings like schools or hospitals, where staff are highly trained and difficult to replace, and need to collaborate in order to get the core work accomplished. Every experienced teacher who decides to leave is likely to be replaced with a less experienced teacher who will require several years before he or she becomes expert. The consequences for students are real: As Borko and Livingston (1989) noted some time ago, "Novices' cognitive schemata are less elaborate, interconnected, and accessible than experts' and . . . their pedagogical reasoning skills are less well developed" (p. 473). The same problems occur when school leader turnover is high (Louis et al., 2010). A recent study of six schools showed that turnover of principals had serious negative effects on schoolwide efforts to confront institutional racism, where progress on difficult changes tended to stop (at least temporarily) when positive leaders departed (Palmer & Louis, 2017).

Fairness: The Basis for an Ethical Climate

When we talk about fairness in the context of organizational climate, we must distinguish it from the broader category of social justice, which often emphasizes finding systemic constraints that (re)produce inequality. Our focus is on the underpinnings of positive psychology, which leads us to emphasize members' collective sense that both they and others are treated fairly, in *procedures*, in access to *opportunities*, and in *interpersonal interactions* (Moorman, 1991; Simons & Roberson, 2003), each of which is related to positive leader behaviors (Bacha & Walker, 2013; Viswesvaran & Ones, 2002). Knippenberg and De Cremer (2008) conclude that there is a connection between positive organizational leadership and organizational justice: "Justice is more strongly related to felt obligation to the organization the higher the quality of the [leader–member system] relationship" (p. 176). Fairness is particularly important in studies that include examining an ethical component in organizational climate and those that are concerned with the increasing diversity of the workforce (Buttner, Lowe, & Billings-Harris, 2012; Shin, 2012). Shin goes further, arguing that the "CEO not only serves as a strong role model for employees, but also affects the . . . firm as a whole by enhancing the ethical leadership of managers and supervisors, which consequently contributes to the formation of an ethical climate" (p. 301).

An important insight from empirical research is that perceived fairness is generalized to trust in the organization as well as to supervisors, and these combine to create an improved environment for job satisfaction, greater commitment, and organizational citizenship behaviors (Aryee, Pawan, & Zhen Xiong, 2002; Bacha & Walker, 2013). Leadership that attends fully to justice is not cost free (often because it is most critical during periods of tension and conflict), but weaker organizational justice may be more costly because of lower satisfaction and commitment, and higher turnover (Cropanzana, Bowen, & Gilliland, 2007; Simons & Roberson, 2003). In schools, a climate characterized by a collective sense of fairness in the behaviors of principals and district office staff may induce trust and allow teachers to be more open to innovations. This is true even where innovations are centrally initiated and quite challenging, such as the implementation of new modes of teacher evaluation (Tuytens & Devos, 2012) or the introduction of total quality management procedures (Louis, 2007).

However, some studies have concluded that obtaining consensus on whether an organizational climate is fair may be more difficult than for the other climate dimensions covered here. Women and people of color tend to rate the promises of fairness and their experience of procedural, distributive, and interpersonal fairness in their settings lower than White men rate them (Buttner, Lowe, & Billings-Harris, 2012). This issue, we argue, will become increasingly important in schools as both student bodies and professional staff become more diverse. In addition, only a few studies have connected perceived organizational justice or fairness directly with productivity and performance (DeConinck & Johnson, 2009; S. K. L. Simon, Schaubroeck, & Aryee, 2002; Simons & Roberson, 2003), and these have used rather different ways of measuring fairness. Although the research base is thinner than for the other climate factors we cover, we include attention to it because of the importance of broader social justice and fairness issues that are embedded in the work of Positive School Leaders.

Engagement: Flourishing Members and Flourishing Organizations

As Rich et al. (2010) note, "Engagement serves as an important mechanism through which the effects of antecedents are transmitted" (pp. 620–621). Employee engagement is, perhaps, the most critical element that links the conditions discussed above to deeper organizational culture and performance. Analysts approach the topic of engagement in various ways. For example, Harter et al. (2002) suggest that "we see engagement occurring when individuals are emotionally connected to others and cognitively vigilant . . . [when they] perceive that they are part of something significant with coworkers whom they trust, and have chances to improve and develop (p. 269). Rich et al. (2010) maintain that "engagement reflects the simultaneous investment of cognitive, emotional, and physical energies in such a way that one is actively and completely involved in the full performance of a role" (p. 622). Other researchers also lay out definitions of engagement as "characterized by vigor, dedication, and absorption . . . that is not focused on any particular object, event, individual, or behavior" (Schaufeli & Bakker, 2004, p. 295). Still others are attentive to the elements or characteristics of engagement, focusing particularly on organizational identity/identification (Schaufeli & Bakker, 2004; Walter & Bruch, 2008).

Engagement is more than an aspect of a positive work environment. It leads to organizational performance. Some studies find a direct relationship in which a higher number of engaged employees leads to higher performance (Christian, Garza, & Slaughter, 2011), while others outline more complex relationships (Bakker, 2011; Salanova, Agut, & Peiró, 2005; Wang, Lu, & Siu, 2015). This is as true in schools as in other kinds of organizations: Engaged teachers create classrooms that engage students and, therefore, increase achievement (Guthrie, Dreher, & Baker, 2000; Louis & Smith, 1991; Skinner & Belmont, 1993). And, we know that engagement—in both schools and other work settings—is linked to positive leadership behaviors (Breevaart, Bakker, Demerouti, & Derks, 2016; Louis & Smith, 1991; D. M. Quinn, 2002). A convincing study, carried out with teachers, suggests that the relationship between organizational resources (a supportive social environment and a clear sense of purpose) and a sense of full engagement in work is recursive (Salanova, Bakker, & Llorens, 2006). Where there are more organizational resources, teachers are more engaged; when teachers are more engaged, they participate in enlarging organizational resources.

POSITIVE LEADERSHIP AND ORGANIZATIONAL CULTURE

The desire to improve the human condition is universal and . . . the capacity to do so is latent in most systems. (Cameron et al., 2003, p. 10)

Transformational leadership . . . affects the goals and the culture of the school, which have direct ties to individual teachers' commitment to change and improvement. (Firestone & Louis, 1999, p. 315)

When individuals are open to change and connecting to work and others, are focused and attentive, and complete rather than fragmented, their systems adopt the same characteristics, collectively. (Kahn, 1992, p. 331)

Research that examines the outcomes of positive leadership also attends to its impacts on *organizational culture*. As noted previously, organizational climate can shift rather quickly based on external events, leadership turnover, and other factors. Organizational culture, which focuses less on feelings and perceptions and more on underlying values, norms of behavior, and core assumptions about organizational purpose, is embedded and can be quite resistant to change (Denison, 1996; Schein, 2010). This is particularly true in schools, whose collective culture and behavioral routines are deeply influenced by the broader assumptions of the teaching profession, as well as by stakeholder expectations about how schools should operate (Firestone & Louis, 1999).

As with organizational climate, observations about the relationship between leadership and organizational culture must be prefaced by the observation that there is little consensus about how to conceptualize or measure it. When one adds the variety of approaches to positive leadership (which we discussed in Chapter 1) and the lack of consensus about what constitutes organizational effectiveness, it is obvious that we are operating outside of precision science (March & Sutton, 1997). However, as part of building a strong case for grounding sustained school improvement in the principles of positive organizational psychology, we are obligated to address school culture.

For the purposes of our synthesis, we draw on the influential perspective developed by Denison and his colleagues (Denison, Haaland, & Goelzer, 2003; Denison & Mishra, 1995; Denison & Spreitzer, 1991; Fey & Denison, 2003), which identifies four core elements of organizational culture—involvement, consistency, adaptability, and mission—that reflect, we believe, the principles of positive organizational theory laid out in Chapter 3. These relationships are shown in Figure 8.1.

In Chapters 6 and 7, we examined the evidence that leadership behaviors and leader–member relations affect individual and team performance, and in Part II we identified some of the most important ways in which leaders help to prepare members to become more committed and potentially more productive. However, as Edgar Schein (2010) and others remind us, leaders can have a large (albeit often indirect) impact on the collective values and taken-for-granted assumptions associated with "how we do things around here." These, then, create more (or less) positive settings for collective work.

Thus, a goal of positive leadership is to create settings in which members behave "organizationally" and therefore can be relied on to become "positive organizers" rather than simply playing by rules that privilege individual preferences (Josephson, 1952; Leithwood & Steinbach, 1991; Weick, 2003). Positive leadership can change the way in which individual members experience

Figure 8.1. Organizational Culture and Principles of Positive School Leadership

Denison's Culture Dimensions (Fey & Denison, 2003, p. 690)	Principles of Positive School Leadership (Chapter 3)
"**Involvement.** Effective organizations empower people, organize around teams, and develop human capability . . . managers, and employees are committed and feel a strong sense of ownership. People at all levels feel that they have input into decisions that will affect their work and see a direct connection to the goals of the organization."	**Relationally Grounded:** Places the development of positive relationships with all stakeholders at the center of leadership work **Growth-Based:** Emphasizes the importance of personal growth and development for all members of the school
"**Consistency.** Effective organizations tend to have 'strong' cultures that are highly consistent, well-coordinated, and well integrated. Behavioral norms are rooted in core values, and leaders and followers are able to reach agreement even with diverse points of view. Consistency is a source of stability and internal integration resulting from a common mindset."	**Asset-Based:** Consistently focused on the assets that all stakeholders bring to the school **Value-Centered:** Clearly and regularly articulates enduring values that are the foundation of an enterprise committed to human development **Virtue-Based:** Consistently models value-based behaviors in ways that others would describe as virtuous
"**Adaptability.** . . . Adaptable organizations are driven by their customers, take risks and learn from their mistakes, and have capability and experience at creating change."	**Means-Focused:** Recognizes the importance of the daily tasks of school leadership as a foundation for positive transformation **Authentic:** Requires self-awareness, transparency, balanced consideration, and self-regulated behavior
"**Mission.** Effective organizations have a clear sense of purpose and direction defining goals and strategic objectives and expressing a vision of the future."	**Transcendent:** Fosters a morally compelling vision that moves others to make commitments to the common good **Service-Grounded:** Emphasizes the stewardship functions of leadership: conserving and nurturing the humanity of all those served by the organization

their work, but it is "collective perceptions of social context [that] are significantly related to individual work resilience" (Meneghel, Borgogni, Miraglia, Salanova, & Martínez, 2016, p. 2047). This assertion holds true in a variety of countries and work settings. A recent study of Indonesian secondary schools found, for example, that principals who interacted more frequently with teachers were seen as moral leaders, and those who provided an intellectually stimulating environment were more likely to create strong consensus around goals—which then led to greater teacher efficacy (Damanik & Aldridge, 2017). Again, we see the line of reasoning that views Positive School Leadership in the center of a virtuous cycle where a flourishing school culture nurtures flourishing individuals—who then reinforce the culture.

This chapter only begins to explore the ways in which positive organizational leadership stimulates a positive culture, and focuses on a selection of cultural features that are associated with long-term performance. We begin by examining how the density of social networks can promote easily observed organizational citizenship behavior. We go on to look at two additional features of organizational culture that are less visible but are important in schools and other settings because they contribute to adaptability and vitality: collective sense of efficacy and innovation. We finally consider a feature of culture that is critical for maintaining consistent values and mission/focus: modes of problem finding and conflict resolution.

Involvement: Building Social Networks

In Chapter 5, we placed relationships at the center of positive organizational and leadership theory. In Chapter 6 we went on to show that positive leadership develops *psychological capital*, including a sense of flourishing (Fredrickson, 2000; T. A. Wright & Bonett, 2007), psychological safety (Rich et al., 2010), "broad minded coping" (Fredrickson, 2000, p. 135), positive self-evaluation (Rich et al., 2010), and overall resilience (Harland et al., 2005). Here we turn from the dyadic relationships that support individual development, to social networks, which are an indicator of how positive social relationships create *social capital* (Bourdieu, 1986; Coleman, 1990; Putnam, 1995), which sustains groups in the same way that psychological capital supports individual thriving.

Collective empowerment and ownership require social connections among members of a group. Maak (2007) draws a clear distinction between psychological and social capital, claiming that the latter requires social connections among members that go beyond dyadic leader–member exchanges. Instead, Maak argues that leaders must be "weavers" of denser relationships that are based in values and mutual commitment; others describe the work as building bridges between people and groups that otherwise might be disconnected (Cross & Parker, 2004).

There is evidence that practices that focus on building networks within and between groups have impacts on both organizational climate and the more longstanding organizational culture (Collins & Clark, 2003). Developing social networks is a leadership responsibility, although the detailed work of maintaining relationships will evolve naturally among members (Cohen & Prusak, 2001). Positive leadership behaviors increase the density of both formal communication and informal friendship networks, both of which are associated with stronger organizations (Zohar & Tenne-Gazit, 2008). In schools, this stimulates natural network density among teachers (Supovitz, Sirinides, & May, 2010), while changes in district incentives for networking and collaboration can support stronger ties within grade levels (Daly et al., 2010).

Networks also contribute to the achievement of goals. The density of personal and social relationships within a group or an organization predicts performance in business (Collins & Clark, 2003; W. R. Evans & Davis, 2005; Nahapiet & Ghoshal, 1998; Youndt & Snell, 2004), government (Boix & Posner, 1998; Knack, 2002), and education (Frank, Zhao, & Borman, 2004; Leana & Pil, 2006; M. Lee, Louis, & Anderson, 2012; Moolenaar, Daly, & Sleegers, 2010; Moolenaar, Sleegers, & Daly, 2012). Networks are particularly important in organizations that are "information rich" or dependent on sharing relevant information. In schools, for example, a 4th-grade teacher who shares information about her students' strengths and weaknesses with the relevant 5th-grade teachers may provide critical insights into what those students need; without such information, the first month of school may require (re)collecting information that already exists.

Involvement and Consistency: Organizational Citizenship Behaviors

One important strand of positive leadership research examines discretionary work behavior (Bommer et al., 2007; Hoffman, Blair, Meriac, & Woehr, 2007;), often referred to as organizational citizenship behavior (OCB). Organizational citizenship behaviors include positive actions that fall outside the scope of required tasks. They are discretionary and voluntary and "in the aggregate promote the effective functioning of the organization" (Bommer et al., 2007, p. 1481). In other words, people do not engage in OCB to enhance personal benefits other than their own intrinsic satisfaction (McNeely & Meglino, 1994). This aspect of organizational culture is important both because there is a wealth of scholarship on this topic and because its application in educational leadership research is increasing (DiPaola & Hoy, 2005a, 2005b; Nutov & Somech, 2017; Somech & Bogler, 2002; Somech & Ron, 2007). This suggests that Positive school leaders cannot afford to ignore it.

OCB often is considered a collective element of a positive, ethically based organizational culture that privileges relational community (Liden et al., 2008; Shin, 2012). Its application to schools' experience is obvious.

As Somech and Ron (2007) note, "The success of schools fundamentally depends on teachers' willingness to go above and beyond the call of duty, namely, to exhibit organizational citizenship behaviors" (p. 38). If teachers collaborate to develop new ways of teaching and supporting students in and out of the classroom, innovation increases. If they go out of their way to care, both students and adults thrive (Louis & Murphy, 2017; Louis, Murphy, & Smylie, 2016). In other words, as in most other professional organizations, administrators, colleagues, and parents assume some level of work activity beyond the job description.

We classify OCB as relevant to the cultural dimensions of involvement and consistency based on the cluster of behaviors identified by Konovsky and Pugh (1994). These include (1) *altruism* (interpersonal helping, including assisting another person with an organizationally relevant task or problem), (2) *conscientiousness* (carrying out role behaviors well beyond the minimum required levels), (3) *sportsmanship* (willingness to accept minor frustrations without complaint), (4) *courtesy* (taking action to prevent problems from occurring by respecting others' needs), and (5) *civic virtue* (responsible workplace participation). Wrzesniewski and Dutton (2001), Caprara and Steca (2007), Liden et al. (2008), and others add to this list by discussing other specific citizenship behaviors, such as generating new ideas for doing work, accepting reasonable orders, sharing, donating, caring, comforting, and helping. In school settings, scholars define teacher OCB in three arenas—work with students, teacher teams, and the school as a whole—while principal OCB would include also work with the community (Nutov & Somech, 2017). Although OCB is broadly defined and variably measured, at least one meta-analysis suggests that all of the individual behaviors are highly associated with one another (LePine, Erez, & Johnson, 2002).

Voluntary organizational citizenship is generative in nature: Once in play, it tends to deepen and flourish (Cooperrider & Sekerka, 2003; Fredrickson, 2000; Gittell & Douglass, 2012), adding to the positive climate and culture of any organization. Miller, Grimes, McMullen, and Vogus (2012), for example, argue that it "overrides a traditional mode of processing costs and benefits and thereby gives way to a prosocial cost-benefit analysis that overcomes the typical individual's reluctance to engage in activities with higher personal risk" (p. 624).

Gittell and Douglass (2012) throw light on this when they confirm that reciprocity runs deep in settings where strong relationships focus on "coproduction" rather than individual task performance, a finding that is reflected in Kruse et al.'s (1995) assumption that high-level teacher collaboration requires coproduction. The underlying argument is that adaptive responses to new challenges are more likely to occur in work settings where there is reciprocity and where people contribute more than what is required in their individual job descriptions. But there are also cultural benefits of organizational citizenship behavior that are traced to the development of stronger human relationships: "Participants treat each other as subjects rather than objects, fostering their attentiveness to each other (Gittell & Douglass, 2012, p. 721). OCB supports, therefore, a culture of respect and civility that incorporates the principles of positive school leadership and positive cultures.

Organizational citizenship does not just add to the organization's culture. Where the culture creates increased pressure for voluntary contributions, personal stress both on and off the job can also increase (Bolino, Turnley, Gilstrap, & Suazo, 2010). Moreover, when organizational citizenship is removed or absent, that also detracts (Detert et al., 2007; Marcus & Schuler, 2004; Robinson & Bennett, 1995) and may induce deviant behavior (Avey, Palanski, & Walumbwa, 2011). Both deviant behavior and stress are more likely to occur in settings where the cultural norms about effort are particularly strong. This means that Positive school leaders must attend both to nurturing voluntary commitments and to preventing overload that occurs because of escalating group expectations.

Whatever list of specific actions is included, there is consensus that positive leadership influences the extent of OCB in every country in which it has been studied, whether through generating stronger leader–member exchanges (Walumbwa, Hartnell, et al., 2010), widespread organizational justice practices (Ehrhart, 2004), and/or more meaningful job designs (Purvanova, Bono, & Dziewczynski, 2006). These relationships seem to be apparent across school cultures as varied as those of the United States (DiPaola & Hoy, 2005a, 2005b), Israel (in the extensive work of Anit Somech), and Tanzania (Nguni, Sleegers, & Denessen, 2006).

Collective organizational citizenship behaviors are associated with both individual and organizational outcomes. We know that they cause people to undertake risks because those risks are consistent with their values, and they promote individual and organizational caring (Fredrickson, 2001; Gittell & Douglass, 2012). Organizational citizenship behavior is connected with both individual and collective job satisfaction (McNeely & Meglino, 1994; Ostroff, 1992); with motivation, turnover, and absenteeism (N. P. Podsakoff, Whiting, Podsakoff, & Blume, 2009); and with organizational climate (DiPaola & Tschannen-Moran, 2014). At the organizational level, OCBs are linked to a wide variety of other measures of longer term organizational outcomes, including general measures of organizational effectiveness, such as student learning (DiPaola & Hoy, 2005a; N. P Podsakoff et al., 2009), organizational learning (Somech & Drach-Zahavy, 2004), financial results (Koys, 2001), productivity (Cameron & Caza, 2002), and customer satisfaction (Detert et al., 2007; Ostroff, 1992).

Adaptability: Building Collective Efficacy

As Ron Heifetz (1994) aptly noted, most of the problems facing modern organizations do not require simple, technical solutions. Instead, they require uncomfortable and often distressing challenges to the status quo that fall squarely into the arena of positive leadership (Heifetz, Grashow, & Linsky, 2009). However, individual heroic action by a few leaders is not enough: To grapple with uncomfortable changes, organizations require a strong sense of the group's capacity to be effective during change.

Alfred Bandura's (1997) enduring contribution to positive psychology emerged with his explication of the idea of an individual sense of efficacy, which, as we saw in Chapter 6, is intertwined with relationships with leaders and peers. Collective efficacy (Bandura, 1997) is, however, distinctive because it reflects a "group's shared belief in its conjoint capabilities to organize and execute courses of action required to produce given levels of attainment" (p. 477). Others argue that this occurs in large measure because individuals' reactions and behaviors, regardless of their own self-efficacy, are deeply affected by the group's beliefs about the power to control processes and outcomes (Tasa, Sears, & Schat, 2011). As Goddard and Salloum (2012) note, group beliefs reflect the self-assurance required to tackle complicated problems more vigorously. They go on to argue that "organizations with effective coping skills effectively build on success . . . and react to stresses in ways that do not emphasize inadequacies. . . . Leaders may play a key role in influencing . . . collective efficacy for various organizational pursuits" (p. 645).

Collective efficacy does not emerge in a vacuum, but is deeply affected by the other aspects of organizational climate and culture described so far. It is, therefore, not surprising that positive leadership is associated with higher levels of collective efficacy. In particular, there is an emerging consensus that positive leadership behaviors promote both collective efficacy and increased communication and collaboration (e.g., stronger social networks and leader–member relationships), which also contribute to effective tackling of challenges (Dumay et al., 2013; Jung & Sosik, 2002; Kark, Shamir, & Chen, 2003). A critical study in education found that teachers' beliefs about their principal's positive support were a stronger predictor of commitment to teaching than their reported influence over school decisions (Ware & Kitsantas, 2007). In addition, it is positive leadership from the top levels of the organization that is most critical to promoting collective (as opposed to individual) efficacy (G. Chen & Bliese, 2002). At least one study concludes that positive (transformational) leadership and collective efficacy together determine the degree to which individuals feel a sense of personal efficacy (Kurt, Duyar, & Çalik, 2011).

Research gives us clues about why developing a culture characterized by strong collective efficacy must be an important priority for positive leaders. Walumbwa, Wang, Lawler, and Shi (2004) found, for example, that transformational leadership had limited effects on job satisfaction, commitment, and retention where collective efficacy was low. To put it positively, a leader's efforts to develop individuals may be more effective if the belief that "we can do it" is ingrained.

The incorporation of collective efficacy has been more visible in community studies and in educational research than in private-sector studies. In community studies, considerable focus is placed on the role of collective efficacy beliefs in preventing violence and promoting health (Ahern, Cerda, Lippman, Tardiff, & Galea, 2013; Browning, Burrington, Leventhal, & Brooks-Gunn, 2008; Browning, Soller, Gardner, & Brooks-Gunn, 2013; Sampson, Raudenbush, & Earls, 1997). In education, one seminal study indicates that variation between schools in individual teacher self-efficacy is fully accounted for by collective efficacy (Goddard & Goddard, 2001). Furthermore, multiple studies suggest that collective efficacy is a powerful predictor of student achievement (Hoy, Sweetland, & Smith, 2002; Moolenaar et al., 2012; Tschannen-Moran & Barr, 2004). While the evidence is still accumulating, research suggests that collective efficacy has a strong impact on performance because it is associated more broadly with positive organizational culture (Hoy, Tarter, & Hoy, 2006), higher levels of value consensus (Ross & Gray, 2006), higher levels of commitment (Ware & Kitsantas, 2007), and lower levels of stress and burnout (Klassen, 2010). In summary, collective efficacy, no matter how difficult it is to assess, must be a focus for Positive School Leaders.

Adaptability: A Culture of Innovation and Change

The association of positive leadership with a culture that also promotes innovation has emerged as a strong and consistent finding across multiple sectors. Before we unpack this generalization, however, we must first tackle what we mean by a culture of innovation. We can begin with the insights of two prolific scholars of organizational change, Karl Weick and Robert Quinn (1999), who distinguish between two different types of change: episodic and continuous. Episodic change refers to innovations that bring something entirely new to the organization. In schools, this might be the elimination of punishment-focused discipline systems and the introduction of restorative justice programs; in business, it might be a completely new product line. Continuous change refers to the honing and reshaping of existing structures and processes. Schools are deeply familiar with continuous change, as they have adapted over long periods to adjustments in the curriculum or internally generated practices of coordinating work across grade levels. Each of these two types of change has different implications for positive leadership and organizational culture.

Leadership scholars often think about continuous change in a framework of organizational learning (J. S. Brown & Duguid, 1991, 2001; Senge, 2002), which is seen as a key characteristic of positive organizations. In order to understand an organization's learning culture, leaders need to adopt the eye of an anthropologist, looking for the details of how work is carried out and then promoting mechanisms to institutionalize the processes that contribute to learning and change (Lipschitz, Popper, & Oz, 1996). Organizational learning occurs in the presence of habituated *searching* for new information, *processing* and *evaluating* information with others, *incorporating* and *using* new ideas, and *generating ideas* within the organization as well as importing them from outside (Louis & Lee, 2016; Louis & Leithwood, 1998; Schechter, 2008). The central processes provide a lever for continuous improvement in innovative practice through frequent and deliberate adjustments of existing practice in response to new ideas or new data, rather than major strategic reorientations (J. S. Brown & Duguid, 1991, 2001; Schechter & Qadach, 2012). In this regard, a continuous improvement change culture is consistent with models of total quality management developed for both private- and public-sector organizations (Detert, Schroeder, & Mauriel, 2000; Hackman & Wageman, 1995). From the perspective of Positive School Leaders, given the rapidly changing environments faced by schools today, this approach to thoughtful, systematic but incremental improvements feels like a welcome return to professional practice rather than reform imposed from above.

In contrast, Berson, Oreg, and Dvir (2008) state that innovation cultures involve an "entrepreneurial orientation, creativity and a risk-taking work environment" (p. 617). "Innovate or die" is another phrase that permeates research on innovation (Lemon & Sahota, 2004). Popular business writing often focuses on this kind of organizational culture, which is associated with successful start-up companies and the renewal of lumbering Fortune 500 firms. Moreover, the language has been applied to the public sector, including schools, which are challenged to be more entrepreneurial and innovative in meeting new demands for rapid change rather than for continuous improvement.

However, an emphasis on the value of entrepreneurship in the public sector has a weak evidentiary base for two reasons. First, many members are "programmed" to ignore new information that challenges their existing practices (Argyris, 1976). Strong cultures in established social service agencies can create "uniformity, loyalty, and commitment to the organization [that inhibits] innovation and organizational ability to respond to change" (Jaskyte & Dressler, 2005, p. 26). In other words, the stronger the collective professional culture, the less likely members are to introduce novel behaviors without consulting with colleagues. Collective wisdom and consistency in practice are valued in most human service agencies and other settings where high reliability in services and outcomes is prized (Stringfield, Reynolds, & Schaffer, 2008).

A second reason is that the entrepreneurial perspective privileges *episodic change* and does not reflect the reality of positive leadership, positive organizational culture, and *continuous change* presented in this chapter. One study of 56 government agencies found, for example, that organizational innovation and organizational learning were positively associated (Hurley & Hult, 1998) and that an organizational learning culture was an important precondition for developing a culture of innovation. This finding has been affirmed by later research as well (Alegre & Chiva, 2008; Jiménez-Jiménez & Sanz-Valle, 2011).

An integration of what we know about the behaviors associated with both organizational learning and innovation is presented in Figure 8.2.

Organizational learning and innovation are connected to other aspects of organizational culture. For example, teachers who already feel good about their teaching (are high in self- and collective efficacy) are more open to learning about ways of getting even better (Camburn, 2010; De Neve, Devos, & Tuytens, 2015), and informal networks of sharing matter a great deal (Mohrman, Tenkasi, & Mohrman, 2003). Tenkasi and Chesmore's (2003) study points out that networks solve two common "problems" of change: weak information sharing within and between teams, and the tendency for common recommended practices to diverge during implementation.

Positive leadership also influences innovation and change, which, in turn, are linked with performance. One large study of manufacturing firms found, for example, a complex set of relationships: "Transformational leadership positively and indirectly influenced organizational innovation through organizational learning and knowledge management. Knowledge management and organizational learning affected organizational performance indirectly by organizational innovation" (Noruzy, Dalfard, Azhdari, Nazari-Shirkouhi, & Rezazadeh, 2013, p. 1). Similar findings characterize the pharmaceutical industry (Garcia-Morales, Matias-Reche, & Hurtado-Torres, 2008), organizations that provide services (Choudhary, Akhtar, & Zaheer, 2013), and even higher education (Abbasi & Zamani-Miandashti, 2013). All of these studies also connect innovation and continuous organizational learning to some measure of productivity.

Maintaining Mission: Managing Difference and Conflict

Even the most positive work settings will not be problem free. As Gelfand, Leslie, Keller, and De Dreu (2012) observe, "Put simply, conflict in organizations is inevitable given that humans therein need to manage their mutual interdependence" (p. 1132). Indeed, conflict avoidance is associated with weak ties among members and poorly functioning organizations, and a "conflict-positive" setting is associated with strength (Tichy, 1983; Tjosvold, 2008). Differences of opinion, whether sharp or easily resolved, are part of the process of organizational and individual self-assessment. However, in order

Figure 8.2. Attributes of Innovation and Change Cultures

BEHAVIORAL INDICATORS

Is it safe to adapt and learn: Do members trust one another? Do they trust their clients/stakeholders? Is innovation/change supported and "risk free" for individuals and teams?

Is there consensus around learning: Do leaders and other members assess whether innovations or change programs make positive contributions to other important components of the culture?

Is there a focus on identifying weaknesses: Do members and leaders know their processes (and clients/stakeholders) well enough to tailor organizational work to their needs? Do they regularly assess what needs to be eliminated and replaced?

Do all members share responsibility for the success of the whole school: Do members focus their personal development and learning on organizational priorities? Are they willing to work with others on significant innovations?

Is current practice open and shared: Do members and leaders share what they are doing—both strong and weak practices—with colleagues?

Do deep conversations connect innovation and learning: Do all members engage in regular and sustained conversations about what they are doing to improve?

---

to manage difference and potential conflicts, positive leaders first must be aware that problems are emerging. Business and education scholars (Marks & Printy, 2003; Mumford, Todd, Higgs, & McIntosh, 2017) agree, based on empirical studies, that problem finding—looking for and anticipating issues that are not yet highly visible and addressing them before they become impediments—is among the most important skills for positive leaders.

But interpersonal conflict and disagreements about how work should be carried out also can be significant distractors from the collective enterprise. When these occur, they create significant challenges for positive leaders, who simultaneously must keep an eye on the organization's mission and on the relationships that support that mission. Dealing with specific conflict episodes ("putting out fires") is not the focus of positive leaders' work; rather, the focus is on diagnosing the accretion of smaller problems or conflicts over time (Mumford et al., 2017; Sheppard, 1992). Problem finding also is particularly relevant for public organizations, where unresolved disagreements frequently arise because of ambiguous and conflicting social expectations about mission (B. E. Wright, 2007). Thus, Positive school leaders must begin from the premise "that conflict exists and that it matters how it is managed" (De Dreu, 2008, p. 10).

One issue with existing positive leadership models is that they avoid discussions of the role of conflict and power, and largely exclude them from much of the research that we have cited so far (Yukl, 1999). The *Oxford Handbook of Positive Organizational Scholarship* (Cameron & Spreitzer, 2012), for example, has only two brief references to conflict in a volume of over 1,000 pages. This omission is surprising, because the topics of conflict and power are prominent in organizational research. However, many early studies focused on the way in which differences were hidden and therefore poorly resolved (Baldridge, 1971; Farrell & Petersen, 1982; Kolb & Bartunek, 1992). The theme of covert conflict—unrecognized and unresolved—has continued in studies of both schools and other organizations, often under the label of micro-politics (Ball, 2012; Morrill, Zald, & Rao, 2003).

Tjosvold (2008) points out that "conflict researchers have contributed to the bad reputation of conflict by confounding conflict and competition and suggesting that the kind of conflict, rather than its management, determines its outcomes" (p. 19). He goes on to argue that positive leadership is important because it promotes quality relationships (see Chapter 4), which "promote constructive conflict that results in employee involvement and performance" (p. 21). Jehn (1995), who found that conflict over tasks was detrimental only when tasks were routine, supports this finding.

In order to consider how conflict management might be part of a Positive School Leader's toolkit, we first must recognize that not all conflicts are alike. Three types of conflict cultures emerge in organizations: (1) a *dominating conflict culture*, which assumes that overt and heated conflict is positive and that members have the ability to "handle" it; (2) a *collaborative conflict culture*, where conflict is also open but the focus is on reaching solutions that are potentially beneficial to all; and (3) an *avoidant conflict culture*, which assumes that conflict is dangerous and prioritizes harmonious relationships (Gelfand et al., 2012). Differences in conflict culture and the ways in which leaders approach conflict account for a variety of organizational outcomes, with collaborative conflict cultures making positive contributions to cohesion and creativity/innovation. In contrast, dominating and avoidant conflict cultures have consistently negative implications for teams and customer satisfaction. In addition, covert conflict, or micro-politics, is increasingly an element in the discussion of workplace diversity and conflict, where differential power and White/male privilege dominate (Guillaume, Dawson, Otaye-Ebede, Woods, & West, 2017). Hogg (2015) points out that "the challenge of intergroup leadership is to construct an *intergroup relational identity* that focuses on collaboration and avoids identity threat" (p. 177) and goes on to suggest that leaders focus on positive actions to build coalitions that incorporate social identity, a perspective that has some empirical base (Rupert, Jehn, van Engen, & de Reuver, 2010).

Overall, however, the absence of a strong research base for positive approaches to conflict management, including conflict arising from demographic diversity, is clearly a gap (Guillaume et al., 2017). Khalifa, Gooden, and

Davis (2016) provide a preliminary perspective, synthesizing the research on culturally responsive school leadership within a positive framework that emphasizes a service focus, moral grounding, and an asset-based approach to social identity. What is distinctive is their emphasis on engagement of communities as full partners.

ORGANIZATIONAL PERFORMANCE AND PRODUCTIVITY

In the world of administration, the means-ends dilemma is a difficult problem. (R. E. Quinn & Rohrbaugh, 1983, p. 370)

Increasingly, research is indicating that the best organizations incorporate, rather than attempt to banish, the ambivalence inherent in human life. (Lewis, 2011, p. 9)

The performance impact criterion is used to differentiate [positive organizational behavior] from both the positive self-development literature and positive psychology itself. (Luthans & Avolio, 2009, p. 299)

We must not ignore the relationship between positive leadership and organizational performance. In schools, this has produced a long and well-established concern with "school effectiveness" as measured by student achievement (Reynolds et al., 2014). In the private sector there is often a focus on growth, return on investment, or profitability, while in public-sector organizations the emphasis is typically on client satisfaction. Because the links between positive leadership and these longer term outcomes are less well established, we will focus only on productivity (including student achievement) and client satisfaction.

The previous chapters articulated underlying mechanisms that leaders use to develop positive organizational settings, beginning with clear personal values and virtues, and building up to their influence on work groups. However valuable these are, focusing only on positive individual experiences and relationships inside the organization may be unconvincing to many. The public and involved stakeholders assess the value of an organization—and therefore its leaders—on a wide variety of outcomes, but whether it is a small nonprofit agency or a large multinational firm, there is always attention to whether "they are doing what they said they were going to do."

It is widely recognized that organizational productivity or performance is never assessed by everyone at every moment according to the same uniform measure of outcomes or productivity (Goodman & Pennings, 1977). R. E. Quinn and Rohrbaugh (1983) captured this in their "competing values" framework, which proposes persistent tensions between developing human resources, creating a stable internal organizational environment, focusing on serving the needs of clients or the public, and meeting other relevant performance goals from different constituencies. In education, the enduring leadership dilemmas related to multiple and equally desirable outcomes are also well documented (Ogawa, Crowson, & Goldring, 1999). Cameron, Quinn, De-Graff, and Thakor (2014) make a strong case that positive leadership demands a focus on managing all of these at the organizational level.

In other words, for both members of the organization and members of the public, productivity or performance is a particularly messy concept. We will not enter the debates about what counts as a "more productive" government bureaucracy or a "more effective" school, but will examine briefly what we know about the links between positive leadership and some desirable outcomes. We emphasize brevity, because this book is about Positive School Leadership, and most productivity and effectiveness studies do not focus in depth on either positive leader behaviors or the way in which these effect desired outcomes.

"Are They Satisfied?"

"Client satisfaction" is a critical measure of organizational performance because most organizations offer services or products. Planning for the future requires looking at how satisfied people are currently with what they believe they have paid for, either directly or indirectly. This is particularly important when the "products" are human services, where satisfaction often depends on the client's relationship with the provider. It is also true in education, where parents often base their satisfaction with a school on how they assess their child's teacher rather than their opinion of the educational system in general. There is ample evidence that "client" assessment of services can be traced to the influence of positive leaders. This is true in nursing homes (Ott & van Dijk, 2005), drug treatment centers (Broome, Knight, Edwards, & Flynn, 2009), and mental health centers (Firth-Cozens & Mowbray, 2001). Koys (2001) points to findings that suggest that customer satisfaction is linked to employee satisfaction, which, as we showed in Chapter 6, is strongly linked to leader–member relationships and positive leadership.

Organizational Productivity/Performance

Another outcome measure is captured by the general idea of "productivity" or "performance." Many important positive organizational leadership scholars have shown that there is a strong relationship between *individual and team performance* and positive organizational leadership. The link between positive leadership and overall organizational performance is, however, indirect in all sectors (Heck & Hallinger, 2014; Leithwood et al., 2004; Luthans & Youssef, 2007; Pratt & Ashforth, 2003). Virtually all studies that link positive leadership to productivity do so by examining individual members' work.

However, it is possible to build up a line of reasoning by linking studies that do not directly address the question of how positive leaders affect productivity. For example, in Chapter 6 we showed that there are direct ties between positive leadership and job satisfaction at the individual level, and in this chapter, at the collective level. An analysis of nearly 8,000 business units by Harter et al. (2002) shows a strong relationship between job satisfaction and business performance and it is, thus, reasonable to conclude that positive leadership affects performance because it shapes individual and collective job satisfaction. Another study shows that transformational and servant leadership both have strong (indirect) relationships with profitability in the private sector (Choudhary et al., 2013).

Similar findings occur in other sectors, including public administration (Andrews & Boyne, 2010; Cho & Ringquist, 2011) and nonprofit organizations (Geer, Maher, & Cole, 2008; Shiva & Suar, 2012). Hitt and Tucker (2016) summarize the evidence of leadership effects on school outcomes in ways that point to positive leadership domains and behaviors. Recent emphasis on instructional leadership, leader coaching, and caring leadership indicates that all have elements of positive psychology as an underpinning and have been associated with student achievement. Overall, the case for effects of positive leadership on productivity remains stronger in education than in other sectors, but studies do not capture the full range of behaviors that were discussed in Chapter 4.

SUMMARY

This chapter culminates our exploration of the potential of positive organizational leadership as a force for improving the lives and the outcomes for professionals who work in school settings. Figure 8.3 shows that outcomes can be of many kinds. Too often, and in too many countries, pundits wish to reduce the power and potential of leadership to a simple linear formula that has a single result (typically a single preferred measure of productivity). Of course, this book cannot change the preference of many for simple solutions to very complex problems. Instead, our goal is to provide meaty arguments for why such simple formulas are not at the heart of leadership work.

We have argued that empirical research connects Positive School Leadership to the climate or "feel" of the organization, and to its deeper cultural patterns and expectations that guide the daily nonroutine work of educating children. We also have indicated that Positive school leaders will make a difference in the degree to which other stakeholders believe their legitimate expectations are met. But, we also have maintained that there is more to be done. As a number of studies indicate, we are not alone in wanting to show that positive leadership is important. However, our sense is that the "state of the art" in understanding the organizational outcomes of positive leadership is, compared with the topics discussed in previous chapters, less well developed, both theoretically and in terms of findings. For Positive school leaders who are interested in improving their work immediately, the good news is that there is a great deal that we can draw on from studies carried out in schools, both in the United States and elsewhere.

Figure 8.3. Organizational Outcomes of Positive Leadership

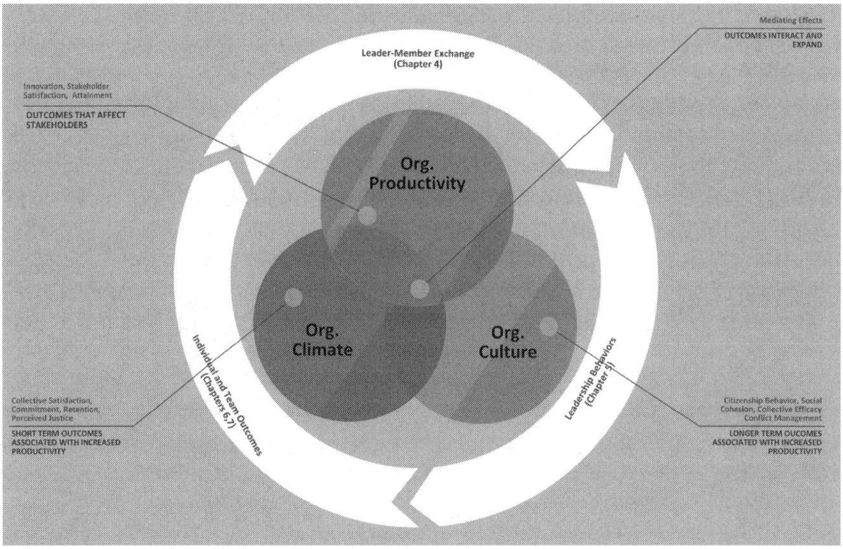

CHAPTER 9

The Case for Positive Leadership in Schools

Our primary motivations for this book were twofold. First, we sought to develop an asset-based theory of positive school leadership from the ground up, avoiding the tendency to leap to general assertions about positivity and leadership practice that were poorly grounded in empirical work. Second, we wanted to introduce the idea of positive school leadership by placing it in the context of the broad and deep work carried out by scholars who are unfamiliar with education, but whose observations connect with what we know about schools. In carrying out the project, we decided to build a model in which leadership provides a broad base for the multiple and varied opportunities for leadership that occur in any busy school context.

A MODEL OF POSITIVE SCHOOL LEADERSHIP

We summarize the logic of our work in Figure 9.1. The broad basis for the principles of positive school leadership formed the content of the first three chapters, where we developed the argument that the principles of positive school leadership are grounded in character, values, and personal attributes. We began there because we believe that the foundations of leadership theory, from cultures around the world, attend to the importance of the person who exercises leadership. From Plato and Confucius to religious texts from all traditions, classical writers emphasize the importance of self-knowledge and adherence to particular ethics and values. The critical grounding of leadership in values and moral behavior was affirmed more recently by James McGregor Burns (1978). As was apparent in the first three chapters, the historical focus on leaders-as-persons has equal resonance today.

Being a "good person" is not enough, however, to create a positive impact on schools. Leadership is always assessed through the eye of the beholder, who cannot see inside a person but draws inferences based on actions. Chapter 4 is, in our view, the pivot that turns leader behaviors into impact, largely through the development of relationships that foster positive reactions in others. According to empirical research, without this foundation of positive relationships between leaders and others in the school, even excellent plans and ambitious aspirations will fall flat. We regard this summary as a hinge not only because of the extensive research that supports this assertion, but because as we look at educational research, much of the attention to leader–member relationships is either assumed or touched on in passing. As a consequence, we argue that too little attention is paid to relationship building in school-leader preparation and professional development programs.

Chapter 5 elaborates on this argument by looking more deeply at the role of leadership as "talent development." We do this by working through studies that examine what leaders actually *do* to create the positive relationships that are the grounding of productive schools (and other organizations). Since the leadership literature is full of recommendations for leaders' actions, we emphasize that we filtered our review of specific behaviors through the lens of positive leadership, using the many terms that capture the positive perspectives that we listed in Chapter 1. We also focused in Chapter 5 on those behaviors that have demonstrable impact on other individuals, supporting them in becoming more productive, engaged, and resilient in carrying out their work. It is significant that, at this juncture in the development of our model, we largely ignored many of the exhortations of the popular transformational literature that emphasize leaders as change makers. This is not because we believe that those aspects of leadership work are unimportant, but we argue that positive organizational research suggests that redirecting and reshaping schools requires that leaders first establish their legitimate relational base.

Chapters 6 and 7 expand on this argument, showing how the positive dyadic relationships between leaders and members have an impact on how formal teams and organizations as a whole function. Attention to teams in school leadership research is relatively recent, because the usual image of schools emphasizes their "flat" organizational structure, with a few designated (licensed) administrators responsible for supervising all teachers. While some research on secondary schools looks at departments as teams, it is not a significant theme in empirical work. Recent attention focuses on professional communities, but studies of how leaders create dynamic and productive relationships within them are limited. In other words, we point to Chapters 6 and 7 as setting the stage for more consideration of team and leadership in elementary, middle, and high schools.

As we demonstrate in Chapter 8, there is significantly more research in education on the way in which leadership behaviors help to develop effective schools, but the most solid research, we argue, is focused on the positive actions and behaviors that are well documented by educational leadership scholars. In addition, educational research, we believe, will be strengthened by incorporating some of the perspectives from other sectors that we cover in that chapter, as well as by developing more complex models of leadership that take account of the research covered in Chapters 1–7.

BROADER SOCIAL OUTCOMES OF POSITIVE LEADERSHIP

There is a modest but robust tradition in organizational studies of looking for "spillover effects," which are defined as events or outcomes that occur as an indirect or unintended consequence of actions or events in another setting. One example is the development of regional economies based on the clustering of technology firms near universities with strong scientific departments in, for example, biology and engineering (Audretch, Lehman, & Warning, 2005). In education, most research on spillover effects looks at how larger social trends (housing availability or patterns of incarceration) affect schools rather than how schools affect their communities (Bowen & Richman, 2002). In addition, much of the emphasis in educational studies has been on harmful spillover effects. These occur, for example, where the more educated members of a community move away from the setting where they received their education, which is associated in multiple studies with subsequent reduced funding for both higher and K–12 education (Strathman, 1994).

However, the positive organizational leadership literature clearly asserts that the model shown in Figure 9.1 will have benefits beyond the performance of a particular organization.

> When a leader creates alignment between the values of the firm and organizational practices such as corporate philanthropy and protection of the environment, leadership extends beyond the company to the entire community. (Reave, 2005, p. 676)

There is growing attention to the spillover effects from positive organizations to more positive social experiences outside of the organizations. Gretchen Spreitzer (2007), one of the prominent scholars in positive organizational studies, argues that "over the last few years, there has been increased interest in understanding how business organizations may contribute to international peace" (p. 1084). Taking advantage of large-scale international databases, she shows that countries with more empowering organizational leadership values are less corrupt and more peaceful, and also demonstrates some support for the hypothesis that a more empowered workers' culture is associated with positive social outcomes. Unanticipated spillover effects also occur at a more micro level, where organizational partnerships may engage members at all levels, leading to denser and more significant relationships (Kolk, van Dolen, & Vock, 2010). In schools, at least one study suggests that these micro-level engagements may have an impact on classrooms and student learning (Gordon & Louis, 2009).

In addition to the unanticipated spillover effects, scholars argue that positive leaders should play a more active role in the settings in which they are located. Feldman and Khademian (2003) point out that this is common

Figure 9.1. The Logic of Positive School Leadership

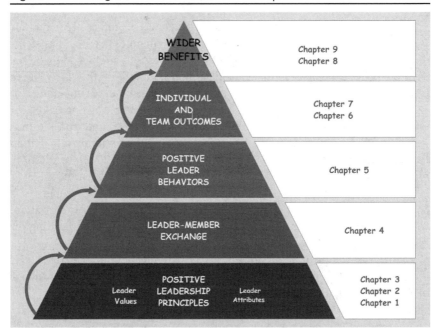

behavior because "many organizations, both public and private, make efforts to engage and improve the communities in which they are located" (p. 344), while a major consulting organization argues that "organizations with surface purpose . . . may miss out on a fundamental element of purpose: its positive impact on society" (Carlesi et al., 2017, p. 3). Indeed, educational scholars have argued for years that positive engagement with communities is a responsibility of schools and school leaders (Deal & Peterson, 1999; J. L. Epstein, 1995; Fullan & Hargreaves, 1996), and many highly touted programs in both the United States and elsewhere are based on community engagement models. The idea is that school leaders can become actors in positive spillover by linking with families and community agencies to enhance out-of-school experiences for students and, thus, youth development.

Joseph and Feldman (2009) argue that school leaders may become even more engaged in developing community assets that support youth although the challenges in doing so are significant. Many of these programs begin with a structural and policy perspective that looks at how formal leaders should engage with the community, and have a tendency to reinforce a hierarchical relationship where school leaders are "in charge" (M. P. Evans & Radina, 2014; Malen, 1994). When community engagement is not premised on an asset perspective, it can create resistance among leaders by creating controversies that are based in "who has the power" (L. Johnson, Carter, & Finn, 2011). Thus, the positive leadership literature suggests that school–community engagement programs may not be enough. Instead, scholars argue for a more organic, relationship-based perspective that begins with relationships inside the organization, but is compatible with the idea of spillovers.

> We suggest that one way to achieve this goal is through the empowerment of employees. We show how enhancing the agency of employees can empower the members of the public they deal with in their work, thus enabling organizations to strengthen the communities in which they operate. (Feldman & Khademian, 2003, pp. 344–345)

In other words, if positive leaders create positive cultures and productivity within the organization, they can have indirect impacts on their communities. In education, this appears as a theme in the research on service learning, where principal support creates and reinforces teacher involvement (S. Hunter & Brisbin, 2000; Markus, Howard, & King, 1993; Scales, Roehlkepartain, Neal, Kielsmeier, & Benson, 2006; Wade, 1997), which leads to increased teacher empowerment and engagement.

Perhaps most important in schools is the assumption that a leader's asset building with teachers and other adults will have internal spillover effects and create more positive youth development experiences (Buck, Carr, & Robertson, 2008), which are related both to student achievement (Scales, Benson, Roehlkepartain, Sesma, & van Dulmen, 2006), and to both immediate and long-term civic engagement (Pasek, Feldman, Romer, & Jamieson, 2008; Torney-Purta, 2002). In other words, positive school leadership enhances leader effects beyond the current focus on formal tested achievement. We are convinced by the logic that suggests how positive school leadership can affect the lives of students and their communities, although surprised by the absence of solid empirical research.

CONCLUSION

> Plato . . . noted that people are not sheep, and leaders are not shepherds; Plato regarded the leader as a weaver, whose main task was to weave together different kinds of people into the fabric of society. (Maak, 2007, p. 340)

Becoming a Positive School Leader is a challenging task. Formal preparation programs cannot guarantee it, and not all leaders demonstrate the positive leadership that we have emphasized throughout this book. Furthermore, there is considerable room even within our model for individual choices about where to place one's positive relational leadership emphasis. To give one example, leaders can choose to focus on empowering and supporting employee autonomy and creativity, or they can emphasize employee engagement, benevolence, or care. A positive school leader might choose to emphasize one over the other depending on the particular circumstances of the school and the challenges facing it. Both types of positive leaders can have organization-wide effects, but they may be different (Berson et al., 2008). In those authors' study of for-profit organizations, autonomy-supporting leaders led more innovative organizations with higher sales; the more benevolence-focused leaders had higher job satisfaction among employees but lower sales. Choosing the route to creating a higher performing school may depend on where the school is starting: It may not be possible to foster high creativity, for example, where members are not already secure and reasonably satisfied with the school's culture and leadership.

This is just one example suggesting that few leaders, in any circumstance, will fit the model perfectly. Furthermore, no leader is consistently relational and positive in all circumstances, and no leader can convince all followers that he or she has all of the elements of positive leadership. Our long trip through the vast literature on positive leadership suggests that both beginning and experienced school leaders at all levels can be enriched by the ideas we have extracted. But, the experience of becoming a positive leader will be both an individual and a collective one. Each school leader's journey will be affected by his or her internal development, but it also will be responsive to the relationships and settings in which the leader finds him- or herself.

References

Abbasi, E., & Zamani-Miandashti, N. (2013). The role of transformational leadership, organizational culture and organizational learning in improving the performance of Iranian agricultural faculties. *Higher Education, 66*(4), 505–519.

Adler, P. S., Kwon, S. W., & Heckscher, C. (2008). Perspective—Professional work: The emergence of collaborative community. *Organization Science, 19*(2), 359–376.

Ahern, J., Cerda, M., Lippman, S. A., Tardiff, K. J., & Galea, S. (2013). Navigating non-positivity in neighbourhood studies: An analysis of collective efficacy and violence. *Journal of Epidemiology and Community Health, 67*(2), 159–165.

Alegre, J., & Chiva, R. (2008). Assessing the impact of organizational learning capability on product innovation performance: An empirical test. *Technovation, 28*(6), 315–326.

Alok, K. (2014). Authentic leadership and psychological ownership: Investigation of interrelations. *Leadership & Organization Development Journal, 35*(4), 266–285.

Anderson, N. R., & West, M. A. (1998). Measuring climate for work group innovation: Development and validation of the team climate inventory. *Journal of Organizational Behavior, 19*(3), 235–258.

Anderson-Butcher, D., & Ashton, D. (2004). Innovative models of collaboration to serve children, youths, families, and communities. *Children & Schools, 26*(1), 39–53.

Andrews, R., & Boyne, G. A. (2010). Capacity, leadership, and organizational performance: Testing the black box model of public management. *Public Administration Review, 70*(3), 443–454.

Aquino, K., & Reed, A., II. (2002). The self-importance of moral identity. *Journal of Personality and Social Psychology, 83*(6), 1423–1440.

Argyris, C. (1976). Theories of action that inhibit individual learning. *American Psychologist, 31*(9), 638.

Arjoon, S. (2000). Virtue theory as a dynamic theory of business. *Journal of Business Ethics, 28*(2), 159–178.

Arnold, K. A., & Connelly, C. E. (2013). Transformational leadership and psychological well-being: Effects on followers and leaders. In H. S. Leonard, R. Lewis, A. M. Freedman, & J. Passmore, (Eds.), *The Wiley Blackwell handbook of the psychology of leadership, change, and organizational development* (pp. 175–194). Hoboken, NJ: Wiley.

Aryee, S., Pawan, S. B., & Zhen Xiong, C. (2002). Trust as a mediator of the relationship between organizational justice and work outcomes: Test of a social exchange model. *Journal of Organizational Behavior, 23*(3), 267–285.

Ashforth B. E., & Humphrey R. H. (1993). Emotional labor in service roles: The influence of identity. *Academy of Management Review, 18*(1) 88–115.

Atkins, P., & Parker, S. (2011). Understanding individual compassion in organizations: The role of appraisals and psychological flexibility. *Academy of Management Review, 74*(4), 524–546.

Atwater, L., & Carmeli, A. (2009). Leader–member exchange, feelings of energy, and involvement in creative work. *The Leadership Quarterly, 20*(3), 264–275.

Audretsch, D. B., Lehmann, E. E., & Warning, S. (2005). University spillovers and new firm location. *Research Policy, 34*(7), 1113–1122.

Avey, J., Hughes, L., Norman, S., & Luthans, K. (2008). Using positivity, transformational leadership and empowerment to combat employee negativity. *Leadership & Organization Development Journal, 29*(2), 110–126.

Avey, J. B., Palanski, M. E., & Walumbwa, F. O. (2011). When leadership goes unnoticed: The moderating role of follower self-esteem on the relationship between ethical leadership and follower behavior. *Journal of Business Ethics, 98*(4), 573–582.

Avolio, B. J., & Gardner, W. L. (2005). Authentic leadership development: Getting to the root of positive forms of leadership. *The Leadership Quarterly, 16*(3), 315–338.

Avolio, B. J., Gardner, W. L., Walumbwa, F. O., Luthans, F., & May, D. R. (2004). Unlocking the mask: A look at the process by which authentic leaders impact follower attitudes and behaviors. *The Leadership Quarterly, 15*(6), 801–823.

Avolio, B. J., Zhu, W., Koh, W., & Bhatia, P. (2004). Transformational leadership and organizational commitment: Mediating role of psychological empowerment and moderating role of structural distance. *Journal of Organizational Behavior, 25*(8), 951–968.

Bacha, E., & Walker, S. (2013). The relationship between transformational leadership and followers' perceptions of fairness. *Journal of Business Ethics, 116*(3), 667–680.

Bakker, A. B. (2011). An evidence-based model of work engagement. *Current Directions in Psychological Science, 20*(4), 265–269.

Bakker, A. B., & Schaufeli, W. B. (2008). Positive organizational behavior: Engaged employees in flourishing organizations. *Journal of Organizational Behavior, 29*(2), 147–154.

Bakker, A. B., & Xanthopoulou, D. (2013). Creativity and charisma among female leaders: The role of resources and work engagement. *International Journal of Human Resource Management, 24*, 2760–2779.

Baldridge, J. V. (1971). *Power and conflict in the university: Research in the sociology of complex organizations.* New York, NY: Wiley.

Bali, V. A. (2016). Evolving trends in public opinion on the quality of local schools. *Educational Policy, 30*(5), 688–720.

Ball, S. J. (2012). *The micro-politics of the school: Towards a theory of school organization.* New York, NY: Routledge.

Bandura, A. (1988). Organizational application of social cognitive theory. *Australian Journal of Management, 13*(2), 275–302.

Bandura, A. (1997). *Self-efficacy: The exercise of control.* New York, NY: Macmillan.

Barnard, C. (1938). *The functions of the executive.* Boston, MA: Harvard University Press.

Bass, B. M. (1990). From transactional to transformational leadership: Learning to share the vision. *Organizational Dynamics, 18*(3), 19–31.

Bass, B. M., & Steidlmeier, P. (1999). Ethics, character, and authentic transformational leadership behavior. *The Leadership Quarterly, 10*(2), 181–217.

Bass, L. (2012). When care trumps justice: The operationalization of black feminist caring in educational leadership. *International Journal of Qualitative Studies in Education, 25*(1), 73–87.

Beck, L. G. (1994). *Reclaiming educational administration as a caring profession.* New York, NY: Teachers College Press. Retrieved from eric.ed.gov/?id=ED394214

Beck, L. G., & Murphy, J. (1998, December). Site-based management and school success: Untangling the variables. *School Effectiveness and School Improvement, 9*(4), 358–385.

Begley, P. T. (2001). In pursuit of authentic school leadership practices. *International Journal of Leadership in Education, 4*(4), 353–365.

Begley, P. T. (2006). Self-knowledge, capacity and sensitivity: Prerequisites to authentic leadership by school principals. *Journal of Educational Administration, 44*(6), 570–589.

Berg, J. M., Dutton, J. E., & Wrzesniewski, A. (2013). Job crafting and meaningful work. In B. J. Dik, Z. S. Byrne, & M. F. Steger (Eds.), *Purpose and meaning in the workplace* (pp. 81–104). Washington, DC: American Psychological Association.

Berkovich, I., & Eyal, O. (2015). Educational leaders and emotions: An international review of empirical evidence 1992–2012. *Review of Educational Research, 85*(1), 129–167.

Berkowitz, M. W., & Bier, M. C. (2007). What works in character education. *Journal of Research in Character Education, 5*(1), 29.

Berson, Y., Oreg, S., & Dvir, T. (2008). CEO values, organizational culture and firm outcomes. *Journal of Organizational Behavior, 29*(5), 615–633.

Black, G. (2010). Correlational analysis of servant leadership and school climate. *Catholic Education: A Journal of Inquiry and Practice, 13*(4), 437–466.

Blau, G. J., & Boal, K. B. (1987). Conceptualizing how job involvement and organizational commitment affect turnover and absenteeism. *Academy of Management Review, 12*(2), 288–300.

Blau, P. M. (1955). *The dynamics of bureaucracy: A study of interpersonal relations in two government agencies.* Chicago, IL: University of Chicago Press.

Blumberg, A., & Greenfield, W. (1986). *The effective principal: Perspectives on school leadership.* Newton, MA: Allyn & Bacon.

Boehm, S. A., Dwertmann, D. J., Bruch, H., & Shamir, B. (2015). The missing link? Investigating organizational identity strength and transformational leadership climate as mechanisms that connect CEO charisma with firm performance. *The Leadership Quarterly, 26*(2), 156–171.

Boerner, S., Eisenbeiss, S. A., & Griesser, D. (2007). Follower behavior and organizational performance: The impact of transformational leaders. *Journal of Leadership & Organizational Studies, 13*(3), 15–26.

Bogler, R., & Somech, A. (2004). Influence of teacher empowerment on teachers' organizational commitment, professional commitment and organizational citizenship behavior in schools. *Teaching and Teacher Education, 20*(3), 277–289.

Boies, K., Fiset, J., & Gill, H. (2015). Communication and trust are key: Unlocking the relationship between leadership and team performance and creativity. *The Leadership Quarterly, 26*(6), 1080–1094.

Boix, C., & Posner, D. N. (1998). Social capital: Explaining its origins and effects on government performance. *British Journal of Political Science, 28*(04), 686–693.

Bolino, M. C., Turnley, W. H., & Bloodgood, J. M. (2002). Citizenship behavior and the creation of social capital in organizations. *Academy of Management Review, 27*(4), 505–522.

Bolino, M. C., Turnley, W. H., Gilstrap, J. B., & Suazo, M. M. (2010). Citizenship under pressure: What's a "good soldier" to do? *Journal of Organizational Behavior, 31*(6), 835–855.

Bolman, L. G., & Deal, T. E. (1991). *Reframing organizations.* San Francisco, CA: Jossey-Bass.

Bolman, L. G., & Deal, T. E. (2003). *Reframing organizations: Artistry, choice, and leadership.* New York, NY: Wiley.

Bolman, L. G., & Deal, T. E. (2010). Reframing the path to school leadership: A guide for teachers and principals. Thousand Oaks, CA: Corwin Press.

Bolman, L. G., & Deal, T. E. (2011). *The wizard and the warrior: Leading with passion and power.* San Francisco, CA: Jossey Bass.

Bommer, W. H., Dierdorff, E. C., & Rubin, R. S. (2007). Does prevalence mitigate relevance? The moderating effect of group-level OCB on employee performance. *Academy of Management Journal, 50*(6), 1481–1494.

Bond, F. W., Flaxman, P. E., & Bunce, D. (2008). The influence of psychological flexibility on work redesign: Mediated moderation of a work reorganization intervention. *Journal of Applied Psychology, 93*(3), 645–654.

Bono, J. E., & Judge, T. A. (2003). Self-concordance at work: Toward understanding the motivational effects of transformational leaders. *Academy of Management Journal, 46*(5), 554–571.

Borko, H., & Livingston, C. (1989). Cognition and improvisation: Differences in mathematics instruction by expert and novice teachers. *American Educational Research Journal, 26*(4), 473–498.

Bourdieu, P. (1986). The forms of capital. In J. G. Richardson (Ed.), *Handbook of Theory and Research for the Sociology of Education* (pp. 241–258). Westport, CT: Greenwood Press.

Bowen, G. L., & Richman, J. M. (2002). Schools in the context of communities. *Children & Schools, 24*(2), 67–71.

Bowie, N. E. (1998). A Kantian theory of meaningful work. *Journal of Business Ethics, 17*(9), 1083–1092.

Bowman, J. S. (2010). The success of failure: The paradox of performance pay. *Review of Public Personnel Administration, 30*(1), 70–88.

Bozeman, B., & Su, X. (2015). Public service motivation concepts and theory: A critique. *Public Administration Review, 75*(5), 700–710.

Breevaart, K., Bakker, A. B., Demerouti, E., & Derks, D. (2016). Who takes the lead? A multi-source diary study on leadership, work engagement, and job performance. *Journal of Organizational Behavior, 37*(3), 309–325. doi: http://onlinelibrary.wiley.com/enhanced/exportCitation/doi/10.1002/job.2041

Bright, D. S. (2006). Forgiveness as an attribute of leadership. In E. D. Hess & K. S. Cameron (Eds.), *Leading with values: Positivity, virtue, and high performance* (pp. 172–193). Cambridge, UK: Cambridge University Press.

Brockbank, A., & McGill, I. (2012). Facilitating reflective learning: Coaching, mentoring and supervision. London, UK: Kogan Page.

Brooks, D. (2017, April 18). Building a thicker community. *The New York Times*, p. A19.

Broome, K. M., Knight, D. K., Edwards, J. R., & Flynn, P. M. (2009). Leadership, burnout, and job satisfaction in outpatient drug-free treatment programs. *Journal of Substance Abuse Treatment, 37*(2), 160–170.

Brower, H. H., Schoorman, F. D., & Tan, H. H. (2000). A model of relational leadership: The integration of trust and leader–member exchange. *The Leadership Quarterly, 11*(2), 227–250.

Brown, J. S., & Duguid, P. (1991). Organizational learning and communities-of-practice: Toward a unified view of working, learning, and innovation. *Organization Science, 2*(1), 40–57.

Brown, J. S., & Duguid, P. (2001). Knowledge and organization: A social-practice perspective. *Organization Science, 12*(2), 198–213.

Brown, K. M., & Wynn, S. R. (2009). Finding, supporting, and keeping: The role of the principal in teacher retention issues. *Leadership and Policy in Schools, 8*(1), 37–63.

Brown, M. E., & Treviño, L. K. (2006). Ethical leadership: A review and future directions. *The Leadership Quarterly, 17*(6), 595–616.

Browning, C. R., Burrington, L. A., Leventhal, T., & Brooks-Gunn, J. (2008). Neighborhood structural inequality, collective efficacy, and sexual risk behavior among urban youth. *Journal of Health and Social Behavior, 49*(3), 269–285.

Browning, C. R., Soller, B., Gardner, M., & Brooks-Gunn, J. (2013). "Feeling disorder" as a comparative and contingent process: Gender, neighborhood conditions, and adolescent mental health. *Journal of Health and Social Behavior, 54*(3), 296–314.

Bryk, A., Camburn, E., & Louis, K. S. (1999). Professional community in Chicago elementary schools: Facilitating factors and organizational consequences. *Educational Administration Quarterly, 35*(5), 751–781.

Bryk, A. S., & Schneider, B. L. (2002). *Trust in Schools: A core resource for school improvement.* New York, NY: Russell Sage Foundation.

Bryson, J. (2010). The future of public and nonprofit strategic planning in the United States. *Public Administration Review, 70*, S255–S267.

Buck, B., Carr, S. R., & Robertson, J. (2008). Positive psychology and student engagement. *Journal of Cross-Disciplinary Perspectives in Education, 1*(1), 28–35.

Buluc, B., & Gunes, A. M. (2014). Relationship between organizational justice and organizational commitment in primary schools. *Anthropologist, 18*(1), 145–152.

Burnier, D. (2003). Other voices/other rooms: Towards a care-centered public administration. *Administrative Theory & Praxis, 25*(4), 529–544.

Burns, J. M. (1978). *Leadership.* New York, NY: Harper Torchback.

Burrello, L., Beitz, L., & Mann, J. (2016). *A positive manifesto: How appreciative schools can transform public education.* Ashford, CT: Elephant Rock Books.

Buttner, E. H., Lowe, K. B., & Billings-Harris, L. (2012). An empirical test of diversity climate: Dimensionality and relative effects on employee of color outcomes. *Journal of Business Ethics, 110*(3), 247–258.

Cain, S. (2013). *Quiet: The power of introverts in a world that can't stop talking.* New York, NY: Broadway Books.

Camburn, E. M. (2010). Embedded teacher learning opportunities as a site for reflective practice: An exploratory study. *American Journal of Education, 116*(4), 463–489.

Cameron, K. S. (2003). Organizational virtuousness and performance. In K. S. Cameron, J. E. Dutton, & R. E. Quinn (Eds.), *Positive organizational scholarship: Foundations of a new discipline* (pp. 49–65). San Francisco, CA: Berrett-Koehler.

Cameron, K. S. (2006). Leadership values that enable extraordinary success. In D. Hess & K.S. Cameron (Eds.), *Leading with values: Positivity, virtue, and high performance* (pp. 132–150). Cambridge, UK: Cambridge University Press.

Cameron, K. S. (2012). *Positive leadership: Strategies for extraordinary performance.* San Francisco, CA: Berrett-Koehler.

Cameron, K. S., & Caza, A. (2002). Organizational and leadership virtues and the role of forgiveness. *Journal of Leadership & Organizational Studies, 9*(1), 33–48.

Cameron, K. S, Dutton, J. E., & Quinn, R. E. (Eds.). (2003). *Positive organizational scholarship: Foundations of a new discipline.* San Francisco, CA: Berrett-Koehler.

Cameron, K. S., Quinn, R. E., DeGraff, J., & Thakor, A. V. (2014). *Competing values leadership, Second Edition.* Cheltenham, UK: Edward Elgar.

Cameron, K. S., & Spreitzer, G. M. (Eds.). (2012). *The Oxford handbook of positive organizational scholarship.* New York, NY: Oxford University Press.

Canrinus, E. T., Helms-Lorenz, M., Beijaard, D., Buitink, J., & Hofman, A. (2012). Self-efficacy, job satisfaction, motivation and commitment: Exploring the relationships between indicators of teachers' professional identity. *European Journal of Psychology of Education, 27*(1), 115–132.

Capen, S. (1947). The teaching profession and labor unions. *The Journal of General Education, 1*(4), 275–278.

Caprara, G. V., & Steca, P. (2007). Prosocial agency: The contribution of values and self-efficacy beliefs to prosocial behavior across ages. *Journal of Social and Clinical Psychology, 26*(2), 218–239.

Cardona, P. (2000). Transcendental leadership. *The Leadership & Organization Development Journal, 21*(4), 201–206.

Carlesi, C., Hemerling, J., Kilmann, J., Meese, D., & Shipman, D. (2017, May 15). Purpose with the power to transform your organization. Retrieved from www.bcg.com/publications/2017/transformation-behavior-culture-purpose-power-transform-organization.aspx

Carmeli, A., Atwater, L., & Levi, A. (2011). How leadership enhances employees' knowledge sharing: The intervening roles of relational and organizational identification. *The Journal of Technology Transfer, 36*(3), 257–274.

Carson, J. B., Tesluk, P. E., & Marrone, J. A. (2007). Shared leadership in teams: An investigation of antecedent conditions and performance. *Academy of Management Journal, 50*(5), 1217–1234.

Cerit, Y. (2009). The effects of servant leadership behaviours of school principals on teachers' job satisfaction. *Educational Management Administration & Leadership, 37*(5), 600–623.

Chaskin, R. J., & Rauner, D. M. (1995). Toward a field of caring. *Phi Delta Kappan, 76*(9), 718.

Chemers, M. (1997). *An integrative theory of leadership*. Mahwah, NJ: Erlbaum.

Chen, G., & Bliese, P. D. (2002). The role of different levels of leadership in predicting self- and collective efficacy: Evidence for discontinuity. *Journal of Applied Psychology, 87*(3), 549.

Chen, G., Kirkman, B. L., Kanfer, R., Allen, D., & Rosen, B. (2007). A multilevel study of leadership, empowerment, and performance in teams. *Journal of Applied Psychology, 92*(2), 331–346.

Chen, Z., Zhu, J., & Zhou, M. (2015). How does a servant leader fuel the service fire? A multilevel model of servant leadership, individual self-identity, group competition climate, and customer service performance. *Journal of Applied Psychology, 100*(2), 511–521.

Cho, Y. J., & Ringquist, E. J. (2011). Managerial trustworthiness and organizational outcomes. *Journal of Public Administration Research and Theory, 21*(1), 53–86.

Choi, Y., & Mai-Dalton, R. R. (1998). On the leadership function of self-sacrifice. *The Leadership Quarterly, 9*(4), 475–501.

Choudhary, A. I., Akhtar, S. A., & Zaheer, A. (2013). Impact of transformational and servant leadership on organizational performance: A comparative analysis. *Journal of Business Ethics, 116*(2), 433–440.

Christian, M. S., Garza, A. S., & Slaughter, J. E. (2011). Work engagement: A quantitative review and test of its relations with task and contextual performance. *Personnel Psychology, 64*(1), 89–136.

Clapp-Smith, R., Vogelgesang, G. R., & Avey, J. B. (2009). Authentic leadership and positive psychological capital: The mediating role of trust at the group level of analysis. *Journal of Leadership & Organizational Studies, 15*(3), 227–240.

Clifton, D. O., & Harter, J. K. (2003). Investing in strengths. In K. S. Cameron, J. E. Dutton, & R. E. Quinn (Eds.), *Positive organizational scholarship: Foundations of a new discipline* (pp. 112–121). San Francisco, CA: Berrett-Koehler.

Cogliser, C. C., & Schriesheim, C. A. (2000). Exploring work unit context and leader–member exchange: A multi-level perspective. *Journal of Organizational Behavior, 21*(5), 487–511.

Cohen, D., & Prusak, L. (2001). In good company: How social capital makes organizations work. Boston, MA: Harvard Business Press.

Cole, N. D., & Latham, G. P. (1997). Effects of training in procedural justice on perceptions of disciplinary fairness by unionized employees and disciplinary subject matter experts. *Journal of Applied Psychology, 82*(5), 699.

Coleman, J. S. (1990). *Foundations of social capital*. Cambridge, MA: Harvard University Press.

Collins, C. J., & Clark, K. D. (2003). Strategic human resource practices, top management team social networks, and firm performance: The role of human resource practices in creating organizational competitive advantage. *Academy of Management Journal, 46*(6), 740–751.

Conger, J., Kanungo, R., & Menon, S. (2000). Charismatic leadership and follower effects. *Journal of Organizational Behavior, 21*, 747–767.

Connelly, S., Gaddis, B., & Helton-Fauth, W. (2013). A closer look at the role of emotions in transformational and charismatic leadership. In B. J. Avolio & F. J. Yammarino (Eds.), *Transformational and charismatic leadership: The road ahead, 10th anniversary edition* (pp. 299–327). Bingley, UK: Emerald.

Cook, R. (1918). Ethics of the teaching profession. *The Journal of Education, 87*(8, 2168), 207–208.

Cooper, T., Scandura, T., & Schriesheim, C. (2005). *Looking forward but learning from our past: Potential challenges to developing authentic leadership theory and authentic leaders.* Coral Gables, FL: Department of Management, School of Business Administration, University of Miami.

Cooperrider, D., & Sekerka, L. (2003). Toward a theory of positive organizational change. In K. S. Cameron, J. E. Dutton, & R. E. Quinn (Eds.), *Positive organizational scholarship: Foundations of a new discipline* (pp. 163–175). San Francisco, CA: Berrett-Koehler.

Corbin, J., & Strauss, A. (1990). Grounded theory research: Procedures, canons, and evaluative criteria. *Qualitative Sociology, 13*(1), 3–21.

Cosner, S. (2011). Teacher learning, instructional considerations and principal communication: Lessons from a longitudinal study of collaborative data use by teachers. *Educational Management Administration & Leadership, 39*(5), 568–589.

Coyle-Shapiro, J. A. M. (2002). A psychological contract perspective on organizational citizenship behavior. *Journal of Organizational Behavior, 23*(8), 927–946.

Cropanzana, R., Bowen, D. E., & Gilliland, S. W. (2007). The management of organizational justice. *The Academy of Management Perspectives, 21*(4), 34–48.

Cross, R. L., & Parker, A. (2004). The hidden power of social networks: Understanding how work really gets done in organizations. Boston, MA: Harvard Business School Press.

Cullen, J. B., Parboteeah, K. P., & Victor, B. (2003). The effects of ethical climates on organizational commitment: A two-study analysis. *Journal of Business Ethics, 46*(2), 127–141.

Cummings, T. G. (1978). Self-regulating work groups: A socio-technical synthesis. *Academy of Management Review, 3*(3), 625–634.

Daly, A. J., Liou, Y. H., & Moolenaar, N. M. (2014). The principal connection: Trust and innovative climate in a network of reform. In D. Van Maele, M. Van Houtte, & P. Forsyth (Eds.), *Trust and school life* (pp. 285–311). Dordrecht, Netherlands: Springer.

Daly, A. J., Moolenaar, N. M., Bolivar, J. M., & Burke, P. (2010). Relationships in reform: The role of teachers' social networks. *Journal of Educational Administration, 48*(3), 359–391.

Damanik, E., & Aldridge, J. (2017). Transformational leadership and its impact on school climate and teachers' self-efficacy in Indonesian high schools. *Journal of School Leadership, 27*(2), 269–295.

Datnow, A., & Hubbard, L. (2016). Teacher capacity for and beliefs about data-driven decision making: A literature review of international research. *Journal of Educational Change, 17*(1), 7–28.

Daus, C. S., & Ashkanasy, N. M. (2005). The case for the ability-based model of emotional intelligence in organizational behavior. *Journal of Organizational Behavior, 26*(4), 453–466.

Day, C., & Hong, J. (2016). Influences on the capacities for emotional resilience of teachers in schools serving disadvantaged urban communities: Challenges of living on the edge. *Teaching and Teacher Education, 59*, 115–125.

De Cremer, D., & Knippenberg, D. (2005). Cooperation as a function of leader self-sacrifice, trust, and identification. *Leadership & Organization Development Journal, 26*(5), 355–369.

De Dreu, C. K. (2008). The virtue and vice of workplace conflict: Food for (pessimistic) thought. *Journal of Organizational Behavior, 29*(1), 5–18.

De Jong, B. A., & Elfring, T. (2010). How does trust affect the performance of ongoing teams? The mediating role of reflexivity, monitoring, and effort. *Academy of Management Journal, 53*(3), 535–549.

De Neve, D., Devos, G., & Tuytens, M. (2015). The importance of job resources and self-efficacy for beginning teachers' professional learning in differentiated instruction. *Teaching and Teacher Education, 47*, 30–41.

De Pree, M. (1997). *Leading without power: Finding hope in serving community* (Vol. 400). San Francisco, CA: Jossey-Bass.

Deal, T. E., & Peterson, K. D. (1994). *The leadership paradox: Balancing logic and artistry in schools.* San Francisco, CA: Jossey-Bass.

Deal, T. E., & Peterson, K. D. (1999). *Shaping school culture: The heart of leadership.* San Francisco, CA: Jossey-Bass.

DeConinck, J. B., & Johnson, J. T. (2009). The effects of perceived supervisor support, perceived organizational support, and organizational justice on turnover among salespeople. *The Journal of Personal Selling and Sales Management, 29*(4), 333–350.

Demirtas, O., & Akdogan, A. A. (2015). The effect of ethical leadership behavior on ethical climate, turnover intention, and affective commitment. *Journal of Business Ethics, 130*(1), 59–67.

Denison, D. R. (1996). What is the difference between organizational culture and organizational climate? A native's point of view on a decade of paradigm wars. *The Academy of Management Review, 21*(3), 619–654.

Denison, D. R., Haaland, S., & Goelzer, P. (2003). Corporate culture and organizational effectiveness: Is there a similar pattern around the world? In J. Osland, M. Li, & M. Mendenhall (Eds.), *Advances in global leadership* (pp. 205–227). Bingley, UK: Emerald.

Denison, D. R., & Mishra, A. K. (1995). Toward a theory of organizational culture and effectiveness. *Organization Science, 6*(2), 204–223.

Denison, D. R., & Spreitzer, G. M. (1991). Organizational culture and organizational development: A competing values approach. *Research in Organizational Change and Development, 5*(1), 1–21.

Dennis, R., & Bocarnea, M. (2005). Development of the servant leadership assessment instrument. *Leadership & Organization Development Journal, 26*(8), 600–615.

Dent, E., Higgins, M., & Wharff, D. (2005). Spirituality and leadership: An empirical review of definitions, distinctions, and embedded assumptions. *The Leadership Quarterly, 16*, 625–653.

Detert, J. R., Schroeder, R. G., & Mauriel, J. J. (2000). A framework for linking culture and improvement initiatives in organizations. *Academy of Management Review, 25*(4), 850–863.

Detert, J. R., Treviño, L. K., Burris, E. R., & Andiappan, M. (2007). Managerial modes of influence and counterproductivity in organizations: A longitudinal business-unit-level investigation. *Journal of Applied Psychology, 92*(4), 993-1005.

Dickson, M. W., Smith, D. B., Grojean, M. W., & Ehrhart, M. (2001). An organizational climate regarding ethics: The outcome of leader values and the practices that reflect them. *The Leadership Quarterly, 12*(2), 197–217.

DiPaola, M. F., & Hoy, W. K. (2005a). Organizational citizenship of faculty and achievement of high school students. *The High School Journal, 88*(3), 35–44.

DiPaola, M. F., & Hoy, W. K. (2005b). School characteristics that foster organizational citizenship behavior. *Journal of School Leadership, 15*(4), 387.

DiPaola, M., & Tschannen-Moran, M. (2014). Organizational citizenship behavior in schools and its relationship to school climate. *Journal of School Leadership, 11*(5), 424.

Dirks, K. T., & Ferrin, D. L. (2002). Trust in leadership: Meta-analytic findings and implications for research and practice. *Journal of Applied Psychology, 87*(4), 611.

Doh, J. P. (2003). Can leadership be taught? Perspectives from management educators. *Academy of Management Learning & Education, 2*(1), 54–67.

Donaldson, G. A., Jr. (2001). *Cultivating leadership in schools: Connecting people, purpose, and practice.* Retrieved from eric.ed.gov/?id=ED459512

Driscoll, C., & McKee, M. (2007). Restorying a culture of ethical and spiritual values: A role for leader storytelling. *Journal of Business Ethics, 73*(2), 205–217.

Druskat, V. U., & Pescosolido, A. T. (2002). The content of effective teamwork mental models in self-managing teams: Ownership, learning and heedful interrelating. *Human Relations, 55*(3), 283–314.

Druskat, V. U., & Wheeler, J. V. (2003). Managing from the boundary: The effective leadership of self-managing work teams. *Academy of Management Journal, 46*(4), 435–457.

DuFour, R. (2004). Schools as learning communities. *Educational Leadership, 61*(8), 6–11.

Duignan, P. (2005). Socially responsible leadership: Schools for a more just and democratic society. *Leading & Managing, 11*(1), 1–13.

Duignan, P. (2012). Educational leadership: Together creating ethical learning environments. Cambridge, UK: Cambridge University Press.

Duignan, P. A., & Bhindi, N. (1997). Authenticity in leadership: An emerging perspective. *Journal of Educational Administration, 35*(3), 195–209.

Dumay, X., Boonen, T., & Van Damme, J. (2013). Principal leadership long-term indirect effects on learning growth in mathematics. *The Elementary School Journal, 114*(2), 225–251.

Dust, S. B., Resick, C. J., & Mawritz, M. B. (2014). Transformational leadership, psychological empowerment, and the moderating role of mechanistic–organic contexts. *Journal of Organizational Behavior, 35*(3), 413–433.

Edmondson, A. (1999). Psychological safety and learning behavior in work teams. *Administrative Science Quarterly, 44*(2), 350–383.

Edú-Valsania, S., Moriano, J. A., & Molero, F. (2016). Authentic leadership and employee knowledge sharing behavior: Mediation of the innovation climate and workgroup identification. *Leadership & Organization Development Journal, 37*(4), 487–506.

Ehrhart, M. G. (2004). Leadership and procedural justice climate as antecedents of unit-level organizational citizenship behavior. *Personnel Psychology, 57*(1), 61–94.

Eisenbeiss, S. A. (2012). Re-thinking ethical leadership: An interdisciplinary integrative approach. *The Leadership Quarterly, 23*(5), 791–808.

Elmore, R. (2005). Knowing the right thing to do: School improvement and performance-based accountability. Retrieved from https://www.nga.org/files/live/sites/NGA/files/pdf/0803KNOWING.pdf

Emerson, R. M. (1976). Social exchange theory. *Annual Review of Sociology, 2,* 335–362.

Emmons, R. A. (2003). Acts of gratitude in organizations. In K. S. Cameron, J. E. Dutton, & R. E. Quinn (Eds.), *Positive organizational scholarship: Foundations of a new discipline* (pp. 81–93). San Francisco, CA: Berrett-Koehler.

English, F. W., & Ehrich, L. C. (2016). *Leading beautifully: Educational leadership as connoisseurship.* New York, NY: Routledge.

Epitropaki, O., & Martin, R. (2005). The moderating role of individual differences in the relation between transformational/transactional leadership perceptions and organizational identification. *The Leadership Quarterly, 16*(4), 569–589.

Epstein, J. L. (1995). School/family/community partnerships. *Phi Delta Kappan, 76*(9), 701.

Epstein, S. (1973). The self-concept revisited: Or a theory of a theory. *American Psychologist, 28*(5), 404.

Erdogan, B., Kraimer, M. L., & Liden, R. C. (2004). Work value congruence and intrinsic career success: The compensatory roles of leader-member exchange and perceived organizational support. *Personnel Psychology, 57*(2), 305–332.

Etzioni, A. (1998). *The new golden rule: Community and morality in a democratic society.* New York, NY: Basic Books.

Evans, M. P., & Radina, R. (2014). Great expectations? Critical discourse analysis of Title I school–family compacts. *School Community Journal, 24*(2), 107.

Evans, W. R., & Davis, W. D. (2005). High-performance work systems and organizational performance: The mediating role of internal social structure. *Journal of Management, 31*(5), 758–775.

Fairholm, G. W. (1991). *Values leadership: Toward a new philosophy of leadership.* New York, NY: Praeger.

Fairholm, G. W. (1996). Spiritual leadership: Fulfilling whole-self needs at work. *Leadership & Organization Development Journal, 17*(5), 11–17.

Fairholm, M. R., & Fairholm, G. (2000). Leadership amid the constraints of trust. *Leadership & Organization Development Journal, 21*(2), 102–109.

Farrell, D., & Petersen, J. C. (1982). Patterns of political behavior in organizations. *The Academy of Management Review, 7*(3), 403–412.

Fassina, N. E., Jones, D. A., & Uggerslev, K. L. (2008). Relationship clean-up time: Using meta-analysis and path analysis to clarify relationships among job satisfaction, perceived fairness, and citizenship behaviors. *Journal of Management, 34*(2), 161–188.

Fehr, R., & Gelfand, M. J. (2012). The forgiving organization: A multilevel model of forgiveness at work. *Academy of Management Review, 37*(4), 664–688

Feldman, M. S., & Khademian, A. M. (2003). Empowerment and cascading vitality. In K. S. Cameron, J. E. Dutton, & R. E. Quinn (Eds.), *Positive organizational scholarship: Foundations of a new discipline* (pp. 343–358). San Francisco, CA: Berrett-Koehler.

Ferch, S. R., & Mitchell, M. M. (2001). Intentional forgiveness in relational leadership: A technique for enhancing effective leadership. *Journal of Leadership & Organizational Studies, 7*(4), 70–83.

Ferris, R. (1988). How organizational love can improve leadership. *Organizational Dynamics, 16*(4), 41–51.

Fey, C. F., & Denison, D. R. (2003). Organizational culture and effectiveness: Can American theory be applied in Russia? *Organization Science, 14*(6), 686–706.

Fineman, S. (2006). On being positive: Concerns and counterpoints. *Academy of Management Review, 31*(2), 270–291.

Firestone, W., & Louis, K. S. (1999). Schools as cultures. In J. Murphy & K. S. Louis (Eds.), *Handbook of research on educational administration* (pp. 297–322). San Francisco, CA: Jossey-Bass.

Firth-Cozens, J., & Mowbray, D. (2001). Leadership and the quality of care. *Quality in Health Care, 10*(Suppl. 2), ii3–ii7.

Foldy, E. G., & Buckley, T. R. (2010). Re-creating street-level practice: The role of routines, work groups, and team learning. *Journal of Public Administration Research and Theory, 20*(1), 23–52.

Foldy, E. G., Rivard, P., & Buckley, T. R. (2009). Power, safety, and learning in racially diverse groups. *Academy of Management Learning & Education, 8*(1), 25–41.

Føllesdal, H., & Hagtvet, K. (2013). Does emotional intelligence as ability predict transformational leadership? A multilevel approach. *The Leadership Quarterly, 24*(5), 747–762.

Fornes, S. L., Rocco, T. S., & Wollard, K. K. (2008). Workplace commitment: A conceptual model developed from integrative review of the research. *Human Resource Development Review 7*(3), 339–357.

Forster, N., Cebis, M., Majteles, S., Mathur, A., Morgan, R., Preuss, J., . . . Wilkinson, D. (1999). The role of story-telling in organizational leadership. *Leadership & Organization Development Journal, 20*(1), 11–17.

Frank, K. A., Zhao, Y., & Borman, K. (2004). Social capital and the diffusion of innovations within organizations: The case of computer technology in schools. *Sociology of Education, 77*(2), 148–171.

Fredrickson, B. L. (2000). Why positive emotions matter in organizations: Lessons from the broaden-and-build model. *The Psychologist-Manager Journal, 4*(2), 131–142.

Fredrickson, B. L. (2001). The role of positive emotions in positive psychology: The broaden-and-build theory of positive emotions. *American Psychologist, 56*(3), 218.

Fredrickson, B. L. (2003). Positive emotions and upward spirals in organizations. In K. S. Cameron, J. E. Dutton, & R. E. Quin (Eds.), *Positive organizational scholarship: Foundations of a new discipline* (pp. 163–175). San Francisco, CA: Berrett-Koehler.

French, J. R. J., & Raven, B. (1959). The bases of social power. In D. Cartwright (Ed.), *Studies in social power* (pp. 150–167). Ann Arbor, MI: Institute for Social Research.

Fridell, M., Newcom Belcher, R., & Messner, P. E. (2009). Discriminate analysis gender public school principal servant leadership differences. *Leadership & Organization Development Journal, 30*(8), 722–736.

Frost, P. (2003). Toxic emotions at work: How compassionate managers handle pain and conflict. Boston, MA: Harvard Business School Press.

Frost, P., Sparrow, S., & Barry, J. (2006). Personality characteristics associated with susceptibility to false memories. *The American Journal of Psychology, 119*(2), 193–204.

Fry, L. (2003). Toward a theory of spiritual leadership. *The Leadership Quarterly, 14,* 693–727.

Frymier, A. B., & Houser, M. L. (2000). The teacher–student relationship as an interpersonal relationship. *Communication Education, 49*(3), 207–219.

Fullan, M., & Hargreaves, A. (1996). *What's worth fighting for in your school?* New York, NY: Teachers College Press.

Furman, G. C., & Shields, C. M. (2005). How can educational leaders promote and support social justice and democratic community in schools? In W. Firestone & C. Riehl (Eds.), *A new agenda for research in educational leadership* (pp. 119–137). New York, NY: Teachers College Press.

Galbraith, J. R. (2002). *Designing organizations: An executive guide to strategy, structure, and processes.* San Francisco, CA: Jossey-Bass.

Garcia-Morales, V. J., Matias-Reche, F., & Hurtado-Torres, N. (2008). Influence of transformational leadership on organizational innovation and performance depending on the level of organizational learning in the pharmaceutical sector. *Journal of Organizational Change Management, 21*(2), 188–212.

Gardner, H. (2012). *Truth, beauty, and goodness reframed: Educating for the virtues in the age of truthiness and Twitter.* New York, NY: Basic Books.

Gardner, W. L., Avolio, B. J., Luthans, F., May, D. R., & Walumbwa, F. (2005). "Can you see the real me?" A self-based model of authentic leader and follower development. *The Leadership Quarterly, 16*(3), 343–372.

Gardner, W. L., & Schermerhorn, J. (2004). Unleashing individual potential: Performance gains through positive organizational behavior and authentic leadership. *Organizational Dynamics, 33*(3), 270–281.

Garvey, B., Stokes, P., & Megginson, D. (2014). *Coaching and mentoring: Theory and practice.* New York, NY: Sage.

Geer, B. W., Maher, J. K., & Cole, M. T. (2008). Managing nonprofit organizations: The importance of transformational leadership and commitment to operating standards for nonprofit accountability. *Public Performance & Management Review, 32*(1), 51–75.

Gelfand, M. J., Leslie, L. M., Keller, K., & De Dreu, C. (2012). Conflict cultures in organizations: How leaders shape conflict cultures and their organizational-level consequences. *Journal of Applied Psychology, 97*(6), 1131–1147.

Giardini, A., & Frese, M. (2008). Linking service employees' emotional competence to customer satisfaction: A multilevel approach. *Journal of Organizational Behavior, 29*(2), 155–170.

Gioia, D. A., & Chittipeddi, K. (1991). Sensemaking and sensegiving in strategic change initiation. *Strategic Management Journal, 12*(6), 433–448.

Gittell, J. H. (2003). A theory of relational coordination. In K. S. Cameron, J. E. Dutton, & R. E. Quinn (Eds.), *Positive organizational scholarship: Foundations of a new discipline* (pp. 279–295). San Francisco, CA: Berrett-Koehler.

Gittell, J. H. (2008). Relationships and resilience: Care provider responses to pressures from managed care. *The Journal of Applied Behavioral Science, 44*(1), 25–47.

Gittell, J. H. (2012). New directions for relationship coordination theory. In K. S. Cameron & G. M. Spreitzer (Eds.), *The Oxford handbook of positive organizational scholarship* (pp. 400–411). New York, NY: Oxford University Press.

Gittell, J. H., & Douglass, A. (2012). Relational bureaucracy: Structuring reciprocal relationships into roles. *Academy of Management Review, 37*(4), 709–733.

Glaser, B., & Strauss, A. (1967). *The discovery of grounded theory: Strategies for qualitative research.* Chicago, IL: Aldine.

Glisson, C., & Hemmelgarn, A. (1998). The effects of organizational climate and interorganizational coordination on the quality and outcomes of children's service systems. *Child Abuse & Neglect, 22*(5), 401–421.

Glynn, M., & Jamerson, H. (2006). Principled leadership: A framework for action. In E. D. Hess & K. S. Cameron (Eds.), *Leading with values: Positivity, virtue, and high performance* (pp. 151–171). New York, NY: Cambridge University Press.

Goddard, R., & Goddard, Y. L. (2001). A multilevel analysis of the relationship between teacher and collective efficacy in urban schools. *Teaching and Teacher Education, 17*(7), 807–818.

Goddard, R., & Salloum, S. (2012). Collective efficacy beliefs, organizational excellence, and leadership. In K. S. Cameron & G. M. Spreitzer (Eds.), *Oxford handbook of positive organizational scholarship* (pp. 642–650). New York, NY: Oxford University Press.

Goh, S.-K., & Zhen-Jie, L. B. (2014). The influence of servant leadership towards organizational commitment: The mediating role of trust in leaders. *International Journal of Business and Management, 9*(1), 17.

Gold, A. (2003). Principled principals? Values-driven leadership: Evidence from ten case studies of 'outstanding' school leaders. *Educational Management & Administration, 31*(2), 127–138.

Goleman, D. (1998). *Working with emotional intelligence.* New York, NY: Bantam.

Goleman, D. (2000). Leadership that gets results. *Harvard Business Review, 78*(2), 4–17.

Goodman, P. S., & Pennings, J. M. (1977). *New perspectives on organizational effectiveness.* San Francisco, CA: Jossey-Bass.

Gooty, J., Connelly, S., Griffith, J., & Gupta, A. (2010). Leadership, affect and emotions: A state of the science review. *The Leadership Quarterly, 21*(6), 979–1004.

Gordon, M. F., & Louis, K. S. (2009). Linking parent and community involvement with student achievement: Comparing principal and teacher perceptions of stakeholder influence. *American Journal of Education, 116*(1), 1–31.

Graham, J. W. (1991). Servant-leadership in organizations: Inspirational and moral. *The Leadership Quarterly, 2*(2), 105–119.

Grant, A. M. (2008). The significance of task significance: Job performance effects, relational mechanisms, and boundary conditions. *Journal of Applied Psychology, 93*(1), 108–124.

Grant, A. M., & Berg, J. M. (2012). Prosocial motivation at work. In K. Cameron & G. M. Spreitzer (Eds.), *The Oxford handbook of positive organizational scholarship* (pp. 28–44). New York, NY: Oxford University Press.

Grant, A. M., Gino, F., & Hofmann, D. A. (2011). Reversing the extraverted leadership advantage: The role of employee proactivity. *The Academy of Management Journal, 54*(3), 528–550.

Greenfield, W. (2004). Moral leadership in schools. *Journal of Educational Administration, 4*(2), 174–196.

Greenleaf, R. (1997). Servant leadership: A journey into the nature of legitimate power and greatness. New York, NY: Paulist Press. (Original work published 1977)

Griffin, M. A., Neal, A., & Parker, S. K. (2007). A new model of work role performance: Positive behavior in uncertain and interdependent contexts. *Academy of Management Journal, 50*(2), 327–347.

Grimshaw, J. (1986). *Philosophy and feminist thinking.* Minneapolis, MN: University of Minnesota Press.

Grissom, J. A. (2011). Can good principals keep teachers in disadvantaged schools? Linking principal effectiveness to teacher satisfaction and turnover in hard-to-staff environments. *Teachers College Record, 113*(11), 2552–2585.

Grojean, M. W., Resick, C. J., Dickson, M. W., & Smith, D. B. (2004). Leaders, values, and organizational climate: Examining leadership strategies for establishing an organizational climate regarding ethics. *Journal of Business Ethics, 55*(3), 223–241.

Guillaume, Y. R., Dawson, J. F., Otaye-Ebede, L., Woods, S. A., & West, M. A. (2017). Harnessing demographic differences in organizations: What moderates the effects of workplace diversity? *Journal of Organizational Behavior, 38*(2), 276–303.

Guthrie, J., Dreher, M. J., & Baker, L. (2000). Why teacher engagement is important to student achievement. In L. Baker, M. J. Dreher, & J. Guthrie (Eds.), *Engaging young readers: Promoting achievement and motivation* (pp. 309–320). New York, NY: Guilford Press.

Hackett, R. D., & Wang, G. (2012). Virtues and leadership: An integrating conceptual framework founded in Aristotelian and Confucian perspectives on virtues. *Management Decision, 50*(5), 868–899.

Hackman, J. R. (1998). Why teams don't work. In S. Tindale (Ed.), *Theory and research on small groups* (pp. 245–267). New York, NY: Springer.

Hackman, J. R. (2002). Leading teams: Setting the stage for great performances: Boston, MA: Harvard Business Press.

Hackman, J. R. (2003). Learning more by crossing levels: Evidence from airplanes, hospitals, and orchestras. *Journal of Organizational Behavior, 24*(8), 905–922.

Hackman, J. R., & Wageman, R. (1995). Total quality management: Empirical, conceptual, and practical issues. *Administrative Science Quarterly, 40,* 309–342.

Hall, D. T. (2004). Self-awareness, identity, and leader development. In D. V. Day, S. J. Zaccaro, & S. M. Halpin (Eds.), *Leader development for transforming organizations: Growing leaders for tomorrow* (pp. 153–176). Mahwah, NJ: Erlbaum.

Hall, D., & Chandler, D. E. (2005). Psychological success: When the career is a calling. *Journal of Organizational Behavior, 26*(2), 155–176.

Hallinger, P., & Heck, R. H. (2011). Exploring the journey of school improvement: Classifying and analyzing patterns of change in school improvement processes and learning outcomes. *School Effectiveness and School Improvement, 22*(1), 1–27.

Hallinger, P., Heck, R., & Murphy, J. (2014). Teacher evaluation and school improvement. *Educational Assessment, Evaluation and Accountability, 26*(1), 5–28.

Halverson, R., & Clifford, M. (2013). Distributed instructional leadership in high schools. *Journal of School Leadership, 23*(2), 389–419.

Hanbury, G. L., Sapat, A., & Washington, C. W. (2004). Know yourself and take charge of your own destiny: The "fit model" of leadership. *Public Administration Review, 64*(5), 566–576.

Hannah, S., Lester, P., & Vogelgesang, G. (2005). Moral leadership: Explicating the moral component of authentic leadership. *Leadership and Management, 3*, 43–81.

Hannah, S. T., Woolfolk, R. L., & Lord, R. G. (2009). Leader self-structure: A framework for positive leadership. *Journal of Organizational Behavior, 30*(2), 269–290.

Hargreaves, A. (1998). The emotional politics of teaching and teacher development: With implications for educational leadership. *International Journal of Leadership in Education, 1*(4), 315–336.

Hargreaves, A. (2000). Mixed emotions: Teachers' perceptions of their interactions with students. *Teaching and Teacher Education, 16*(8), 811–826.

Hargreaves, A. (2005). Educational change takes ages: Life, career and generational factors in teachers' emotional responses to educational change. *Teaching and Teacher Education, 21*(8), 967–983.

Harland, L., Harrison, W., Jones, J., & Reiter-Palmon, R. (2005). Leadership behaviors and subordinate resilience. *Journal of Leadership and Organizational Studies, 11*(2), 2–14.

Harris, A., Leithwood, K., Day, C., Sammons, P., & Hopkins, D. (2007). Distributed leadership and organizational change: Reviewing the evidence. *Journal of Educational Change, 8*(4), 337–347.

Harter, J. K., Schmidt, F. L., & Hayes, T. L. (2002). Business-unit-level relationship between employee satisfaction, employee engagement, and business outcomes: A meta-analysis. *Journal of Applied Psychology, 87*(2), 268–279.

Harter, J. K., Schmidt, F. L., & Keyes, C. L. (2003). Well-being in the workplace and its relationship to business outcomes: A review of the Gallup studies. *Flourishing: Positive Psychology and the Life Well-Lived, 2*, 205–224.

Hassan, S., Wright, B. E., & Yukl, G. (2014). Does ethical leadership matter in government? Effects on organizational commitment, absenteeism, and willingness to report ethical problems. *Public Administration Review, 74*(3), 333–343.

Heck, R., & Hallinger, P. (2014). Modeling the longitudinal effects of school leadership on teaching and learning. *Journal of Educational Administration, 52*(5), 653–681.

Heifetz, R. (1994). *Leadership without easy answers.* Cambridge, MA: Harvard University Press.

Heifetz, R., Grashow, A., & Linsky, M. (2009). *The practice of adaptive leadership.* Boston, MA: Harvard Business School Press.

Hensley, P. A., & Burmeister, L. (2008). Leadership connectors: A theoretical construct for building relationships. *Educational Leadership and Administration: Teaching and Program Development, 20*, 125–134.

Herman, S. (2002). How work gains meaning in contractual time: A narrative model for reconstructing the work ethic. *Journal of Business Ethics, 38*(1/2), 65–79.

Hersey, P., & Blanchard, K. H. (1969). Life cycle theory of leadership. *Training & Development Journal, 23*(5), 26–34.

Hitt, D. H., & Tucker, P. D. (2016). Systematic review of key leader practices found to influence student achievement: A unified framework. *Review of Educational Research, 86*(2), 531–569.

Hochschild, A. (1983). *The managed heart: Commercialization of human feeling*. Berkeley: University of California Press.

Hoffman, B. J., Blair, C. A., Meriac, J. P., & Woehr, D. J. (2007). Expanding the criterion domain? A quantitative review of the OCB literature. *Journal of Applied Psychology, 92*(2), 555.

Hogg, M. A. (2015). Constructive leadership across groups: How leaders can combat prejudice and conflict between subgroups. In E. Lawler (Ed.), *Advances in group processes* (Vol. 32, pp. 177–207). Bingley, UK: Emerald.

Hon, A. H. Y., Bloom, M., & Crant, J. M. (2011). Overcoming resistance to change and enhancing creative performance. *Journal of Management, 40*(3), 919–941.

Hood, J. (2003). The relationship of leadership style and CEO values to ethical practices in organizations. *Journal of Business Ethics, 43*, 263–273.

Houghton, J. D., & Yoho, S. K. (2005). Toward a contingency model of leadership and psychological empowerment: When should self-leadership be encouraged? *Journal of Leadership & Organizational Studies, 11*(4), 65–83.

Howell, J. M., & Hall-Merenda, K. E. (1999). The ties that bind: The impact of leader–member exchange, transformational and transactional leadership, and distance on predicting follower performance. *Journal of Applied Psychology, 84*(5), 680.

Hoy, W. K., & Hannum, J. W. (1997). Middle school climate: An empirical assessment of organizational health and student achievement. *Educational Administration Quarterly, 33*(3), 290–311.

Hoy, W. K., Smith, P. A., & Sweetland, S. R. (2002). The development of the organizational climate index for high schools: Its measure and relationship to faculty trust. *The High School Journal, 86*(2), 38–49.

Hoy, W., & Sweetland, S. (2001). Designing better schools: The meaning and measure of enabling school structures. *Educational Administration Quarterly, 37*(3), 296–321.

Hoy, W. K., Sweetland, S. R., & Smith, P. A. (2002). Toward an organizational model of achievement in high schools: The significance of collective efficacy. *Educational Administration Quarterly, 38*(1), 77–93.

Hoy, W. K., & Tarter, C. J. (2011). Positive psychology and educational administration: An optimistic research agenda. *Educational Administration Quarterly, 47*(3), 427–445.

Hoy, W. K., Tarter, C. J., & Hoy, A. W. (2006). Academic optimism of schools: A force for student achievement. *American Educational Research Journal, 43*(3), 425–446.

Hoy, W. K., Tarter, C. J., & Kottkamp, R. B. (1991). *Open schools, healthy schools: Measuring organizational climate*. Thousand Oaks, CA: Corwin Press.

Hsieh, C.-C., & Wang, D.-S. (2015). Does supervisor-perceived authentic leadership influence employee work engagement through employee-perceived authentic leadership and employee trust? *The International Journal of Human Resource Management, 26*(18), 2329–2348.

Huang, L.-C., Ahlstrom, D., Lee, A. Y.-P., Chen, S.-Y., & Hsieh, M.-J. (2016). High performance work systems, employee well-being, and job involvement: An empirical study. *Personnel Review, 45*(2), 296–314.

Huberman, M., & Miles, M. B. (2002). *The qualitative researcher's companion*. Thousand Oaks, CA: Sage.

Hülsheger, U. R., Anderson, N., & Salgado, J. F. (2009). Team-level predictors of innovation at work: A comprehensive meta-analysis spanning three decades of research. *Journal of Applied Psychology, 94*(5), 1128.

Humphrey, R. H., Burch, G. F., & Adams, L. L. (2016). The benefits of merging leadership research and emotions research. *Frontiers in Psychology, 7*. Retrieved from: https://www.ncbi.nlm.nih.gov/pmc/articles/PMC4934170/

Humphrey, S. E., Nahrgang, J. D., & Morgeson, F. P. (2007). Integrating motivational, social, and contextual work design features: A meta-analytic summary and theoretical extension of the work design literature. *Journal of Applied Psychology, 92*(5), 1332.

Hunter, E. M., Neubert, M. J., Perry, S. J., Witt, L., Penney, L. M., & Weinberger, E. (2013). Servant leaders inspire servant followers: Antecedents and outcomes for employees and the organization. *The Leadership Quarterly, 24*(2), 316–331.

Hunter, S., & Brisbin, R. A. (2000). The impact of service learning on democratic and civic values. *PS: Political Science & Politics, 33*(3), 623–626.

Hurley, R. F., & Hult, G. T. M. (1998). Innovation, market orientation, and organizational learning: An integration and empirical examination. *The Journal of Marketing*, pp. 42–54.

Ilies, R., Morgeson, F. P., & Nahrgang, J. D. (2005). Authentic leadership and eudaemonic well-being: Understanding leader–follower outcomes. *The Leadership Quarterly, 16*(3), 373–394.

Ilies, R., Nahrgang, J. D., & Morgeson, F. P. (2007). Leader–member exchange and citizenship behaviors: A meta-analysis. *Journal of Applied Psychology, 92*(1), 269–277.

Ingersoll, R. M. (2001). Teacher turnover and teacher shortages: An organizational analysis. *American Educational Research Journal, 38*(3), 499–534.

Ingrid, M. N., & Edmondson, A. C. (2006). Making it safe: The effects of leader inclusiveness and professional status on psychological safety and improvement efforts in health care teams. *Journal of Organizational Behavior, 27*(7), 941–966.

Jacobs, R., & Washington, C. (2003). Employee development and organizational performance: A review of literature and directions for future research. *Human Resource Development International, 6*(3), 343–354.

Jaskyte, K., & Dressler, W. W. (2005). Organizational culture and innovation in nonprofit human service organizations. *Administration in Social Work, 29*(2), 23–41.

Jehn, K. A. (1995). A multimethod examination of the benefits and detriments of intragroup conflict. *Administrative Science Quarterly, 40*(2), 256–282.

Jiménez-Jiménez, D., & Sanz-Valle, R. (2011). Innovation, organizational learning, and performance. *Journal of Business Research, 64*(4), 408–417.

Johnson, G., Dempster, N., & Wheeley, E. (2016). Distributed leadership: Theory and practice dimensions in systems, schools, and communities. In G. Johnson & N. Dempster (Eds.), *Leadership in diverse learning contexts* (pp. 3–31). Basel, Switzerland: Springer.

Johnson, L., Carter, J., & Finn, M. (2011). Parent empowerment through organizing for collective action. In C. M. Hands & L. Hubbard (Eds.), *Including families and communities in urban education* (pp. 69–95). Charlotte, NC: Information Age.

Johnson, S. M., Kraft, M. A., & Papay, J. P. (2012). How context matters in high-need schools: The effects of teachers' working conditions on their professional satisfaction and their students' achievement. *Teachers College Record, 114*(10), 1–39.

Joseph, M., & Feldman, J. (2009). Creating and sustaining successful mixed-income communities: Conceptualizing the role of schools. *Education and Urban Society, 41*(6), 623-652.

Josephson, E. (1952). Irrational leadership in formal organizations. *Social Forces, 31*(2), 109–117.

Judge, T. A., Piccolo, R. F., & Kosalka, T. (2009). The bright and dark sides of leader traits: A review and theoretical extension of the leader trait paradigm. *The Leadership Quarterly, 20*(6), 855–875.

Jung, D. I., & Sosik, J. J. (2002). Transformational leadership in work groups: The role of empowerment, cohesiveness, and collective-efficacy on perceived group performance. *Small Group Research, 33*(3), 313–336.

Kaczmarski, K. M., & Cooperrider, D. L. (1997). Constructionist leadership in the global relational age: The case of the Mountain Forum. *Organization & Environment, 10*(3), 235–258.

Kahn, W. A. (1990). Psychological conditions of personal engagement and disengagement at work. *Academy of Management Journal, 33*(4), 692–724.

Kahn, W. A. (1992). To be fully there: Psychological presence at work. *Human Relations, 45*(4), 321–349.

Kark, R., Shamir, B., & Chen, G. (2003). The two faces of transformational leadership: Empowerment and dependency. *Journal of Applied Psychology, 88*(2), 246.

Keiser, N. M., & Shen, J. (2000). Principals' and teachers' perceptions of teacher empowerment. *Journal of Leadership Studies, 7*(3), 115–121.

Kelchtermans, G. (2005). Teachers' emotions in educational reforms: Self-understanding, vulnerable commitment and micropolitical literacy. *Teaching and Teacher Education, 21*(8), 995–1006.

Kellerman, B. (2004). *Bad leadership: What it is, how it happens, why it matters.* Boston, MA: Harvard Business Press.

Kelsey, M. T. (1981). *Caring: How can we love one another?* New York, NY: Paulist Press.

Khalifa, M. A., Gooden, M. A., & Davis, J. E. (2016). Culturally responsive school leadership: A synthesis of the literature. *Review of Educational Research, 86*(4), 1272–1311.

Kim, S. (2002). Participative management and job satisfaction: Lessons for management leadership. *Public Administration Review, 62*(2), 231–241.

Kirby, P. C., Paradise, L. V., & King, M. I. (1992). Extraordinary leaders in education: Understanding transformational leadership. *The Journal of Educational Research, 85*(5), 303–311.

Kirkman, B. L., & Rosen, B. (1999). Beyond self-management: Antecedents and consequences of team empowerment. *Academy of Management Journal, 42*(1), 58–74.

Kirkman, B. L., & Shapiro, D. L. (2001). The impact of cultural values on job satisfaction and organizational commitment in self-managing work teams: The mediating role of employee resistance. *Academy of Management Journal, 44*(3), 557–569.

Kirkpatrick, S., & Locke, E. (1996). Direct and indirect effects of three core charismatic leadership components on performance and attitudes. *Journal of Applied Psychology, 81*(1), 36–51.

Klar, H. W., Huggins, K. S., Hammonds, H. L., & Buskey, F. C. (2016). Fostering the capacity for distributed leadership: A post-heroic approach to leading school improvement. *International Journal of Leadership in Education, 19*(2), 111–137.

Klassen, R. M. (2010). Teacher stress: The mediating role of collective efficacy beliefs. *The Journal of Educational Research, 103*(5), 342–350.

Knack, S. (2002). Social capital and the quality of government: Evidence from the states. *American Journal of Political Science, 46*(4), 772–785.

Knight, J. (2009). Coaching: Approaches and perspectives. Thousand Oaks, CA: Corwin Press.

Knippenberg, D., & De Cremer, D. (2008). Leadership and fairness: Taking stock and looking ahead. *European Journal of Work and Organizational Psychology, 17*(2), 173–179.

Kohlberg, L., & Hersh, R. H. (1977). Moral development: A review of the theory. *Theory into Practice, 16*(2), 53–59.

Kolb, D. (2014). *Experiential learning: Experience as the source of learning and development.* Englewood Cliffs, NJ: Prentice Hall.

Kolb, D., & Bartunek, J. (1992). *Hidden conflict in organizations: Uncovering behind-the-scenes disputes.* Thousand Oaks, CA: Sage.

Kolk, A., van Dolen, W., & Vock, M. (2010). Trickle effects of cross-sector social partnerships. *Journal of Business Ethics, 94*, 123–137.

Konovsky, M. A., & Pugh, S. D. (1994). Citizenship behavior and social exchange. *Academy of Management Journal, 37*(3), 656–669.

Kotter, J. P. (2008). *Force for change: How leadership differs from management.* New York, NY: Simon & Schuster.

Kouzes, J. M., & Posner, B. Z. (1999). *Encouraging the heart: A leader's guide to rewarding and recognizing others.* San Francisco, CA: Jossey-Bass.

Kouzes, J. M., & Posner, B. Z. (2002). *The leadership challenge: How to get extraordinary things done in organizations.* San Francisco, CA: Jossey-Bass.

Koys, D. J. (2001). The effects of employee satisfaction, organizational citizenship behavior, and turnover on organizational effectiveness: A unit-level, longitudinal study. *Personnel Psychology, 54*(1), 101–114.

Kozlowski, S. W., & Bell, B. S. (2013). Work groups and teams in organizations: Review updates. In N. Schmitt & S. Highhouse (Eds.), *Handbook of psychology* (Vol. 12, pp. 412–469). Hoboken, NJ: Wiley.

Kropiewnicki, M. I., & Shapiro, J. P. (April 2001). *Female leadership and the ethic of care: Three case studies.* Paper presented at the annual meeting of the American Educational Research Association, Seattle, WA.

Kroth, M., & Keeler, C. (2009). Caring as a managerial strategy. *Human Resource Development Review, 8*(4), 506–531.

Kruse, S., Louis, K. S., & Bryk, A. (1995). An emerging framework for analyzing school-based professional community. In K. S. Louis & S. Kruse (Eds.), *Professionalism and community: perspectives on reforming urban schools* (pp. 23–44). Thousand Oaks, CA: Corwin Press.

Kurt, T., Duyar, I., & Çalik, T. (2011). Are we legitimate yet? A closer look at the casual relationship mechanisms among principal leadership, teacher self-efficacy and collective efficacy. *Journal of Management Development, 31*(1), 71–86.

Kvale, S. (2008). *Doing interviews*. Thousand Oaks, CA: Sage.

LaBresh, J., Watters, M., & Chandhoke, S. (2017). *The smart and simple way to empower the public sector*. Cambridge, MA: Boston Consulting Group. Retrieved from www.bcgperspectives.com/content/articles/smart-and-simple-way-to-empower-the-public-sector/?utm_source=201702&utm_medium=Email&utm_campaign=Ealert

Larsen, D. E., & Hunter, J. E. (2014). Separating wheat from chaff: How secondary school principals' core values and beliefs influence decision-making related to mandates. *International Journal of Educational Leadership Preparation, 9*(2), 71–90.

Lave, J., & Wenger, E. (1991). *Situated learning: Legitimate peripheral participation*. New York, NY: Cambridge University Press.

Leana, C. R., & Pil, F. K. (2006). Social capital and organizational performance: Evidence from urban public schools. *Organization Science, 17*(3), 353–366.

Learning Forward. (2011). *Standards for professional learning*. Oxford, OH: Author.

Lee, A. N., & Nie, Y. (2017). Teachers' perceptions of school leaders' empowering behaviours and psychological empowerment: Evidence from a Singapore sample. *Educational Management Administration & Leadership, 45*(2), 260–283.

Lee, M., Louis, K. S., & Anderson, S. (2012). Local education authorities and student learning: The effects of policies and practices. *School Effectiveness and School Improvement, 23*(2), 123–138.

Lee, V. E., & Smith, J. B. (1996). Collective responsibility for learning and its effects on gains in achievement for early secondary school students. *American Journal of Education, 104*(2), 103–147.

Lee, F., Caza, A., Edmondson, A., & Thomke, S. (2003). New knowledge creation in organizations. In K. S. Cameron, J. E. Dutton, & R. E. Quinn (Eds.), *Positive organizational scholarship: Foundations of a new discipline* (pp. 194–206). San Francisco, CA: Berrett-Koehler.

Leithwood, K. (2016). Department-head leadership for school improvement. *Leadership and Policy in Schools, 15*(2), 117–140.

Leithwood, K., & Azah, V. N. (2016). Characteristics of effective leadership networks. *Journal of Educational Administration, 54*(4) 409–433.

Leithwood, K., & Beatty, B. (Eds). (2007). *Leading with teacher emotions in minds*. Thousand Oaks, CA: Corwin Press.

Leithwood, K., Harris, A., & Hopkins, D. (2008). Seven strong claims about successful school leadership. *School Leadership and Management, 28*(1), 27–42.

Leithwood, K., Jantzi, D., & Steinbach, R. (1999). *Changing leadership for changing times*. London, UK: McGraw-Hill Education.

Leithwood, K., Louis, K. S., Anderson, S., & Wahlstrom, K. (2004). *Review of research: How leadership influences student learning*. Retrieved from: http://www.wallacefoundation.org/WF/KnowledgeCenter/KnowledgeTopics/EducationLeadership/HowLeadershipInfluencesStudentLearning.htm

Leithwood, K., Mascall, B., & Strauss, T. (2009). *Distributed leadership: According to the evidence*. New York, NY: Routledge.

Leithwood, K., & Menzies, T. (1998). Forms and effects of school-based management: A review. *Educational Policy, 12*(3), 325–346.

Leithwood, K., & Riehl, C. (2005). What we know about successful school leadership. In W. Firestone & C. Riehl (Eds.), *A new agenda: Directions for research on educational leadership* (pp. 12–27). New York, NY: Teachers College Press.

Leithwood, K., & Steinbach, R. (1991). Indicators of transformational leadership in the everyday problem solving of school administrators. *Journal of Personnel Evaluation in Education, 4*(3), 221–244.

Leithwood, K., & Steinbach, R. (1995). *Expert problem solving: Evidence from school and district leaders.* Albany: State University of New York Press.

Lemon, M., & Sahota, P. S. (2004). Organizational culture as a knowledge repository for increased innovative capacity. *Technovation, 24*(6), 483–498.

Lennick, D., & Kiel, F. (2007). *Moral intelligence: Enhancing business performance and leadership success.* Upper Saddle River, NJ: Pearson Prentice Hall.

LePine, J. A., Erez, A., & Johnson, D. E. (2002). The nature and dimensionality of organizational citizenship behavior: A critical review and meta-analysis. *Journal of Applied Psychology, 87*(1), 52–65.

Leroy, H., Palanski, M. E., & Simons, T. (2012). Authentic leadership and behavioral integrity as drivers of follower commitment and performance. *Journal of Business Ethics, 107*(3), 255–264.

Lewis, S. (2011). *Positive psychology at work: How positive leadership and appreciative inquiry create inspiring organizations.* Hoboken, NJ: Wiley.

Liden, R. C., Erdogan, B., Wayne, S. J., & Sparrowe, R. T. (2006). Leader–member exchange, differentiation, and task interdependence: Implications for individual and group performance. *Journal of Organizational Behavior, 27*(6), 723–746.

Liden, R. C., Wayne, S. J., Liao, C., & Meuser, J. D. (2014). Servant leadership and serving culture: Influence on individual and unit performance. *Academy of Management Journal, 57*(5), 1434–1452.

Liden, R. C., Wayne, S. J., & Sparrowe, R. T. (2000). An examination of the mediating role of psychological empowerment on the relations between the job, interpersonal relationships, and work outcomes. *Journal of Applied Psychology, 85*(3), 407–416.

Liden, R. C., Wayne, S. J., Zhao, H., & Henderson, D. (2008). Servant leadership: Development of a multidimensional measure and multi-level assessment. *The Leadership Quarterly, 19*(2), 161–177.

Liedtka, J. M. (1996). Feminist morality and competitive reality: A role for an ethic of care? *Business Ethics Quarterly, 6*(2), 179–200.

Liedtka, J. (1999). Linking competitive advantage with communities of practice. *Journal of Management Inquiry, 8*(1), 5–16.

Lind, E. A., Kanfer, R., & Earley, P. C. (1990). Voice, control, and procedural justice: Instrumental and noninstrumental concerns in fairness judgments. *Journal of Personality and Social Psychology, 59*(5), 952.

Lippitt, R. (1939). Field theory and experiment in social psychology: Autocratic and democratic group atmospheres. *American Journal of Sociology, 45*(1), 26–49.

Lipschitz, R., Popper, M., & Oz, S. (1996). Building learning organizations: The design and implementation of organizational learning mechanisms. *Journal of Applied Behavioral Science, 32*(3), 292–305.

Little, J. W. (1990). The persistence of privacy: Autonomy and initiative in teachers' professional relations. *Teachers College Record, 91*(4), 509–536.

Little, J. W. (1993). Teachers' professional development in a climate of educational reform. *Educational Evaluation and Policy Analysis, 15*(2), 129–151.

Little, L. M., Gooty, J., & Williams, M. (2016). The role of leader emotion management in leader–member exchange and follower outcomes. *The Leadership Quarterly, 27*(1), 85–97.

Logan, D. C., & Fischer-Wright, H. (2006, August 4). *Rhetoric and the rise of tribes: Using organizational alchemy* (Part 3 of 3 in the rhetoric series) (Barbados Group Working Paper No. 06-07; iHEA 2007 6th World Congress: Explorations in Health Economics Paper). Retrieved from: https://papers.ssrn.com/sol3/papers.cfm?abstract_id=922314%20

Loi, R., Chan, K. W., & Lam, L. W. (2014). Leader–member exchange, organizational identification, and job satisfaction: A social identity perspective. *Journal of Occupational and Organizational Psychology, 87*(1), 42–61.

Lord, R. G., & Brown, D. J. (2001). Leadership, values, and subordinate self-concepts. *The Leadership Quarterly, 12*, 133–152.

Lord, R. G., Brown, D. J., & Freiberg, S. J. (1999). Understanding the dynamics of leadership: The role of follower self-concepts in the leader/follower relationship. *Organizational Behavior and Human Decision Processes, 78*(3), 167–203.

Lotto, L. S., & Murphy, J. (1990). Cognition and sensemaking in schools. In L. S. Lotto & P. W. Thurston (Eds.), *Advances in educational administration: Changing perspectives on the school.* (Vol. 1, Part B). Greenwich, CT: JAI Press.

Louis, K. S. (1998). Effects of teacher quality of work life in secondary schools on commitment and sense of efficacy. *School Effectiveness and School Improvement, 9*(1), 1–27.

Louis, K. S. (2007). Trust and improvement in schools. *Journal of School Change, 8*(1), 1–24.

Louis, K. S., & Lee, M. (2016). Teachers' capacity for organizational learning: The effects of school culture and context. *School Effectiveness and School Improvement, 27*(4), 534–556.

Louis, K. S., & Leithwood, K. (1998). From organizational learning to professional learning communities. In K. Leithwood & K. S. Louis (Eds.), *Organizational learning in schools* (pp. 275–285). Lisse, Netherlands: Swets & Zeitlinger.

Louis, K. S., Leithwood, K., Wahlstrom, K. L., Anderson, S. E., Michlin, M., & Mascall, B. (2010). Learning from leadership: Investigating the links to improved student learning. *Center for Applied Research and Educational Improvement/University of Minnesota and Ontario Institute for Studies in Education/University of Toronto.* Retrieved from www.wallacefoundation.org/WF/KnowledgeCenter/Knowledge-Topics/EducationLeadership/HowLeadershipInfluencesStudentLearning.htm

Louis, K. S., & Murphy, J. (2017). Trust, caring and organizational learning: The leader's role. *Journal of Educational Administration, 55*(1), 103–126.

Louis, K. S., Murphy, J. F., & Smylie, M. (2016). Caring leadership in schools: Findings from exploratory analyses. *Educational Administration Quarterly, 52*(2), 1–37.

Louis, K. S., & Robinson, V. (2012). External mandates and instructional leadership: Principals as mediating agents. *Journal of Educational Administration, 50*(5), 629–665.

Louis, K. S., & Smith, B. (1991). Restructuring, teacher engagement and school culture: Perspectives on school reform and the improvement of teacher's work. *School Effectiveness and School Improvement, 2*(1), 34–52.

Louis, K. S., Thomas, E., & Anderson, S. (2010). How do states influence leadership in small districts? *Educational Policy and Leadership, 9*(3) 328–366.

Louis, K. S., & van Velzen, B. (Eds.). (2012). *Educational policy in an international context: Political culture and its effects.* New York, NY: Palgrave/Macmillan.

Lurie, Y. (2004). Humanizing business through emotions: On the role of emotions in ethics. *Journal of Business Ethics, 49*(1), 1–11.

Luthans, F. (2002a). The need for and meaning of positive organizational behavior. *Journal of Organizational Behavior, 23*(6), 695–706.

Luthans, F. (2002b). Positive organizational behavior: Developing and managing psychological strengths. *The Academy of Management Executive, 16*(1), 57–72.

Luthans, F., Avey, J. B., & Patera, J. L. (2008). Experimental analysis of a web-based training intervention to develop positive psychological capital. *Academy of Management Learning & Education, 7*(2), 209–221.

Luthans, F., & Avolio, B. J. (2003). Authentic leadership development. In K. S. Cameron, J. E. Dutton, & R. E. Quinn (Eds.), *Positive organizational scholarship: Foundations of a new discipline* (pp. 242–258). San Francisco, CA: Berrett-Koehler.

Luthans, F., & Avolio, B. J. (2009). The "point" of positive organizational behavior. *Journal of Organizational Behavior, 30*(2), 291–307.

Luthans, F., & Church, A. (2002). Organizational behavior: Developing and managing psychological strengths. *The Academy of Management Executive, 16*(1), 57–75.

Luthans, F., Luthans, K. W., & Luthans, B. C. (2004). Positive psychological capital: Beyond human and social capital. *Business Horizons, 47*(1), 45–50.

Luthans, F., Norman, S. M., Avolio, B. J., & Avey, J. B. (2008). The mediating role of psychological capital in the supportive organizational climate—employee performance relationship. *Journal of Organizational Behavior, 29*(2), 219–238.

Luthans, F., Vogelgesang, G. R., & Lester, P. B. (2006). Developing the psychological capital of resiliency. *Human Resource Development Review, 5*(1), 25–44.

Luthans, F., & Youssef, C. M. (2007). Emerging positive organizational behavior. *Journal of Management, 33*(3), 321–349.

Luthans, F., Youssef, C. M., & Avolio, B. J. (2007). *Psychological capital: Developing the human competitive edge.* Oxford, UK: Oxford University Press.

Maak, T. (2007). Responsible leadership, stakeholder engagement, and the emergence of social capital. *Journal of Business Ethics, 74*(4), 329–343.

Mackay, F. (2001). *Love and politics: Women politicians and the ethics of care.* London, UK: Bloomsbury.

Madden, L. T., Duchon, D., Madden, T. M., & Plowman, D. A. (2012). Emergent organizational capacity for compassion. *Academy of Management Review, 37*(4), 689–708.

Maitlis, S., & Christianson, M. (2014). Sensemaking in organizations: Taking stock and moving forward. *The Academy of Management Annals, 8*(1), 57–125.

Malen, B. (1994). Enacting site-based management: A political utilities analysis. *Educational Evaluation and Policy Analysis, 16*(3), 249–267.

Mannix, E., & Neale, M. A. (2005). What differences make a difference? The promise and reality of diverse teams in organizations. *Psychological Science in the Public Interest, 6*(2), 31–55.

March, J. G., & Sutton, R. I. (1997). Crossroads—organizational performance as a dependent variable. *Organization Science, 8*(6), 698–706.

Marcus, B., & Schuler, H. (2004). Antecedents of counterproductive behavior at work: A general perspective. *Journal of Applied Psychology, 89*(4), 647.

Markow, F., & Klenk, K. (2005). The effects of personal meaning and calling on organizational commitment: An empirical investigation of spiritual leadership. *International Journal of Organizational Analysis, 13*(1), 8–27.

Marks, H. M., & Louis, K. S. (1999). Teacher empowerment and the capacity for organizational learning. *Educational Administration Quarterly, 35*(5), 707–750.

Marks, H. M., & Printy, S. M. (2003). Principal leadership and school performance: An integration of transformational and instructional leadership. *Educational Administration Quarterly, 39*(3), 370–397.

Markus, G. B., Howard, J. P., & King, D. C. (1993). Integrating community service and classroom instruction enhances learning: Results from an experiment. *Educational Evaluation and Policy Analysis, 15*(4), 410–419.

Masten, A. S., & Coatsworth, J. D. (1998). The development of competence in favorable and unfavorable environments: Lessons from research on successful children. *American Psychologist, 53*(2), 205.

Maxwell, J. C. (2001). *The 17 irrefutable laws of teamwork.* Nashville, TN: Thomas Nelson.

May, D. R., Chan, A., Hodges, T., & Avolio, B. (2003). Developing the moral component of authentic leadership. *Organizational Dynamics, 32*(3), 247–260.

May, D. R., Gilson, R. L., & Harter, L. M. (2004). The psychological conditions of meaningfulness, safety and availability and the engagement of the human spirit at work. *Journal of Occupational and Organizational Psychology, 77*(1), 11–37.

Mayer, D. M., Kuenzi, M., Greenbaum, R., Bardes, M., & Salvador, R. B. (2009). How low does ethical leadership flow? Test of a trickle-down model. *Organizational Behavior and Human Decision Processes, 108*(1), 1–13.

Mayer, R. C., Davis, J. H., & Schoorman, F. D. (1995). An integrative model of organizational trust. *Academy of Management Review, 20*(3), 709–734.

Mayeroff, M. (1971). *On caring.* New York, NY: HarperCollins.

Mayrowetz, D., Smylie, M., Murphy, J., & Louis, K. S. (2007, November). *Micropolitics and the development of distributed leadership.* Paper presented at the annual conference of the University Council for Educational Administration, Arlington, VA.

McAllister, D. J., & Bigley, G. A. (2002). Work context and the definition of self: How organizational care influences organization-based self-esteem. *Academy of Management Journal, 45*(5), 894–904.

McGregor, D. (1960). *The human side of enterprise.* Chicago, IL: University of Chicago Press.

McLaughlin, M. W., & Talbert, J. E. (2001). *Professional communities and the work of high school teaching*. Chicago, IL: University of Chicago Press.

McLaughlin, M. W., & Talbert, J. E. (2006). *Building school-based teacher learning communities: Professional strategies to improve student achievement.* New York, NY: Teachers College Press.

McMurray, A., Pirola-Merlo, A., Sarros, J., & Islam, M. (2010). Leadership, climate, psychological capital, commitment, and wellbeing in a non-profit organization. *Leadership & Organization Development Journal, 31*(5), 436–457.

McNeely, B. L., & Meglino, B. M. (1994). The role of dispositional and situational antecedents in prosocial organizational behavior: An examination of the intended beneficiaries of prosocial behavior. *Journal of Applied Psychology, 79*(6), 836–844.

Melrose, K. (2003). Putting servant leadership into practice. In K. S. Cameron, J. E. Dutton, & R. E. Quinn (Eds.), *Positive organizational scholarship: Foundations of a new discipline* (pp. 279–296). San Francisco, CA: Berrett-Koehler.

Meneghel, I., Borgogni, L., Miraglia, M., Salanova, M., & Martínez, I. M. (2016). From social context and resilience to performance through job satisfaction: A multilevel study over time. *Human Relations, 69*(11), 2047–2067.

Miller, T. L., Grimes, M. G., McMullen, J. S., & Vogus, T. J. (2012). Venturing for others with heart and head: How compassion encourages social entrepreneurship. *Academy of Management Review, 37*(4), 616–640.

Mizell, H., Hord, S., Killion, J., & Hirsh, S. (2011). New standards put the spotlight on professional learning. *Journal of Staff Development, 32*(4), 10.

Mohrman, S. A., Tenkasi, R. V., & Mohrman, A. M. J. (2003). The role of networks in fundamental organizational change: A grounded analysis. *The Journal of Applied Behavioral Science, 39*(3), 301–323.

Møller, J., Eggen, A., Fuglestad, O. L., Langfeldt, G., Presthus, A.-M., Skrøvset, S., . . . Vedøy, G. (2007). Successful leadership based on democratic values. In C. Day & K. Leithwood (Eds.), *Successful principal leadership in times of change: An international perspective* (pp. 71–86). Dordrecht, Netherlands: Springer.

Moolenaar, N. M., Daly, A. J., & Sleegers, P. J. (2010). Occupying the principal position: Examining relationships between transformational leadership, social network position, and schools' innovative climate. *Educational Administration Quarterly, 46*(5), 623–670.

Moolenaar, N. M., Sleegers, P. J., & Daly, A. J. (2012). Teaming up: Linking collaboration networks, collective efficacy, and student achievement. *Teaching and Teacher Education, 28*(2), 251–262.

Moorman, R. H. (1991). Relationship between organizational justice and organizational citizenship behaviors: Do fairness perceptions influence employee citizenship? *Journal of Applied Psychology, 76*(6), 845.

Morgan, G. (1986). *Images of organization.* Newbury Park, CA: Sage.

Morgeson, F. P. (2005). The external leadership of self-managing teams: Intervening in the context of novel and disruptive events. *Journal of Applied Psychology, 90*(3), 497.

Morieux, Y., & Tollman, P. (2014). *Six simple rules: How to manage complexity without getting complicated.* Cambridge, MA: Boston Consulting Group.

Morrill, C., Zald, M. N., & Rao, H. (2003). Covert political conflict in organizations: Challenges from below. *Annual Review of Sociology, 29*, 391–415.

Mowday, R. T., Porter, L. W., & Steers, R. M. (1982). Employee–organizational linkages: The psychology of commitment, absenteeism, and turnover. New York, NY: Academic Press.

Moye, M. J., Henkin, A. B., & Egley, R. J. (2005). Teacher-principal relationships: Exploring linkages between empowerment and interpersonal trust. *Journal of Educational Administration, 43*(3), 260–277.

Mullen, C. (2012). Mentoring: An overview. In A. Fletcher & C. Mullen (Eds.), *The Sage handbook of mentoring and coaching in education* (pp. 7–23). Thousand Oaks, CA: Sage.

Mumford, M. D., Todd, E. M., Higgs, C., & McIntosh, T. (2017). Cognitive skills and leadership performance: The nine critical skills. *The Leadership Quarterly, 28*(1), 24–39.

Murphy, J. (1988). Methodological, measurement, and conceptual problems in the study of administrator instructional leadership. *Educational Evaluation and Policy Analysis, 10*(2), 117–139.

Murphy, J. (2005). *Connecting teacher leadership and school improvement.* Thousand Oaks, CA: Corwin Press.

Murphy, J. (2006). *Preparing school leaders: An agenda for research and action.* Lanham, MD: Rowman & Littlefield.

Murphy, J. (2014). *Creating productive cultures in schools: For students, teachers, and parents.* Thousand Oaks, CA: Corwin Press.

Murphy, J. (2015). Creating communities of professionalism: Addressing cultural and structural barriers. *Journal of Educational Administration, 53*(2), 154–176.

Murphy, J. (2016a). Teacher as unit leader: Defining and examining the effects of care and support on children. A review of the research. *Journal of Human Resource and Sustainability Studies, 4*(3), 243–279.

Murphy, J. (2016b). *Understanding schooling through the eyes of students.* Thousand Oaks, CA: Corwin Press.

Murphy, J., & Beck, L. G. (1995). *School-based management as school reform: Taking stock.* Newbury Park, CA: Corwin Press.

Murphy, J., Beck, L. G., Crawford, M., & Hodges, A. (2001). *The productive high school: Creating personalized academic communities.* Thousand Oaks, CA: Corwin Press.

Murphy, J., Hallinger, P., & Heck, R. (2013, September). Leading via teacher evaluation: The case of the missing clothes. *Educational Researcher, 42*(6), 349–354.

Murphy, J., Louis, K. S., & Smylie, M. (2017). Positive school leadership: How the professional standards for educational leaders can be brought to life. *Phi Delta Kappan, 99*(1), 21–24.

Murphy, J., Smylie, M., Mayrowetz, D., & Louis, K. S. (2009, April). The role of the principal in fostering the development of distributed leadership. *School Leadership & Management, 29*(2), 181–214.

Murphy, J., & Torre, D. (2014). *Creating productive cultures in schools: For students, teachers, and parents.* Thousand Oaks, CA: Corwin Press.

Nahapiet, J., & Ghoshal, S. (1998). Social capital, intellectual capital, and the organizational advantage. *Academy of Management Review, 23*(2), 242–266.

Nahrgang, J. D., Morgeson, F. P., & Ilies, R. (2009). The development of leader–member exchanges: Exploring how personality and performance influence leader and member relationships over time. *Organizational Behavior and Human Decision Processes, 108*(2), 256–266.

Narvaez, D. (2008). Human flourishing and moral development: Cognitive and neurobiological perspectives of virtue development. In L. Nucci & D. Narvaez, *Handbook of moral and character education* (pp. 310–327). Mahwah, NJ: Erlbaum.

Nasomboon, B. (2014). The relationship among leadership commitment, organizational performance, and employee engagement. *International Business Research, 7*(9), 77.

National Policy Board for Educational Administration. (2015). *Professional standards for educational leaders 2015.* Reston, VA: Author.

Neal, K. W. (1999). *Developing and sustaining teacher communities: Caring as central in teachers' negotiation of reading instruction and curriculum implementation.* Retrieved from eric.ed.gov/?id=ED436527

Newman, A., Ucbasaran, D., Zhu, F., & Hirst, G. (2014). Psychological capital: A review and synthesis. *Journal of Organizational Behavior, 35*(Suppl. 1), S120–S138.

Nguni, S., Sleegers, P., & Denessen, E. (2006). Transformational and transactional leadership effects on teachers' job satisfaction, organizational commitment, and organizational citizenship behavior in primary schools: The Tanzanian case. *School Effectiveness and School Improvement, 17*(2), 145–177.

Nobel, C. (2010). Introverts: The best leaders for proactive employees. *Harvard Business School Working Knowledge*, pp. 1–2.

Noblit, G. W., Rogers, D. L., & McCadden, B. M. (1995). In the meantime: The possibilities of caring. *Phi Delta Kappan, 76*(9), 680–685.

Noruzy, A., Dalfard, V. M., Azhdari, B., Nazari-Shirkouhi, S., & Rezazadeh, A. (2013). Relations between transformational leadership, organizational learning, knowledge management, organizational innovation, and organizational performance: An empirical investigation of manufacturing firms. *The International Journal of Advanced Manufacturing Technology, 64*(5–8)pp. 1–13.

Nutov, L., & Somech, A. (2017). Principals going above and beyond: Understanding organizational citizenship behavior among school principals. *Journal of School Leadership, 27*(2), 186–214.

O'Connor, K. E. (2008). "You choose to care": Teachers, emotions and professional identity. *Teaching and Teacher Education, 24*(1), 117–126.

Ogawa, R. T., Crowson, R. L., & Goldring, E. B. (1999). Enduring dilemmas of school organization. *Handbook of research on educational administration, 2*, 277–295.

Oldham, G. R., & Hackman, J. R. (2010). Not what it was and not what it will be: The future of job design research. *Journal of Organizational Behavior, 31*(2/3), 463–479.

Oplatka, I. (2007). Managing emotions in teaching: Toward an understanding of emotion displays and caring as nonprescribed role elements. *Teachers College Record, 109*(6), 1374–1400.

Ostroff, C. (1992). The relationship between satisfaction, attitudes, and performance: An organizational level analysis. *Journal of Applied Psychology, 77*(6), 963–974.

Ott, M., & van Dijk, H. (2005). Effects of HRM on client satisfaction in nursing and care for the elderly. *Employee Relations, 27*(4), 413–424.

Owens, B. P., & Hekman, D. R. (2012). Modeling how to grow: An inductive examination of humble leader behaviors, contingencies, and outcomes. *Academy of Management Journal, 55*(4), 787–818.

Palanski, M. E., & Yammarino, F. J. (2009). Integrity and leadership: A multi-level conceptual framework. *The Leadership Quarterly, 20*(3), 405–420.

Palanski, M. E., & Yammarino, F. J. (2011). Impact of behavioral integrity on follower job performance: A three-study examination. *The Leadership Quarterly, 22*(4), 765–786.

Palmer, E., & Louis, K. S. (2017). Talking about race: Overcoming fear in the process of change. *Journal of School Leadership, 27*(5), 591–611.

Park, N., & Peterson, C. M. (2003). Virtues and organizations. In K. Cameron, J. Dutton, & R. E. Quinn (Eds.), *Positive organizational scholarship: Foundations of a new discipline* (pp. 33–47). San Francisco, CA: Berrett-Koehler.

Parris, M. A., & Vickers, M. H. (2005). Working in teams: The influence of rhetoric—from sensemaking to sadness. *Administrative Theory & Praxis, 27*(2), 277–300.

Pasek, J., Feldman, L., Romer, D., & Jamieson, K. H. (2008). Schools as incubators of democratic participation: Building long-term political efficacy with civic education. *Applied Development Science, 12*(1), 26–37.

Penuel, W. R., Riel, M., Krause, A., & Frank, K. A. (2009). Analyzing teachers' professional interactions in a school as social capital: A social network approach. *Teachers College Record, 111*(1), 124–163.

Perry, J. L. (1996). Measuring public service motivation: An assessment of construct reliability and validity. *Journal of Public Administration Research and Theory, 6*(1), 5–22.

Peterson, C., Park, N., Hall, N., & Seligman, M. E. (2009). Zest and work. *Journal of Organizational Behavior, 30*(2), 161–172.

Peterson, S. J., & Byron, K. (2008). Exploring the role of hope in job performance: Results from four studies. *Journal of Organizational Behavior, 29*(6), 785–803.

Peterson, S. J., Galvin, B. M., & Lange, D. (2012). CEO servant leadership: Exploring executive characteristics and firm performance. *Personnel Psychology, 65*(3), 565–596.

Peterson, S. J., Luthans, F., Avolio, B. J., Walumbwa, F. O., & Zhang, Z. (2011). Psychological capital and employee performance: A latent growth modeling approach. *Personnel Psychology, 64*(2), 427–450.

Piccolo, R. F., & Colquitt, J. A. (2006). Transformational leadership and job behaviors: The mediating role of core job characteristics. *Academy of Management Journal, 49*(2), 327–340.

Pless, N., & Maak, T. (2011). Responsible leadership: Pathways to the future. *Journal of Business Ethics, 98*, 3–13.

Plowman, D. A., Solansky, S., Beck, T. E., Baker, L., Kulkarni, M., & Travis, D. V. (2007). The role of leadership in emergent, self-organization. *The Leadership Quarterly, 18*(4), 341–356.

Podsakoff, N. P., Whiting, S. W., Podsakoff, P. M., & Blume, B. D. (2009). Individual- and organizational-level consequences of organizational citizenship behaviors: A meta-analysis. *Journal of Applied Psychology, 94*(1), 122.

Podsakoff, P. M., MacKenzie, S. B., & Ahearne, M. (1997). Moderating effects of goal acceptance on the relationship between group cohesiveness and productivity. *Journal of Applied Psychology, 82*(6), 974–983.

Podsakoff, P. M., MacKenzie, S. B., & Bommer, W. H. (1996). Transformational leader behaviors and substitutes for leadership as determinants of employee satisfaction, commitment, trust, and organizational citizenship behaviors. *Journal of Management, 22*(2), 259–298.

Pratt, M. G., & Ashforth, B. E. (2003). Fostering meaningfulness in working and at work. In K. S. Cameron & J. E. Dutton (Eds.), *Positive organizational scholarship: Foundations of a new discipline* (pp. 309–326). San Francisco, CA: Berrett-Koehler.

Price, H. E. (2011). Principal–teacher interactions. *Educational Administration Quarterly, 48*(1), 39–85.

Printy, S. M. (2014). Insights for an integrated leadership school. *Journal of School Public Relations, 35*(2), 298–316.

Purvanova, R. K., Bono, J. E., & Dzieweczynski, J. (2006). Transformational leadership, job characteristics, and organizational citizenship performance. *Human Performance, 19*(1), 1–22.

Putnam, R. D. (1995). Bowling alone: America's declining social capital. *Journal of Democracy, 6*(1), 65–78.

Quick, J. C., & Quick, J. D. (2004). Healthy, happy, productive work: A leadership challenge. *Organizational Dynamics, 33*(4), 329–337.

Quinn, D. M. (2002). The impact of principal leadership behaviors on instructional practice and student engagement. *Journal of Educational Administration, 40*(5), 447–467.

Quinn, R. E. (2010). Deep change: Discovering the leader within. Hoboken, NJ: Wiley.

Quinn, R. E., & Rohrbaugh, J. (1983). A spatial model of effectiveness criteria: Towards a competing values approach to organizational analysis. *Management Science, 29*(3), 363–377.

Quinn, R. E., Spreitzer, G. M., & Brown, M. V. (2000). Changing others through changing ourselves: The transformation of human systems. *Journal of Management Inquiry, 9*(2), 147–164.

Rapp, T. L., Gilson, L. L., Mathieu, J. E., & Ruddy, T. (2016). Leading empowered teams: An examination of the role of external team leaders and team coaches. *The Leadership Quarterly, 27*(1), 109–123.

Rauner, D. M. (2000). *They still pick me up when I fall: The role of caring in youth development and community life*. New York, NY: Columbia University Press.

Ravitch, D. (2011). *Life and death of the great American school*. New York, NY: Basic Books.

Reave, L. (2005). Spiritual values and practices related to leadership effectiveness. *The Leadership Quarterly, 16*, 655–687.

Reitzug, U. C., West, D. L., & Angel, R. (2008). Conceptualizing instructional leadership: The voices of principals. *Education and Urban Society, 40*(6), 694–714.

Reynolds, D., Creemers, B., Nesselrodt, P. S., Shaffer, E., Stringfield, S., & Teddlie, C. (2014). *Advances in school effectiveness research and practice*. New York, NY: Elsevier.

Rice, E. M., & Schneider, G. T. (1994). A decade of teacher empowerment: An empirical analysis of teacher involvement in decision making, 1980–1991. *Journal of Educational Administration, 32*(1), 43–58.

Rich, B. L., Lepine, J. A., & Crawford, E. R. (2010). Job engagement: Antecedents and effects on job performance. *Academy of Management Journal, 53*(3), 617–635.

Riggio, R. E., Zhu, W., Reina, C., & Maroosis, J. A. (2010). Virtue-based measurement of ethical leadership: The leadership virtues questionnaire. *Consulting Psychology Journal: Practice and Research, 62*(4), 235–250.

Riketta, M. (2005). Organizational identification: A meta-analysis. *Journal of Vocational Behavior, 66*(2), 358–384.

Robertson, J. L., & Barling, J. (2013). Greening organizations through leaders' influence on employees' pro-environmental behaviors. *Journal of Organizational Behavior, 34*(2), 176–194.

Robinson, S. L., & Bennett, R. J. (1995). A typology of deviant workplace behaviors: A multidimensional scaling study. *Academy of Management Journal, 38*(2), 555–572.

Rosenholtz, S. J. (1985). Effective schools: Interpreting the evidence. *American Journal of Education, 93*(3), 352–388.

Ross, J. A., & Gray, P. (2006). Transformational leadership and teacher commitment to organizational values: The mediating effects of collective teacher efficacy. *School Effectiveness and School Improvement, 17*(2), 179–199.

Rothmann, S., & Coetzer, E. P. (2003). The big five personality dimensions and job performance. *SA Journal of Industrial Psychology, 29*(1), 68.

Rupert, J., Jehn, K. A., van Engen, M. L., & de Reuver, R. S. M. (2010). Commitment of cultural minorities in organizations: Effects of leadership and pressure to conform. *Journal of Business and Psychology, 25*(1), 25–37.

Russell, R. F. (2001). The role of values in servant leadership. *Leadership & Organization Development Journal, 22*(2), 76–83.

Ryan, R. M., & Deci, E. L. (2003). On assimilating identities to the self: A self-determination theory perspective on internalization and integrity within cultures. In M. R. Leary & J. P. Tanguay (Eds.), *Handbook of self and identity* (pp. 253–272). New York, NY: Guilford Press.

Rynes, S. L., Bartunek, J. M., Dutton, J. E., & Margolis, J. D. (2012). Care and compassion through an organizational lens: Opening up new possibilities. *Academy of Management Review, 37*(4), 503–523.

Salanova, M., Agut, S., & Peiró, J. M. (2005). Linking organizational resources and work engagement to employee performance and customer loyalty: The mediation of service climate. *Journal of Applied Psychology, 90*(6), 1217–1227.

Salanova, M., Bakker, A. B., & Llorens, S. (2006). Flow at work: Evidence for an upward spiral of personal and organizational resources. *Journal of Happiness Studies, 7*(1), 1–22.

Salovey, P., & Mayer, J. D. (1990). Emotional intelligence. *Imagination, Cognition and Personality, 9*(3), 185–211.

Sama, L., & Shoaf, V. (2008). Ethical leadership for the professions: Fostering a moral community. *Journal of Business Ethics, 78*(1/2), 39–46.

Sampson, R. J., Raudenbush, S. W., & Earls, F. (1997). Neighborhoods and violent crime: A multilevel study of collective efficacy. *Science, 277*(5328), 918–924.

Sanchez-Burks, J., & Huy, Q. N. (2009). Emotional aperture and strategic change: The accurate recognition of collective emotions. *Organization Science, 20*(1), 22–34.

Sandage, S. J., & Hill, P. C. (2001). The virtues of positive psychology: The rapprochement and challenges of an affirmative postmodern perspective. *Journal for the Theory of Social Behaviour, 31*(3), 241–260.

Santoro, D. (2011). Good teaching in difficult times: Demoralization in the pursuit of good work. *American Journal of Education, 118*(1), 1–23.

Sarros, J. C., Cooper, B. K., & Santora, J. C. (2008). Building a climate for innovation through transformational leadership and organizational culture. *Journal of Leadership & Organizational Studies, 15*(2), 145–158.

Scales, P. C., Benson, P. L., Roehlkepartain, E. C., Sesma, A., & van Dulmen, M. (2006). The role of developmental assets in predicting academic achievement: A longitudinal study. *Journal of Adolescence, 29*(5), 691–708.

Scales, P. C., Roehlkepartain, E. C., Neal, M., Kielsmeier, J. C., & Benson, P. L. (2006). Reducing academic achievement gaps: The role of community service and service-learning. *Journal of Experiential Education, 29*(1), 38–60.

Scandura, T. A. (1992). Mentorship and career mobility: An empirical investigation. *Journal of Organizational Behavior, 13*(2), 169–174.

Schaubroeck, J., Lam, S. S., & Peng, A. C. (2011). Cognition-based and affect-based trust as mediators of leader behavior influences on team performance. *Journal of Applied Psychology, 96*(4), 863.

Schaufeli, W. B., & Bakker, A. B. (2004). Job demands, job resources, and their relationship with burnout and engagement: A multi-sample study. *Journal of Organizational Behavior, 25*(3), 293–315.

Schechter, C. (2008). Organizational learning mechanisms: The meaning, measure, and implications for school improvement. *Educational Administration Quarterly, 44*(2), 155–186.

Schechter, C., & Qadach, M. (2012). Toward an organizational model of change in elementary schools: The contribution of organizational learning mechanisms. *Educational Administration Quarterly, 48*(1), 116–153.

Schein, E. H. (2010). *Organizational culture and leadership* (2nd ed.). San Francisco, CA: Jossey-Bass.

Schneider, B., Ehrhart, M. G., & Macey, W. H. (2013). Organizational climate and culture. *Annual Review of Psychology, 64*, 361–388.

Seashore, S. E. (1954). *Group cohesiveness in the industrial work group.* Ann Arbor: University of Michigan, Institute for Social Research.

Seligman, M. (2010, October 7). *Flourish: Positive psychology and positive interventions.* The Tanner lectures on human values. University of Michigan, Ann Arbor. Retrieved from pdfs.semanticscholar.org/0ae0/150c87dcc82e7455ef4237d911f-55fac9ba0.pdf

Senge, P. (1977). Afterword. In *Servant leadership: A journey into the nature of legitimate power and greatness.* New York, NY: Paulist Press.

Senge, P. (2002). *The fifth discipline: The art and practice of the learning organization.* New York, NY: Currency Doubleday.

Sergiovanni, T. (1992). *Moral leadership: Getting to the heart of school improvement.* San Francisco, CA: Jossey-Bass.

Sergiovanni, T. (1994). *Building community in schools.* San Francisco, CA: Jossey-Bass.

Shaked, H., & Schechter, C. (in press). *Holistic school leadership: Systems thinking for educational leaders.* London, UK: Springer.

Shapira-Lishchinsky, O., & Tsemach, S. (2014). Psychological empowerment as a mediator between teachers' perceptions of authentic leadership and their withdrawal and citizenship behaviors. *Educational Administration Quarterly, 50*(4), 675–712.

Shapiro, J., & Stefkovich, J. (1997). The ethics of justice, critique and care: Preparing educational administrators to lead democratic and diverse schools. In L. G. Beck & J. Murphy, (Eds.), *Ethics in educational leadership programs: Emerging models* (pp. 109–140). Charlottesville, VA: The University Council for Educational Administration.

Shaw, J. D., Dineen, B. R., Fang, R., & Vellella, R. F. (2009). Employee-organization exchange relationships, HRM practices, and quit rates of good and poor performers. *The Academy of Management Journal, 52*(5), 1016–1033.

Sheppard, B. H. (1992). Conflict research as schizophrenia: The many faces of organizational conflict. *Journal of Organizational Behavior, 13*(3), 325–334.

Shin, Y. (2012). CEO ethical leadership, ethical climate, climate strength, and collective organizational citizenship behavior. *Journal of Business Ethics, 108*(3), 299–312.

Shipton, H. J., West, M. A., Parkes, C. L., Dawson, J. F., & Patterson, M. G. (2006). When promoting positive feelings pays: Aggregate job satisfaction, work design features, and innovation in manufacturing organizations. *European Journal of Work and Organizational Psychology, 15*(4), 404–430.

Shiva, M. S. A. M., & Suar, D. (2012). Transformational leadership, organizational culture, organizational effectiveness, and programme outcomes in non-governmental organizations. *Voluntas: International Journal of Voluntary and Nonprofit Organizations, 23*(3), 684–710.

Short, P. M. (1994). Defining teacher empowerment. *Education, 114*(4), 488–493.

Shuffler, M. L., DiazGranados, D., & Salas, E. (2011). There's a science for that: Team development interventions in organizations. *Current Directions in Psychological Science, 20*(6), 365–372.

Simola, S. K., Barling, J., & Turner, N. (2010). Transformational leadership and leader moral orientation: Contrasting an ethic of justice and an ethic of care. *The Leadership Quarterly, 21*(1), 179–188.

Simon, H. A. (1972). Theories of bounded rationality. *Decision and Organization, 1*(1), 161–176.

Simon, S. K. L., Schaubroeck, J., & Aryee, S. (2002). Relationship between organizational justice and employee work outcomes: A cross-national study. *Journal of Organizational Behavior, 23*(1), 1–18.

Simons, T. L. (1999). Behavioral integrity as a critical ingredient for transformational leadership. *Journal of Organizational Change Management, 12*(2), 89–104.

Simons, T., & Roberson, Q. (2003). Why managers should care about fairness: The effects of aggregate justice perceptions on organizational outcomes. *Journal of Applied Psychology, 88*(3), 432.

Skinner, E. A., & Belmont, M. J. (1993). Motivation in the classroom: Reciprocal effects of teacher behavior and student engagement across the school year. *Journal of Educational Psychology, 85*(4), 571.

Sluss, D. M., & Ashforth, B. E. (2008). How relational and organizational identification converge: Processes and conditions. *Organization Science, 19*(6), 807–823.

Sluss, D. M., Klimchak, M., & Holmes, J. J. (2008). Perceived organizational support as a mediator between relational exchange and organizational identification. *Journal of Vocational Behavior, 73*(3), 457–464.

Smircich, L., & Morgan, G. (1982). Leadership: The management of meaning. *Journal of Applied Behavioral Science, 18*(3), 257–273.

Smith, B., Montagno, R., & Kuzmenko, T. (2004). Transformational and servant leadership: Content and contextual comparisons. *Journal of Leadership and Organizational Studies, 10*(4), 80–91.

Smith, T. M., & Rowley, K. J. (2005). Enhancing commitment or tightening control:

The function of teacher professional development in an era of accountability. *Educational Policy, 19*(1), 126–154.

Smylie, M., Murphy, J., & Louis, K. S. (2016). Caring school leadership: A multi-disciplinary, cross-occupational model, *American Journal of Education, 123*(1). Retrieved from: https://www.journals.uchicago.edu/doi/abs/10.1086/688166

Solomon, D., Schaps, E., Watson, M., & Battistich, V. (1992). Creating caring school and classroom communities for all students. In R. A. Villa, J. S. Thousand, W. Stanback, & S. Stanback (Eds.), *Restructuring for caring and effective education: An administrative guide to creating heterogeneous schools* (pp. 41–60). Baltimore, MD: Brookes.

Somech, A., & Bogler, R. (2002). Antecedents and consequences of teacher organizational and professional commitment. *Educational Administration Quarterly, 38*(4), 555–577.

Somech, A., & Drach-Zahavy, A. (2004). Exploring organizational citizenship behaviour from an organizational perspective: The relationship between organizational learning and organizational citizenship behaviour. *Journal of Occupational and Organizational Psychology, 77*(3), 281–298.

Somech, A., & Ron, I. (2007). Promoting organizational citizenship behavior in schools: The impact of individual and organizational characteristics. *Educational Administration Quarterly, 43*(1), 38–66.

Somech, A., & Wenderow, M. (2006). The impact of participative and directive leadership on teachers' performance: The intervening effects of job structuring, decision domain, and leader–member exchange. *Educational Administration Quarterly, 42*(5), 746–772.

Spears, L. C. (1998). Tracing the growing impact of servant leadership. In L. C. Spears (Ed.), *Insights on leadership: Service, stewardship, spirit and servant-leadership.* New York, NY: Wiley.

Spillane, J. P., Hallett, T., & Diamond, J. B. (2003). Forms of capital and the construction of leadership: Instructional leadership in urban elementary schools. *Sociology of Education, 76*(1), 1–17.

Spreitzer, G. M. (1995). Psychological empowerment in the workplace: Dimensions, measurement, and validation. *The Academy of Management Journal, 38*(5), 1442–1465.

Spreitzer, G. (2007). Giving peace a chance: Organizational leadership, empowerment, and peace. *Journal of Organizational Behavior, 28*(8), 1077–1095.

Spreitzer, G. M. (2008). Taking stock: A review of more than twenty years of research on empowerment at work. In C. Cooper & J. Barling (Eds.), *Handbook of organizational behavior* (pp. 54–72). Thousand Oaks, CA: Sage.

Spreitzer, G. M., Kizilos, M. A., & Nason, S. W. (1997). A dimensional analysis of the relationship between psychological empowerment and effectiveness, satisfaction, and strain. *Journal of Management, 23*(5), 679–704.

Stajkovic, A. D., & Luthans, F. (1998). Self-efficacy and work-related performance: A meta-analysis. *Psychological Bulletin, 124*(2), 240–261.

Starrett, R. J. (1991). Building an ethical school: A theory for practice in educational leadership. *Educational Administration Quarterly, 27*(2), 185–202.

Stephens, J. P., & Carmeli, A. (2016). The positive effect of expressing negative emotions on knowledge creation capability and performance of project teams. *International Journal of Project Management, 34*(5), 862–873.

Stephenson, M. (2007). The "permanent things" and the role of the moral imagination in organizational life: Revisiting the foundations of public and nonprofit leadership. *Administrative Theory & Praxis, 29*(2), 260–277.

Sternberg, R. J., & Vroom, V. (2002). The person versus the situation in leadership. *The Leadership Quarterly, 13*(3), 301–323.

Steyrer, J., Schiffinger, M., & Lang, R. (2008). Organizational commitment—a missing link between leadership behavior and organizational performance? *Scandinavian Journal of Management, 24*(4), 364–374.

Stockard, J., & Lehman, M. (2004). Influences on the satisfaction and retention of lst-year teachers: The importance of effective school management. *Educational Administration Quarterly, 40*(5), 742–771.

Strathman, J. G. (1994). Migration, benefit spillovers and state support of higher education. *Urban Studies, 31*(6), 913–920.

Strauss, A., & Corbin, J. (1998). *Basics of qualitative research.* Thousand Oaks, CA: Sage.

Stringfield, S., Reynolds, D., & Schaffer, E. C. (2008). Improving secondary students' academic achievement through a focus on reform reliability: 4- and 9-year findings from the High Reliability Schools project. *School Effectiveness and School Improvement, 19*(4), 409–428.

Sun, L.-Y., Aryee, S., & Law, K. S. (2007). High-performance human resource practices, citizenship behavior, and organizational performance: A relational perspective. *Academy of Management Journal, 50*(3), 558–577.

Sundstrom, E., De Meuse, K. P., & Futrell, D. (1990). Work teams: Applications and effectiveness. *American Psychologist, 45*(2), 120–133.

Supovitz, J., Sirinides, P., & May, H. (2010). How principals and peers influence teaching and learning. *Educational Administration Quarterly, 46*(1), 31–56.

Takeuchi, R., Chen, G., & Lepak, D. P. (2009). Through the looking glass of a social system: Cross-level effects of high-performance work systems on employees' attitudes. *Personnel Psychology, 62*(1), 1–29.

Tasa, K., Sears, G. J., & Schat, A. C. H. (2011). Personality and teamwork behavior in context: The cross-level moderating role of collective efficacy. *Journal of Organizational Behavior, 32*(1), 65–85.

Taylor, T., Martin, B. N., Hutchinson, S., & Jinks, M. (2007). Examination of leadership practices of principals identified as servant leaders. *International Journal of Leadership in Education, 10*(4), 401–419.

Tenkasi, R. V., & Chesmore, M. C. (2003). Social networks and planned organizational change: The impact of strong network ties on effective change implementation and use. *The Journal of Applied Behavioral Science, 39*(3), 281–300.

Thomas, K. W., & Velthouse, B. A. (1990). Cognitive elements of empowerment: An "interpretive" model of intrinsic task motivation. *Academy of Management Review, 15*(4), 666–681.

Thomas, T., Thomas, J., & Firestone, H. (2015). Mentoring, coaching, and counseling: Toward a common understanding. *Military Review, 95*(4), 50–55.

Thompson, A. D., Grahek, M., Phillips, R. E., & Fay, C. L. (2008). The search for worthy leadership. *Consulting Psychology Journal: Practice and Research, 60*(4), 366–382.

Tichy, N. M. (1983). Managing strategic change: Technical, political, and cultural dynamics. New York, NY: Wiley.

Tjosvold, D. (2008). The conflict-positive organization: It depends upon us. *Journal of Organizational Behavior, 29*(1), 19–28.

Torney-Purta, J. (2002). The school's role in developing civic engagement: A study of adolescents in twenty-eight countries. *Applied Developmental Science, 6*(4), 203–212.

Treviño, L. K., & Brown, M. (2004). Managing to be ethical: Debunking five business ethics myths. *The Academy of Management Executive, 18*(2), 69–81.

Treviño, L. K., Brown, M., & Hartman, L. P. (2003). A qualitative investigation of perceived executive ethical leadership: Perceptions from inside and outside the executive suite. *Human Relations, 56*(1), 5–37.

Treviño, L. K., Hartman, L. P., & Brown, M. (2000). Moral person and moral manager: How executives develop a reputation for ethical leadership. *California Management Review, 42*(4), 128–142.

Tronto, J. C. (1994). Moral boundaries: A political argument for an ethic of care. New York, NY: Routledge.

Truxillo, D. M., Bauer, T. N., & Sanchez, R. J. (2001). Multiple dimensions of procedural justice: Longitudinal effects on selection system fairness and test-taking self-efficacy. *International Journal of Selection and Assessment, 9*(4), 336–349.

Tschannen-Moran, M. (2014). *Trust matters: Leadership for successful schools.* Hoboken, NJ: Wiley.

Tschannen-Moran, M., & Barr, M. (2004). Fostering student learning: The relationship of collective teacher efficacy and student achievement. *Leadership and Policy in Schools, 3*(3), 189–209.

Tschannen-Moran, M., & Gareis, C. R. (2015). Faculty trust in the principal: An essential ingredient in high-performing schools. *Journal of Educational Administration, 53*(1), 66–92.

Tuytens, M., & Devos, G. (2012). The effect of procedural justice in the relationship between charismatic leadership and feedback reactions in performance appraisal. *The International Journal of Human Resource Management, 23*(15), 3047–3062.

Tuytens, M., & Devos, G. (2014). How to activate teachers through teacher evaluation? *School Effectiveness and School Improvement, 25*(4), 509–530.

van Dierendonck, D., & Patterson, K. (2015). Compassionate love as a cornerstone of servant leadership: An integration of previous theorizing and research. *Journal of Business Ethics, 128*(1), 119–131.

Van Kleef, G. A., Homan, A. C., Beersma, B., Van Knippenberg, D., Van Knippenberg, B., & Damen, F. (2009). Searing sentiment or cold calculation? The effects of leader emotional displays on team performance depend on follower epistemic motivation. *The Academy of Management Journal, 52*(3), 562–580.

Van Maele, D., & Van Houtte, M. (2015). Trust in school: A pathway to inhibit teacher burnout? *Journal of Educational Administration, 53*(1), 93–115.

van Veen, K., & Sleegers, P. (2009). Teachers' emotions in a context of reforms: To a deeper understanding of teachers and reforms. In P. A. Schutz & M. Zembylas (Eds.), *Advances in teacher emotion research* (pp. 233–251). New York, NY: Springer.

Van Wingerden, J., Derks, D., & Bakker, A. B. (2017). The impact of personal resources and job crafting interventions on work engagement and performance. *Human Resource Management, 56*(1), 51–67.

Vancouver, J. B., & Schmitt, N. W. (1991). An exploratory examination of person–organization fit: Organizational goal congruence. *Personnel Psychology, 44*(2), 333–352.

Vekeman, E., Devos, G., & Tuytens, M. (2015). The influence of teachers' expectations on principals' implementation of a new teacher evaluation policy in Flemish secondary education. *Educational Assessment, Evaluation and Accountability, 27*(2), 129–151.

Viswesvaran, C., & Ones, D. S. (2002). Examining the construct of organizational justice: A meta-analytic evaluation of relations with work attitudes and behaviors. *Journal of Business Ethics, 38*(3), 193–203.

Voelkel, R. H., Jr., & Chrispeels, J. H. (2017). Within-school differences in professional learning community effectiveness: Implications for leadership. *Journal of School Leadership, 27*(3), 424–453.

Vogelgesang, G. R., Leroy, H., & Avolio, B. J. (2013). The mediating effects of leader integrity with transparency in communication and work engagement/performance. *The Leadership Quarterly, 24*(3), 405–413.

Wade, R. C. (1997). Teachers of service-learning. In A. Waterman (Ed.), *Service-learning: Applications from the research* (pp. 77–93). Mahwah, N.J.: Erlbaum.

Wageman, R. (2001). How leaders foster self-managing team effectiveness: Design choices versus hands-on coaching. *Organization Science, 12*(5), 559–577.

Wageman, R., & Fisher, C. (2014). Who's in charge here? The team leadership implications of authority. In D. V. Day (Ed.), *The Oxford handbook of leadership and organizations* (pp. 455–481). New York, NY: Oxford University Press.

Wagner, S. H., Parker, C. P., & Christiansen, N. D. (2003). Employees that think and act like owners: Effects of ownership beliefs and behaviors on organizational effectiveness. *Personnel Psychology, 56*(4), 847–871.

Wahlstrom, K. L., & Louis, K. S. (2008). How teachers experience principal leadership: The roles of professional community, trust, efficacy, and shared responsibility. *Educational Administration Quarterly, 44*(4), 458–495.

Wahlstrom, K., & Louis, K. S. (November 2015). *Principals as transcultural leaders: Making authentic connections that enhance teaching and learning.* Paper presented at the University Council for Educational Administration, San Diego, CA.

Waldman, D. A., Ranier, G. G., House, R. J., & Puranam, P. (2001). Does leadership matter? CEO leadership attributes and profitability under conditions of perceived environmental uncertainty. *The Academy of Management Journal, 44*(1), 134–143.

Walter, F., & Bruch, H. (2008). The positive group affect spiral: A dynamic model of the emergence of positive affective similarity in work groups. *Journal of Organizational Behavior, 29*(2), 239–261.

Walter, F., Cole, M. S., & Humphrey, R. H. (2011). Emotional intelligence: Sine qua non of leadership or folderol? *Academy of Management Perspectives, 25*(1), 45–59.

Walumbwa, F. O., Avolio, B. J., Gardner, W. L., Wernsing, T. S., & Peterson, S. J. (2008). Authentic leadership: Development and validation of a theory-based measure. *Journal of Management, 34*(1), 89–126.

Walumbwa, F. O., Avolio, B. J., & Zhu, W. (2008). How transformational leadership weaves its influence on individual job performance: The role of identification and efficacy beliefs. *Personnel Psychology, 61*(4), 793–825.

Walumbwa, F. O., Cropanzano, R., & Goldman, B. M. (2011). How leader–member exchange influences effective work behaviors: Social exchange and internal–external efficacy perspectives. *Personnel Psychology, 64*(3), 739–770.

Walumbwa, F. O., Cropanzano, R., & Hartnell, C. A. (2009). Organizational justice, voluntary learning behavior, and job performance: A test of the mediating effects of identification and leader–member exchange. *Journal of Organizational Behavior, 30*(8), 1103–1126.

Walumbwa, F. O., Hartnell, C. A., & Oke, A. (2010). Servant leadership, procedural justice climate, service climate, employee attitudes, and organizational citizenship behavior: A cross-level investigation. *Journal of Applied Psychology, 95*(3), 517–529.

Walumbwa, F. O., Mayer, D. M., Wang, P., Wang, H., Workman, K., & Christensen, A. L. (2011). Linking ethical leadership to employee performance: The roles of leader–member exchange, self-efficacy, and organizational identification. *Organizational Behavior and Human Decision Processes, 115*(2), 204–213.

Walumbwa, F. O., Peterson, S. J., Avolio, B. J., & Hartnell, C. A. (2010). An investigation of the relationships among leader and follower psychological capital, service climate, and job performance. *Personnel Psychology, 63*(4), 937–963.

Walumbwa, F. O., & Schaubroeck, J. (2009). Leader personality traits and employee voice behavior: Mediating roles of ethical leadership and work group psychological safety. *Journal of Applied Psychology, 94*(5), 1275–1286.

Walumbwa, F. O., Wang, P., Lawler, J., & Shi, K. (2004). The role of collective efficacy in the relations between transformational leadership and work outcomes. *Journal of Occupational and Organizational Psychology, 77*, 515–530.

Wang, H., Law, K., Hackett, R., Wang, D., & Chen, Z. (2005). Leader–member exchange as a mediator of the relationship between transformational leadership and followers' performance and organizational citizenship behavior. *Academy of Management Journal, 48*(3), 420–432.

Wang, H., Lu, C., & Siu, O. (2015). Job insecurity and job performance: The moderating role of organizational justice and the mediating role of work engagement. *Journal of Applied Psychology, 100*(4), 1249–1258.

Wang, H., Sui, Y., Luthans, F., Wang, D., & Wu, Y. (2014). Impact of authentic leadership on performance: Role of followers' positive psychological capital and relational processes. *Journal of Organizational Behavior, 35*(1), 5–21.

Wanous, J. P., & Lawler, E. E. (1972). Measurement and meaning of job satisfaction. *Journal of Applied Psychology, 56*(2), 95.

Ware, H., & Kitsantas, A. (2007). Teacher and collective efficacy beliefs as predictors of professional commitment. *The Journal of Educational Research, 100*(5), 303–310.

Weick, K. E. (1979). *The psychology of sensemaking.* New York, NY: Random House.

Weick, K. E. (1993). The collapse of sensemaking in organizations: The Mann Gulch Disaster. *Administrative Science Quarterly, 38*(4), 628–652.

Weick, K. E. (2003). Positive organizing and organizational tragedy. In K. S. Cameron, J. E. Dutton, & R. E. Quinn (Eds.), *Positive organizational scholarship: Foundations of a new discipline* (pp. 66–80). San Francisco, CA: Berrett-Kohler.

Weick, K. E., & Quinn, R. E. (1999). Organizational change and development. *Annual Review of Psychology, 50*(1), 361–386.

West, M. A. (1990). The social psychology of innovation in groups. In M. A. West & J. L. Farr (Eds.), *Innovation and creativity at work* (pp. 4–36). New York, NY: Wiley.

White, P. A. (1992). Teacher empowerment under "ideal" school-site autonomy. *Educational Evaluation and Policy Analysis, 14*(1), 69–82.

Williams, C. (1938). How professional are teachers? *Peabody Journal of Education, 16*(2), 117–120.

Wilson, S. M., & Ferch, S. R. (2005). Enhancing resilience in the workplace through the practice of caring relationships. *Organization Development Journal, 23*(4), 45–60.

Wilson, T. S. (2016). Contesting the public school: Reconsidering charter schools as counterpublics. *American Educational Research Journal, 53*(4), 919–952.

Witherspoon, N., & Arnold, B. M. (2010). Pastoral care: Notions of caring and the Black female principal. *The Journal of Negro Education*, pp. 220–232.

Wood, R., & Bandura, A. (1989). Social cognitive theory of organizational management. *The Academy of Management Review, 14*(3), 361–384.

Woolley, A. W., Aggarwal, I., & Malone, T. W. (2015). Collective intelligence in teams and organizations. In T. W. Malone & M. S. Bernstein (Eds.), *Handbook of collective intelligence* (pp. 143–168). Cambridge, MA: MIT Press.

Woolley, L., Caza, A., & Levy, L. (2010). Authentic leadership and follower development. *Journal of Leadership & Organizational Studies, 18*(4), 438–448.

Wright, B. E. (2007). Public service and motivation: Does mission matter? *Public Administration Review, 67*(1), 54–64.

Wright, T. A., & Bonett, D. G. (2007). Job satisfaction and psychological well-being as nonadditive predictors of workplace turnover. *Journal of Management, 33*(2), 141–160.

Wright, T. A., & Goodstein, J. (2007). Character is not "dead" in management research: A review of individual character and organizational-level virtue. *Journal of Management, 33*(6), 928–958.

Wrzesniewski, A., & Dutton, J. E. (2001). Crafting a job: Revisioning employees as active crafters of their work. *Academy of Management Review, 26*(2), 179–201.

Wu, J. H., Hoy, W. K., & Tarter, C. J. (2013). Enabling school structure, collective responsibility, and a culture of academic optimism: Toward a robust model of school performance in Taiwan. *Journal of Educational Administration, 51*(2), 176–193.

Wu, V., & Short, P. M. (1996). The relationship of empowerment to teacher job commitment and job satisfaction. *Journal of Instructional Psychology, 23*(2), 83–89.

Wyness, M., & Lang, P. (2016). The social and emotional dimensions of schooling: A case study in challenging the 'barriers to learning'. *British Educational Research Journal, 42*(6), 1041–1055.

Xu, X., Yu, F., & Shi, J. (2011). Ethical leadership and leaders' personalities. *Social Behavior and Personality: An International Journal, 39*(3), 361–368.

Yammarino, F. J., Salas, E., Serban, A., Shirreffs, K., & Shuffler, M. L. (2012). Collectivistic leadership approaches: Putting the "we" in leadership science and practice. *Industrial and Organizational Psychology, 5*(4), 382–402.

Yariv, E. (2009). The appraisal of teachers' performance and its impact on the mutuality of principal-teacher emotions. *School Leadership and Management, 29*(5), 445–461.

Ybema, J. F., van der Meer, L., & Leijten, F. R. (2016). Longitudinal relationships between organizational justice, productivity loss, and sickness absence among older employees. *International Journal of Behavioral Medicine, 23*(5), 645–654.

York-Barr, J., & Duke, K. (2004). What do we know about teacher leadership? Findings from two decades of scholarship. *Review of Educational Research, 74*(3), 255–316.

Youndt, M. A., & Snell, S. A. (2004). Human resource configurations, intellectual capital, and organizational performance. *Journal of Managerial Issues, 16*(3), 337–360.

Youngs, P., & King, M. B. (2002). Principal leadership for professional development to build school capacity. *Educational Administration Quarterly, 38*(5), 643–670.

Youssef, C. M., & Luthans, F. (2007). Positive organizational behavior in the workplace: The impact of hope, optimism, and resilience. *Journal of Management, 33*(5), 774–800.

Yukl, G. (1999). An evaluation of conceptual weaknesses in transformational and charismatic leadership theories. *The Leadership Quarterly, 10*(2), 285–305.

Zaccaro, S. J., Rittman, A. L., & Marks, M. A. (2002). Team leadership. *The Leadership Quarterly, 12*(4), 451–483.

Zembylas, M. (2010). Teachers' emotional experiences of growing diversity and multiculturalism in schools and the prospects of an ethic of discomfort. *Teachers and Teaching: Theory and Practice, 16*(6), 703–716.

Zembylas, M., & Papanastasiou, E. C. (2005). Modeling teacher empowerment: The role of job satisfaction. *Educational Research and Evaluation, 11*(5), 433–459.

Zhang, X., & Bartol, K. M. (2010). Linking empowering leadership and employee creativity: The influence of psychological empowerment, intrinsic motivation, and creative process engagement. *Academy of Management Journal, 53*(1), 107–128.

Zhu, W., May, D., & Avolio, B. (2004). The impact of ethical leadership behavior on employee outcomes: The roles of psychological empowerment and authenticity. *Journal of Leadership and Organizational Studies, 11*(1), 16–26.

Zhu, W., Sosik, J. J., Riggio, R. E., & Yang, B. (2012). Relationships between transformational and active transactional leadership and followers' organizational identification: The role of psychological empowerment. *Journal of Behavioral and Applied Management, 13*(3), 186–212.

Zimmerman, M. A. (1995). Psychological empowerment: Issues and illustrations. *American Journal of Community Psychology, 23*(5), 581–599.

Zohar, D., & Tenne-Gazit, O. (2008). Transformational leadership and group interaction as climate antecedents: A social network analysis. *Journal of Applied Psychology, 93*(4), 744–757.

Index

NAME

Abbasi, E., 132
Adams, L. L., 84–85
Adler, P. S., 21–22, 33, 35
Aggarwal, I., 101, 110–111
Agut, S., 122
Ahearne, M., 54
Ahern, J., 130
Ahlstrom, D., 119
Akdogan, A. A., 119
Akhtar, S. A., 132, 137
Aldridge, J., 125
Alegre, J., 132
Allen, D., 5, 14, 47, 70, 93
Alok, K., 92
Anderson, N., 105
Anderson, N. R., 106
Anderson, S., 61, 66, 81, 120, 126, 137
Anderson, S. E., 116
Anderson-Butcher, D., 55, 109
Andiappan, M., 61–62, 95, 128
Andrews, R., 137
Angel, R., 72
Aquino, K., 87
Argyris, C., 131
Arjoon, S., 8
Arnold, B. M., 60
Arnold, K. A., 92
Aryee, S., 120–121
Ashforth, B. E., 45, 48, 51, 55, 81, 85, 90, 118, 137
Ashkanasy, N. M., 85
Ashton, D., 55, 109
Atkins, P., 76–77, 79
Atwater, L., 86, 91
Audretsch, D. B., 141
Avey, J., 14, 18–19, 30–31, 56, 80, 93
Avey, J. B., 7, 19, 92, 128
Avolio, B., 9, 13, 22–23, 29.34, 37, 40, 49, 60, 67, 69–70, 74

Avolio, B. J., 6, 9, 47–48, 50–51, 63–64, 66, 71, 74–78, 80, 83–84, 86–90, 92, 135
Azah, V. N., 37
Azhdari, B., 132

Bacha, E., 120–121
Baker, L., 65, 122
Bakker, A. B., 9–10, 56, 93–94, 96, 122
Baldridge, J. V., 134
Bali, V. A., 30
Ball, S. J., 134
Bandura, A., 87, 129
Bardes, M., 49, 69, 71, 73
Barling, J., 21, 119
Barnard, C., 48–49, 115
Barr, M., 130
Barry, J., 57
Bartol, K. M., 89
Bartunek, J., 134
Bartunek, J. M., 62, 66
Bass, B. M., 17, 19, 21–22, 24–27, 31, 33–35, 37, 39–41, 44, 60
Bass, L., 79
Battistich, V., 80
Bauer, T. N., 88
Beatty, B., 84, 85n1
Beck, L. G., 63, 66, 70, 73, 80, 90, 111
Beck, T. E., 65
Beersma, B., 104
Begley, P. T., 40, 75
Beijaard, D., 63, 91
Beitz, L., 18–19, 23, 26, 31, 36–38, 41
Bell, B. S., 102
Belmont, M. J., 122
Bennett, R. J., 128
Benson, P. L., 143
Berg, J. M., 36, 93–94
Berkovich, I., 85, 97
Berkowitz, M. W., 20

SUBJECT

Culture(s) (*continued*)
  of innovation and change, 130–132, 133f
  organizational, positive leadership and,
    122–135, 124f, 133f

Decision making, data-based, 72, 72n1
Denison's culture dimensions, PSL
    principles and, 123, 124f
Departmental cohesiveness, 101–102
Design, of teams, 110–112
Deviant behavior, 128
Differences/Disagreements, managing,
    132–135
Disengagement, 104
Diversity, in teams, 112
Dominating conflict culture, 134
Dyadic relationships
  collective social learning and, 81
  development of, 52–54, 56
  LMX theory and, 47–49, 56. *See also*
    Leader-member exchanges
  role stages in, 52

Economic exchanges, in work
    relationships, 48. *See also* Exchanges,
    workplace relationships and
Efficacy. *See* Collective efficacy; Self-
    efficacy
Emotional aperture, of groups, 105
Emotional intelligence (EI), 85
Emotions
  implications for leaders, 86
  managing, strategies for, 85–86
  positive, 83–86
  positive leadership and, 84–86
  of teachers, 84, 84n1
  of teams, 103–105
Empowerment
  collective, 125
  leader-member exchanges and, 57
  leadership behavior and, 69–70
  psychological, 89–90
  trust and, 70, 107
Enabling behavior, of leaders, 67–69
Engagement
  antecedents and, 121–122
  disengagement and, 104
  in professional community, 116
  school–community, 142–143
  of teachers, 122
Entrepreneurship, 131–132
Episodic change, 132
Ethical leaders/leadership, 28

modeling of, 73–74
Every Student Succeeds Act, 9n4
Exchanges, workplace relationships and
  economic vs. social, 48
  quality of, 46–47, 51–55
  theory, 45–46. *See also* Leader-member
    exchange (LMX) theory
Expectations
  collective performance, 66
  work-related, 116
Extraversion, 56, 57

Factory image, of organization, 8–9
Fairness
  in leader-member exchanges, 50
  organizational climate and, 120–121
Four D's approach in organizations, 9

GDP of, 70
Gender differences, in perceived sense of
    fairness, 121
Good/Goodness, 17–18
  individual vs. collective, 8
  moral orientation and, 20
Grounded theory
  methods in, 5–7
  models of, 1, 1n1
Group(s). *See also* Team(s)
  assessing performance of, 83
  context of, in leader-member exchanges,
    55
  emotional aperture of, 105
Growth
  organizational, 24–25
  personal. *See* Personal growth
  professional, 24
Growth-based leadership, 23–24, 23n3
  characteristics of, 30f, 38–39
  organizational culture dimension and,
    124f

Humility, collective, 22

Identity
  intergroup relational, 134
  leader development of, 90–91, 96
  organizational, importance of, 116
Incentives, competition vs., 115
Inconsistency, boundary conditions and,
    14
Individual well-being, in organizations,
    83–98
Individual-incentive systems, 115

About the Authors

Joseph F. Murphy is the Frank W. Mayborn Chair of Education and Associate Dean at Peabody College of Education of Vanderbilt University. He has also been a faculty member at the University of Illinois and The Ohio State University, where he was the William Ray Flesher Professor of Education. Murphy was the Founding Chair of the Interstate School Leaders Licensure Consortium. He also chaired the teams that produced revisions to the national standards in 2008 and 2015 (Professional Standards for Educational Leaders). He led the team that developed the specifications with ETS for the School Leaders Licensure Assessment (SLLA). He is also one of the four co-creators of the Vanderbilt Assessment of Leadership in Education (VAL-ED).

Karen Seashore Louis is a regents professor and Robert H. Beck Chair in the Department of Organizational Policy, Leadership, and Development at the University of Minnesota. She has also served as the Director of the Center for Applied Research and Educational Improvement at the University of Minnesota, Department Chair, and Associate Dean of the College of Education and Human Development. Her research focuses on school improvement and reform, school effectiveness, leadership in school settings, and the politics of knowledge use in education. She is a fellow of the American Educational Research Association, where she also served as a Vice-President representing Division A (Educational Administration), and as an Executive Board member of the University Council for Educational Administration. She has received numerous awards, including the lifetime Contributions to Staff Development award from the National Staff Development Association (2007), the Campbell Lifetime Achievement Award from the University Council for Educational Administration (2009), and a life-time achievement award from the International Congress for School Effectiveness and School Improvement (2014).